Inside Stories

Inside Stories

Diaries of British Film-makers at Work

Edited by Duncan Petrie
Assistant Editor: Nick Pettigrew

BRITISH FILM INSTITUTE

BFI PUBLISHING

First published in 1996 by the
British Film Institute,
21 Stephen St, London W1P 2LN

The British Film Institute exists to promote appreciation, enjoyment,
protection and development of moving image culture in and throughout
the whole of the United Kingdom. Its activities include the National Film
and Television Archive; the National Film Theatre; the Museum of the
Moving Image; the London Film Festival; the production and distribution
of film and video; funding and support for regional activities; Library and
Information Services; Stills, Posters and Designs; Research; Publishing
and Education; and the monthly *Sight and Sound* magazine.

Set in Plantin by Fakenham Photosetting, Norfolk
Printed and bound in Italy

British Library Cataloguing-in-Publication Data
A catalogue record for this book is available from the British Library
ISBN 0–85170–584–7
     0–85170–583–9 pbk

Contents

Editor's Acknowledgments

Many thanks to all the contributors who laboured long and hard in their diary writing and made this book possible. Thanks also to BFI Chairman Jeremy Thomas for his efforts in setting up the project, to *Screen International* for advertising it to the Trade, to Colin MacCabe and Richard Paterson for their guidance and support and to all my former colleagues in BFI Research and Education for convincing me this project was worth it – particularly during moments of despair.

Special thanks to Jacintha Cusack and Sarah Armour whose help kept the project ticking along smoothly for more than a year.

Finally, thanks to Nick Pettigrew, my Assistant Editor, who assumed responsibility for the book on my departure from the Institute and who assisted in the final edit of this volume.

Foreword

The contents of this volume are drawn from diaries contributed to the British Film Institute's 'Chronicle of Cinema in Britain' initiated in 1995. This project was based on the participation of individuals actively involved in the film industry in a variety of capacities, from the production process through distribution and exhibition to related industry bodies and journalism. These individuals were invited to submit a monthly diary dealing with their current projects, key events and more general reflection on pertinent issues. The project had two major aims. First, it was conceived of in the context of the Centenary of Cinema celebrations. These tended towards recalling and reassessing founding moments, or constructing a panoramic sweep of one hundred years of history. However, it is important to recognise that the cinema continues to occupy a key position in contemporary cultural life, suggesting the necessity for a project that, in the Centenary year, concentrated on the contemporary rather than the historical. The idea of a diary seemed a perfect way of tapping into this continuously unfolding present, as experienced by individuals at the centre of the various activities that constitute the British film industry. The second aim was to use the project as a way of 'lifting the lid' off of what is still a rather opaque set of industrial and aesthetic practices. Again, the personalised format of the diary seemed particularly appropriate to revealing the day-to-day 'nuts and bolts' of the industry, from the germination of an idea to the presentation of a finished product to an audience. Moreover, the wide range of jobs represented by those taking part in the project – including writers, directors, actors, producers, cinematographers, designers, editors, distributors and cinema managers – reveals the essentially *collaborative* and *multi-faceted* nature of the filmic process. This offers an alternative perspective to the continuing obsession with the director as auteur and the star system in both scholarly writing and popular journalism.

The book is divided into sections according to the positions individuals occupy within the industry. The main body of the volume is preceded by two brief introductory pieces by two of the key figures in current British film production. Stephen Woolley of Scala Productions, whose credits include *The Company of Wolves, Scandal, Backbeat, The Crying Game* and *Interview with the Vampire*, has been one of the most consistently exciting and ambitious producers working in British cinema since the early 80s when he set up Palace Pictures with Nik Powell. David Aukin, Head of Drama at Channel Four, is responsible for one of the most important sources of finance for British film-makers. Since the channel was set up in 1982 it has become increasingly difficult to talk about British cinema without simultaneously talking about television. Institutionally they are extremely close – without funding from Channel Four and the BBC there would be no British film industry to speak of. By the same token many actors, directors and technicians work regularly across both media, and this is reflected in many of the diaries.

If the term 'cinema' is problematic, then so too is the concept 'British'. For many involved in film-making, their work is fundamentally international in nature, frequently taking them overseas to work for months or even years at a time. Hollywood is still a major lure for members of the British film community, particularly those whose achievements and ambitions cannot be contained within the rather limited opportunities offered by an indigenous industry which, despite occasional periods of optimism, is still prone to economic instability. Consequently, this book includes diaries from several ex-pats currently resident in Los Angeles, including director Michael Apted, writer Alan Shiach and actor Alfred Molina. In addition, there are many top technicians who may live in the UK but who work regularly on American films and are represented here by among others cinematographer Peter Suschitzky, costume designer John Bloomfield and editor Mick Audsley.

Inside Stories comprises extracts from the diaries of twenty-seven of the forty-eight individuals who took part. Due to strict limitations on space these extracts deal with only some of the projects and events recounted in the diaries – most of the producers and directors represented here for example were involved with several projects at once. The space problem also necessitated at times rather ruthless selectivity. Therefore I would like to express my sincere thanks to those diarists who could not be included in this volume despite producing fascinating accounts of their year. They are Edward Bazalgette, Maureen Blackwood, Peter Broughan, Mark Cosgrove, Oliver Curtis, Michael Eaton, Sandra Hebron, Simon Kaye, James Mackay, John Mahony, Derek Malcolm, Kelvin Nel, Wendy Palmer, Linda Pariser, Caroline Anne Potts, Jonathan Romney, Iain Softley, Bill Weir, Sheila Whitaker, Ian Wilson and Adrian Wootton.

However, it was always the intention that the 'Chronicle' would have two major outcomes, and in addition to this publication, all of the (complete) diaries have been brought together as a major special collection housed in the BFI Library. Indeed, this volume represents only a fraction of the rich array of material contained in the collection which comprises a much more extensive account of a very special year in the history of film.

One hundred years after its official 'birth', the cinema is indisputably *the* popular art of the 20th century. *Inside Stories* presents a unique insight into the inner workings of an industry, breaking open the toy which, like no other aesthetic form, retains the power to entertain, move and stimulate its audience.

Duncan Petrie
University of Exeter, January 1996

Introductions

Stephen Woolley

For me 1995 was the year of Dublin and *Michael Collins*, the year of hopeful peace in Ireland, the year when positive (Irish) tax incentives contrasted with British short-sightedness and confusion, and the year I realised that documenting a producer's role runs the danger of opening so many Pandora's boxes that self-censorship comes into play and blandness ensues.

However much we might wish to avoid the Machiavellian label, there are times when even a good producer, who at his or her best is a seamless diplomat, can seem a lying, duplicitous hypocrite. I would certainly hesitate to apply the latter description to myself, but in writing a diary you begin to map out a world where so much is left unsaid, unwritten and unacknowledged that the lines between diplomat and hypocrite become blurred. In August I decided that keeping the diary was, alas, a series of compromises. In a letter written to Duncan Petrie at the time I wrote:

> I have a real pragmatic problem in keeping a diary at the moment, simply because of the time restriction imposed upon us all working a six-day week. However, more seriously I am facing a huge philosophical dilemma which was underlined by the publication of excerpts from Nik Powell's diary in *Empire* magazine. This confirmed my greatest fears that articulating what a producer, or in Nik's case, an executive producer, gets up to does not win friends or influence people.
>
> The producer's job is to take the truth on the chin, but quite frankly the truth hurts for a lot of the key people involved in film-making. The final straw that proved that publication of a producer's role can be detrimental was a profile recently published in the *Telegraph*. This article came three weeks into production, and attempted to glamorise and individualise my role in the production of various films, *Michael Collins* included, which is not to say that it was deliberately mean spirited or intentionally vindictive. It just doesn't always pay to be honest, not in this business, and I would only want to publish the truth or nothing.

Later that year Ireland took centre stage of the raging European production debate, showing that far from being an idyllic backwater the Irish film scene vibrated with activity. While the world scoffed at the activities of an Englishman abroad suffering from one 'divine intervention', another almost blew Michael D. Higgins, the brave, high-profile Irish Arts

1

Minster off the political map. This was *Divine Rapture*, the troubled Brando/Depp/Winger project that never got beyond the first few weeks. While the Section 35 tax investment incentive was cleared of primary blame for this unfortunate setback, it did show that producers could not take advantage of the benefits in Ireland without careful financial planning.

Despite key advantages to filming a long-neglected story of an Irish hero in his native land, progress to the shoot became tricky due to the scarcity of skilled labour and construction expertise. Building the biggest exterior set ever envisaged in Irish cinema (O'Connell Street in 1916, the Mansion House and the ruined GPO building all featured) wasn't easy, particularly when another film, *Moll Flanders*, had already nabbed the cream of the Irish technicians. In a year or two, with continuing Section 35 support, there will undoubtedly be a large pool of experienced workers, but we had to begin by importing the knowledge from the UK and supplementing this with semi-experienced local talent. Over the years Pinewood and Shepperton have honed talents that cannot be duplicated overnight. Hotel per diems and a stubborn union pushed our budget up to a point where the benefits of Section 35 simply became awash in our budget.

As soon as we began shooting however, I realised we were blessed. Every cloudless day gave way to clear night followed by another glorious dawn. No producer in Europe shooting on exteriors had grounds for complaint that year, and as well as the convivial atmosphere created by the crew, cast and people of Dublin, the sun poured its warmth into all of our veins. *Michael Collins* became the most joyful production I have ever worked on.

These of course are just my reflections; an actor, a rigger, a driver, or caterer may have had the worst summer of their lives. Within the fabric of a shoot each contributor views the process with different eyes; the resulting collage of images and memories is the fascination of this collection of celluloid snapshots recalling 1995. As Kurosawa's masterpiece, *Rashomon*, demonstrates, our singular and collective memories can often reveal more about ourselves than the events we attempt to recount. This is a collection that calls upon the reader to study what lies between the lines as much as the printed text itself; an exercise in detection is called for.

David Aukin

For British film-makers these are, as the Chinese would wish, 'interesting times'. In case anyone has forgotten, it is scarcely three years since a British feature film was such a rarity that the UN was about to classify it as an endangered species. Today we are on the threshold of something exciting and a future that, among other things, holds the possibility that a film-maker can have a career making films *in this country*; when was the last time anyone could have said that without being immediately labelled an innocent, a fool or a madman? Memories of Goldcrest are still sufficiently vivid to set us on guard against complacency and act as a reminder of the fragility of the fortunes of British films. If people still have the ambition to 'take on Hollywood' instead of just trying to make successful British films, then our fortunes will suffer another, probably terminal, collapse.

One of the minor but significant events of 1995 was the success of *Shallow Grave*. Its significance lies not so much in its good performance abroad – many British films have achieved this over the years – but in the fact that it was able to recoup its costs within the UK without its success here being powered by an initial success in the USA, as was the case with *Four Weddings and a Funeral*. *Shallow Grave* was followed by other similar successes, including *The Madness of King George*. The conclusion I draw is that we can now make films for ourselves; that occasionally these films will 'travel'; that we need no longer feel overwhelmingly dependent on overseas markets to finance our films; and that we can remain true to our stories, to our casting and to our way of making films. The proviso is that the films must be made for a price that can be recouped from our own audiences. The paradox is that the truer we are to ourselves, the more likely we are to make films that will also appeal to the rest of the world.

Another significant achievement of 1995 has been the sheer quantity of feature films made. In the autumn Channel Four had some twenty films in production – that is, films that were either actually shooting, in active pre-production or in post-production. We are finally achieving 'critical mass', by which I mean that the minimum number of films are being financed to allow for the real possibility of some successful films. And while the strike rate in Hollywood is something like one in nine, ours is higher. Without taking risks there can be no successes, and every risk carries the potential for disaster. We have the necessary numbers but we also have the inevitable attendant problems, such as the danger of spreading the talent too thinly, and the recognition that the well of talent itself is not infinite.

Another new and positive phenomenon to emerge has been the Lottery Fund. From my own experience I can offer the following example of the Lottery in action. One of its first awards was £1 million for *The Wood-landers*, the balance of the £4.5 million budget being provided by Channel Four and the French company Chargeurs. *The Woodlanders* is the first feature by the distinguished documentary film-maker Phil Agland, shot, mainly on location, in Dorset (where Thomas Hardy's novel is set). To represent all the seasons – something which is crucial to the story – Phil needed to plan a split shoot, which is of course an expensive way of making a film. Most of the companies we approached for co-finance thought us at best eccentric, but Phil believes, and I share his conviction, that the film has, as a consequence, an authenticity that marks it out as something very special. It is an approach that Hollywood executives do not really understand and with which they would certainly not go along. It is thanks to the Lottery and to our partners, Chargeurs, that Phil's vision can be realised.

There are some enticing prospects in 1996, including new films from Mike Leigh, Danny Boyle, Peter Greenaway, Angela Pope, Gillies MacKinnon and Mark Herman. No doubt there will be troubles and controversies, perhaps over Thaddeus O'Sullivan's *Nothing Personal* or Danny Boyle's *Trainspotting*. At least if we are attacked about these films we shall be able to defend them not only on principle but in the knowledge that they are both fine films.

The Producer

Nik Powell

Nik Powell is an experienced producer who, together with partner Stephen Woolley, established Palace as a major independent producer and distributor during the 80s. After Palace were forced into receivership in the early 90s, Powell and Woolley bounced back with their new company Scala Productions. During 1996 several feature projects were in development, and the following extracts concentrate on the financing and production of one of these, The Hollow Reed, *and some of the preliminary meetings on one other,* Vicious Circles.

Eurimages, mentioned in the diary and others that follow, has the objective of stimulating film and audio-visual production by partly financing the co-production, distribution and exhibition of European films. In the 1995 budget, the British government pulled out of the fund. The European Media Guarantee Company (Euromedia Garanties) offers to share the risks with film-financiers by guaranteeing their bank loans through a public and private fund. British Screen is a private company aided by a government grant which exists primarily to support new talent in commercially viable productions for the cinema which might find difficulty in attracting mainstream commercial funding. Euroscript is the European Script Fund, which provides development loans for film and television fiction with European appeal. Script funding is awarded to companies developing a range of projects for international audiences.

March 20–26 Working feverishly to finish off the financing of *The Hollow Reed*. Several weeks ago we committed to full pre-production on the back of the following: Senator Film (in Berlin) have signed a deal memo to put up approximately £670,000 of the budget; Channel Four have committed in principle to £1 million; and British Screen to £400,000. The Berliner Bank have agreed in principle to advance the balance, but conditional to (1) a guarantee from the European Media Guarantee Company; (2) either a successful Eurimages application or a guarantee from someone else should that application fail; and (3) over £120,000 of deferments of fees and salaries. However, major problems have arisen, some of which I have foreseen, and some of which were unforeseeable except in the sense that of the twenty-five or more film financings I have done, there have always been unforeseen difficulties – never, alas, the same ones.

This time round the main problems are as follows: Channel Four hates the deal that I have done with Senator, so much so that they want either to pull out or replace Senator. But I have already signed Senator up, and Hanno Huth, its six-foot-four, very German boss, sees little reason to

5

change the deal. Nevertheless, I have to enter into negotiations (or more accurately, renegotiations) at the behest of first Channel Four and then the Berliner Bank.

Then there was the fact that British Screen's commitment of £400,000, if it were to sit beside Channel Four's £1 million, was subject to BSkyB's not exercising the option that they have over the pay TV rights under a quite separate deal they have in place with British Screen. I hadn't previously given it much thought because BSkyB have never exercised this particular option and I assumed that they would 'pass' on *Hollow Reed*, just as they had 'passed' on *The Neon Bible* in similar circumstances last year, thus clearing the way for British Screen to invest alongside Channel Four. However, David Elstein has decided on this occasion not to pass but to match Channel Four's offer. Furthermore, he has announced this to the press, and reports of this have appeared in both *Variety* and *Screen International*. Our relationship is firmly with Channel Four (with whom we have produced over ten films), and there's no way we could jump ship to BSkyB for whom we have never produced a film. So I'm obliged to persuade Colin Leventhal and David Aukin at Channel Four to replace British Screen's investment. This brings me into an unwanted potential conflict with British Screen's chief executive.

The next difficulty is to do with the Eurimages application. The board of Eurimages meets only ten days before we are due to start principal photography (on 24 April), so our bankers, Berliner, have required that we obtain replacement financing in case our application is unsuccessful. After all, the odds are stacked firmly against us – there are more than a hundred applications of which only fifteen to twenty will be successful. Our application is the only one from the UK where we are 'majority' producer. However, we have little German content or involvement (our German partners were our principal European co-producer) and this works against us. We have never done a Eurimages application before and have applied for £500,000. I spent most of early March lining up some kind of replacement/finance guarantee to be utilised if our application is unsuccessful, and found an Israeli financier who seemed willing to provide the replacement finance. But around mid-March, he went 'quiet', failing to return my phone calls or respond to my letters. This is making me very nervous.

There are other problems as well. Our Euromedia guarantee is still not in place, and the negotiations for the £120,000 deferments are proving much tougher than I would have liked.

March 27 I call the Israeli financier and finally elicit a response – a fax saying he's 'too busy' to provide the guarantee that I have negotiated with him. I know that 'too busy' is not the reason. He has decided he doesn't want to do the deal. Anyway he's out, and I'm in trouble. I quickly make a list of people to replace him, some of whom I have already been talking to. But they all have their problems. Screen Partners (with whom I worked on *Dark Blood* and *The Neon Bible*) would love to help out but Berliner will not work with them, and vice versa. Maybe I can set something up by which I route their guarantee/insurance policy through a third party. Then there's Chrysalis, our 49-per-cent shareholder. However, they are new to the business and have only just put their business plan through the holding company board – in short, it's probably too early for them to consider even the pretty watertight deal that I can offer them. But I decide to approach them anyway. I also call our lawyer and comrade in New York, Janet Jacobson. She's great. Within half an hour she has produced a list of potential replacement investors. At the same time I decide to reopen negotiations with Canal+ [French production and cable company] and others in France. Canal+ love it but won't make a big enough offer.

March 29 The closing of the finance for *The Hollow Reed* really begins with a big meeting of principals and lawyers and our bankers. What essentially happens is that over several hours we hammer out what is required for the bank to start advancing cash. At the first meeting the list of requirements is very long. Everyone is very sceptical about whether it can be done at all, let alone before 24 April when we start shooting. I calculate that I have enough cash for the next two weeks – the £200,000 from our Chrysalis facility plus the £75,000 overdraft I have recently negotiated with Coutts for the company, and the £100,000 that I believe Channel Four can be persuaded to part with (at this meeting they swear they will not go a dime over £50,000 but I choose not to believe them!). The recently publicised interest of BSkyB in acquiring the film has certainly helped boost confidence in the financing hugely.

Later I go round the corner to see Lyndsey Posner of Chrysalis to fill her in on *The Hollow Reed* and to see if Chrysalis will put up the guarantee. She signs off her deferral (God bless her) but is not at all encouraging about the guarantee. I think to myself: 'I'd prefer it the other way round – do the guarantee, forget about the deferral.' I promise to put it all in writing the following morning.

April 3 I meet with the head of Chrysalis's newly established foreign sales outfit. He is charming and interested in what we are doing. Chrysalis do not have any rights over our projects, but I hope a close relationship will evolve that could be good and useful for us in the future. I brief him with regard to the guarantee I have asked Chrysalis for. I don't get the feeling that he will be able to support it, and I'm right!

April 5 Maddening negotiations with Senator's lawyer, who is visiting London, concerning their million-dollar investment in *Hollow Reed*. Almost two hours to negotiate less than one line, and all the time I could not figure out what was going on. Why was he wilfully and transparently misunderstanding both the English and German translations (both my lawyers speak German)? It was very bizarre, but somehow we work something out.

April 6 Big contract meeting with Channel Four and their lawyers in

Whitfield Street. I have brought Janet (my lawyer) in from New York to help me complete the transaction before our monies run out. There are more than five Channel Four documents for us to agree to, and a further twenty or so for them to agree line by line with the banks, with Senator and with our Spanish distributors Sogapaq. The going is made easier by the fact that we, Berliner and Channel Four have done this many times before. But although we have all done it several times with Senator in a small way – on *Crying Game*, *Backbeat* and *The Neon Bible* – this is our first big deal with them.

I speak to Yani at Lakeshore in LA about possibly putting up *The Hollow Reed* guarantee. He is positive. Liz Karlsen, the producer of *The Hollow Reed*, is screaming at me for money. I arrange to drawdown our Chrysalis facility to enable pre-production to continue while our negotiations continue. I pray that she can make it last long enough.

April 7   This is a kind of 'D-Day' for me as I'm off on holiday to Spain in the morning and things must be in good enough shape to allow me to go. I already know that I will spend most of the holiday on the phone, but I'd rather do that and see my children than not see them at all. 3 pm is the big one – when I have arranged for all the financiers and their lawyers to meet at my bankers in the City to negotiate with them as short as possible a list of things to be achieved before (1) drawdown of the 'interim' finance (worth £200,000) to us and (2) full drawdown. After a lot of argument a shorter list is agreed which Janet and I feel is achievable on our side. Janet will finish the Channel Four and Berliner documentation. We will jointly (and gently) tease from Senator and Sogapaq the documents the bank requires.

I feel confident enough to take my children to Spain the following morning.

April 9–17   I spend each day from around 11 am to 6 pm on the phone and fax which my girlfriend has kindly installed at her house in the south of Spain. Unfortunately my much-prized Euro mobile doesn't yet work in Spain so from Monday through to Friday I am very much housebound. My girlfriend and children are very understanding and supportive. My children clap and cheer at the end of each day when I finish on the phone. They also do very funny imitations of my telephone manner. I think they are a little surprised at how much I have to fight and argue to get our films made. 'Dad, if your films win so many awards and do so well, how come its such a fight to get the money for them? How come they don't just give it to you? – I would!', says my twelve-year-old daughter. I ponder this thought.

Good news arrives on Tuesday afternoon. After an impassioned plea from our Eurimages board member, Timothy Burrill, *Hollow Reed* is successful in its application for funds.

April 18   We start principal photography in five days and we still don't have a cent from our bankers. We have had £42,000 from Channel Four. The rest has come from Scala's own resources. Channel Four have agreed to send a further £50,000 which will be in our bank account on Friday morning. They also pay half of the completion guarantor's fee. This is real progress. Berliner have promised to send £100,000 if the now correct letter of credit is confirmed by not one but two other banks and if Senator sign a side letter which they don't want to sign. Eventually I persuade Senator to sign the side letter. However, when it comes through, it is completely illegible – not a single word can be read. My heart sinks as I call the bank to persuade them to accept this illegible document. I amaze myself by succeeding, but I promise to get a legible one.

April 20 I am still attempting to prise the first £200,000 from Berliner Bank, and Janet and I are also trying to persuade Sogapaq to sign a 'notice of assignment' for the banks. We succeed with Senator over a conference call at 9 am on Friday but not with Sogapaq. The letters of credit are confirmed. The bank wires £100,000 to our bank account on Friday morning. We start shooting Friday afternoon up at Burnham Beeches. The Steadicam operator trips and falls and destroys the camera. The footage is fine but the operator is injured. Though we haven't paid the insurance premiums, I am assured we are covered for this. In any case the operator isn't badly hurt. What a start! We decide that we can start shooting officially on Monday 24 April, even though we don't have full drawdown. We need a further £1 million by the end of next week. I reassure everyone that we will complete the documentation in a few days and the million pounds will be sent.

April 24 To obtain full drawdown of the cash we need for *The Hollow Reed*, we still have a lot to do. The bank requires Eurimages to sign a mutual funding letter, issued to them last week. The lawyer there is very awkward but Angela Jackson (whom I have hired to take care of this for me) does a brilliant job and the agreement is amended and signed. Sogapaq too come on board at long last and sign the additional documents the bank needs. Ditto the others. The bank holds out till the very last moment, always asking for extra things. The first day of photography on *Hollow Reed* has gone well.

April 25 More of the same with one big difference – the bank agrees to fund. One million pounds is sent to the production bank account and I secretly whoop for joy. The pressure is off for the moment. I decide that this weekend I will go to Bath (where they are shooting) to see what Angela Pope (the director), Liz Karlsen (the producer) and everyone are doing with such hard-won cash!

April 27 Marin Karmitz of MK2 and producer of all the recent Kieslowski movies has his head of acquisitions Christine Rau telephone us to tell us that they love *The Hollow Reed* and would like to meet with me about it. I send him and Christine a press kit. It is also the Euroscript script incentive funding application deadline. We were awarded a large one last year and have found the Euroscript fund an absolute lifesaver for developing projects independently. We have already put four Euroscript-funded projects into production and expect to put at least another one before the cameras this year.

April 29–30 I am driven down to Bath with my family to see Liz (Karlsen), meet the members of the cast whom I have not yet met, and see the results of our labours. On arrival I see about an hour's worth of rushes. They are impressive – confident, well lit, and the performances are already coming through: the boy (Sam Bould) is, I think, going to make it. I go to the set which today is a motorway construction site where the actor Jason Flemyng is showing Sam what he does at work. Jason is very funny – showing us a mechanical penis! Martin Donovan (who plays the lead role) also arrives for the last shot. We just get that shot in before Sam has to stop work.

May 3 Los Angeles. Meeting with Jeff Berg, the head of ICM who loves *The Neon Bible* and would like to represent it for North America. We discuss terms (same as for *The Crying Game*), and then he takes, in our presence, a long call from Madonna, about the arrangements for her preparations for Alan Parker's new film *Evita* – fascinating stuff. Jeff is a sophisticated man – strangely un-agentlike. Meetings with him are always short, civilised and productive. Phone conversations (other than with Madonna) never last more than a minute.

May 14 London. I watch selected rushes of *The Hollow Reed* in Channel Four's state-of-the-art projection room with David Aukin (Head of Drama) and the writer Paula Milne. We know that Angela is unhappy with one shot – the penultimate shot of the film in fact. We decide to edit together the film and then decide the whys and wherefores of reshooting it. David loves the rushes, which is very important.

May 17 I started the day with my first breakfast meeting for some months (I try to avoid them, preferring, when pushed, lunches and dinners). But I agree to do this one as the person I'm meeting – Mike 'I'll finance your film' Mendelsohn, head of the film department at the LA arm of the French bank Paribas – is a very elusive man. I have to meet him now as I'll probably never get him on his own at Cannes. I have to know whether he will provide the balance of the finance on *Vicious Circles* (an erotic thriller set in Paris). I already have an offer for a deal for three-quarters of a million dollars from Trimark [US production company]. He tells me that if I can get Trimark to increase their offer, then he will provide the balance. I ponder this. Should I put my new Trimark relationship at risk on the word of Mendelsohn that he will provide the balance unconditionally. I decide to think about it.

When I return to my office in Soho, it's pointed out to me that my friend Michael Kuhn [President of Polygram Filmed Entertainment] has written an article for *The Independent* – 'a mogul's view' of Cannes. Michael tells readers that if they want expert advice on how to get into Cannes parties and dinner uninvited they should 'ask producer Nik Powell'. I fax Michael claiming I'm hurt by his implication that (a) I'm not invited to the parties I want to go to so I have to crash them and (b) that I'm an expert on such matters. I tell him that I already have invites from Troma, Trimark and the BFI. I decide not to invite him to our exclusive *Neon Bible* dinner, but rather to give him expert advice on how to crash it – 'Just turn up, Michael.'

May 18   After a one and a half hour wait on the tarmac at Heathrow we take off for Cannes and arrive just in time for me to make my first meeting at Cannes with Senator's lawyers to reach detailed agreement on the outstanding contracts for *The Hollow Reed*. There are six more to be agreed and signed and it will take the next ten days to achieve this.

May 19   I have a meeting with the French co-producers of our low-budget Paris-set thriller *Vicious Circles*. Then it's my first trip down the Croisette, the strip of seafront that connects all the big hotels – the Martinez, Carlton, Noga, Hilton, Grand and Majestic – to the 'new' Palais at its far end. That means a lot of glad-handing and awkward smiling, with people only half-recognising each other. As I am also being followed by a TV camera it is particularly slow and embarrassing.

My next meeting is with Ian Jessel, one of the pioneers of the independent film pre-sales market. He has just formed a new company, Condor, and wants six to eight pictures a year in the $10–20 million budget range. I present *Vicious Circles*, which, after I explain the story, his acquisitions executive seems keen to read. The story involves a kind of sex harness. She jokes that she has three such harnesses and invites me to check them out in case we want to borrow them for the film.

I finish off the afternoon by having a drink with Emma Clarke, Fineline's London rep who might be interested in buying *The Hollow Reed* for North America. Erica, my girlfriend, meets me at the Majestic bar and we go off to Michael Kuhn's party for *The Usual Suspects*. I'm not invited. At least I thought I wasn't. But I wanted to go to Michael's party precisely because I wasn't invited. I figured that after his comments in *The Independent* he felt he didn't need to invite me. Anyway he's very welcoming when I arrive. Stewart Till (now the number two at PolyGram films) invites me to the Pamela Anderson dinner at the PolyGram villa. I accept with great relief. My twelve-year-old daughter arrives tomorrow and would kill me if she couldn't go. I go to the toilet and while I'm in the cubicle my daughter calls me to ask what she should bring. I tell her about Pamela Anderson.

May 20   There are several big events today. After a couple of meetings in the morning, my bankers, Berliner Bank, arrive at the Majestic to meet with EMG, a Paris-based financial organisation. Conversation isn't easy – my bankers speak English and German, I speak English and 'Anglo-French' (English vocabulary given a French pronunciation) and EMG's senior executive speaks no English at all. After the remaining technicalities have been sorted out, I attempt to cross the language barriers by trying to tell my favourite Cannes stories in French. One of them is about Lenny Henry, who, having been invited by a US distributor to David Bowie's boat, arrives to find no Bowie there. He asks the US distributor where the Thin White Duke is, and is told that David couldn't make it to Cannes this year but always sends his boat. Next year, replies Lenny, I think I'll send my car! This goes down well.

I take my daughter, stepdaughter and girlfriend to the Pamela Anderson party. Pamela Anderson is everything she's cracked up to be. Her husband, Tommy, a rock n'roll drummer is either glued lip to lip to her or throwing up in the toilet. They really are the classic beauty-and-the-beast couple. Tommy, by all accounts, has cleared a bottle of Old Kentucky in the limo from Hotel du Cap to the villa. Someone asks me why PolyGram are backing *Barb Wire*. But when you see radiant Michael Kuhn standing between Pamela and her lookalike manager, you know why he's making the film. The wife of Michael Hamlyn (producer of *Priscilla*) says she just wants to feel Anderson's breasts in the interests of science. There was a large transfer image of Anderson in her movie pose somehow stuck to the bottom of the pool. Michael invites the journalists to ask Pamela, if not about Brecht, then about her role in the movie. The journalists (and Pamela apparently) think he said 'breasts'. Perhaps they haven't heard of Brecht.

May 22   I have my second lunch in a month with Stephen Dorrell [then Secretary of State for National Heritage]. He is in relaxed form. Naturally he can't tell us what he will announce on 6 June. But it is clear that there has been a change of heart – he now accepts that this is a vibrant, outward-looking, international industry, full of small producer-entrepreneurs who are making a worldwide impact with their films – not a dying industry full of moaning minnies asking for handouts. This is quite a sea change for us.

Then it's back down the Croisette to Trimark to finish off my North American deal for *Vicious Circles* and to see if they are interested in the foreign distribution rights. I'm successful.

May 23   The world premiere of Terence Davies' *The Neon Bible*. It has already been screened to the press this morning, to both cheers and some boos. In the afternoon it gets a reasonable reception. We all climb the traditional red carpet. Gena Rowlands is a sensation. The film is projected in an auditorium of almost total silence. It is one of the toughest screenings I've ever attended. Terence's work demands a faith that is difficult to sustain in such a large and potentially belligerent auditorium. We survive nevertheless, and it is warmly received.

June 2   London. Over to Channel Four to catch up with the rushes from *The Hollow Reed*, which continue to move towards revealing the heart of the film. I then discuss with my bankers my new post-Cannes finance plan for *Vicious Circles*. They are not yet satisfied with it. This is fortunate as it saves

12

me having to tell them that last night one of the major financiers (Trimark) withdrew their offer for 'foreign' (not North America) upon which the finance plan is based. This enables me simply to tell my bankers that I will 'rejig' the finance plan to accord more closely with their requirements and come up with another way to do it.

June 6   I go down to Channel Four to see *The Hollow Reed* rushes. We are all a little concerned about the scene where the mother (Joely Richardson) first catches her boyfriend beating up the child. I feel we need more tension, that we may need to film more inserts or something. I call Liz Karlsen and explain my worries, telling her that if we are going to reshoot anything then it has to be done before the kitchen set is taken down. She says they are going to try to have another go at the scene.

June 9   More *Hollow Reed* rushes. They are very encouraging. That afternoon filming is going well. Liz and I discuss the deal for the sound-track. It's to be done by Zbigniew Preisner who did the Kieslowski *Three Colours* trilogy. We discuss ideas for songs and who might re-record them. We have a new and appropriate demo from Elvis Costello which we would like Angela to use in the film.

July 4   I meet with my bankers in order to move forward the financing of *Vicious Circles*. They are very keen but want a full foreign-sales report on *The Neon Bible* from Miramax before committing to *Vicious Circles*.

July 5   Today is Eurimages day and we have to get our application finished. I have arranged for Frank, my business affairs assistant, to jump on a plane to Strasbourg to make sure it gets there on time. I meet with Heather Mansfield from Screen Partners in order to determine which bank we will be doing *Vicious Circles* with if we do it with Heather rather than Berliner. We decide to speak with both Robert Morrice of Royal Bank of Canada and Daiwa, both of whom apparently accept Screen Partners' insured estimates guarantee.

July 6   First myself and then Frank go over the deal memo we need Trimark to sign in order to do 'foreign' on *Vicious Circles*. There are, I should explain, four or five different ways to complete the funding of *Vicious Circles* and all of them will be appearing in the diary. The funding is as follows: Trimark are putting up $750,000 for North America (this is signed); Polygram $300,000 for France (under negotiation); Ibero $125,000 for Spain (sort of signed); BSkyB $150,000 for the UK pay TV; and EMG a guarantee against the rest of British rights. This means we need around $1 million from the rest of 'foreign'. My options are as follows: (1) Berliner cash flow it against Trimark's estimates (in this scenario Trimark to up an extra $250,000 for North America); (2) Kuzui put up the balance via a Japanese presale plus equity (this might take too long); (3) Screen Partners together with either Royal Bank of Canada or Daiwa put up the

13

balance (this is both complicated and expensive but nevertheless a possibility; (4) Condor put up a guarantee for foreign, although they would want script changes which I have not had the opportunity to address with my writer/director; (5) Eurimages, in which case I would need to put back my start date – and it's not enough.

At 6 pm we screen the latest cut of *The Hollow Reed*, making sure that we have invited one or two people who haven't seen it before. We retire afterwards to the pub opposite Twickenham Studios (where it's being cut). The big question is should the mother know right from the beginning that her boyfriend is threatening her child (as in the shooting draft of the script), or should she find this out suddenly and shockingly? I urge the latter on the basis that the audience will more fully understand her subsequent turmoil – not only is she shocked by the discovery itself but she also realises how totally she has been deceived, as much by her own desire to be deceived as by the deception itself. Joely Richardson plays this impossible role quite brilliantly and we must give the audience all the help we can by structuring the cut properly. We agree to do this.

July 7 I visit Timothy Burrill with Frank to review our Eurimages application. As the UK's board member his support is vital to a successful application. He offers his help in getting *The Hollow Reed* Eurimages monies cash-flowed but is pessimistic about having any effect. I tell him that this one is difficult because it's the first time they have done a Scala project and had to deal with Scala-style financing. I am sure that, once a boilerplate contract is worked out, any future productions will flow much more easily – famous last words!

July 8 Los Angeles. I arrive at the apartment where I am to stay and where both Sandy Whitelaw and Penny Du Pont (director and casting director of *Vicious Circles*) have been seeing actresses all week. Sandy shows me a fifteen-minute exert of Angelina Jolie acting in a very, very low-budget movie. She is something else. We all agree that Angelina is head and shoulders above all the others we have seen so far. She really can act. She's exciting. She's sexy. Unfortunately, I discover she also has a reputation for being 'difficult'. She is the lead in Iain Softley's new movie *Hackers*. I call Iain who confirms this but recommends her unreservedly. We agree to arrange another meeting between Angelina and Sandy as both Angelina and Sandy still have reservations.

July 10 I spend all morning down at Trimark since they are heavily involved in *Vicious Circles*. I get both Barry Barnholtz (head of acquisitions) and Sergio Aquerra (foreign) to approve Angelina Jolie.

July 11 Sandy and I meet with Angelina. I arrive late. Angelina hands us a neatly written two-page note headed 'Concerns re the nude scenes'. Angelina (or rather her mother as it turns out; later there is another revelation – Angelina's father is Jon Voight) has counted the number of

14

nude scenes. There are fifteen of them. The note suggests that her body only be gradually revealed – perhaps her breasts should first appear, Angelina suggests, in scene thirty-six when she first tries on the sex harness (which is such a big feature of the film). Sandy and myself are not opposed to such a gradual revelation. However, she will not do any pubic nudity, nor will she consent to a body double. Sandy argues that this is absolutely essential. In a European-set sex thriller we see no reason to pull our punches. Her objections are not political or feminist, but personal. She just does not want to see herself or others to see her, or in the case of a body double, think they see her, nude. In any event, her strong-mindedness is, I think, quite a shock to Sandy. Most actresses either pass on the material completely because of the nudity or else agree to it.

July 18 London. Another screening of *The Hollow Reed*. It is really beginning to work now (although I miss the first ten minutes). The structure is now almost right, so proper editing can at last begin.

August 21 Los Angeles. First I have to meet with Frank Agrama, chairman of the TV company New Harmony, and Ian Jessel, head of Condor, its film subsidiary. We 'line-by-line' the draft deal memo I had sent them for *Vicious Circles* the previous week. This painstaking task is done not without humour. I feel very pleased with myself because both Berliner's offer letter and Trimark's long-promised contract have materialised. My agreement with them cuts out other complex financing and has everything I want: a flexible approach that gives me the freedom to make my own deals, should I so choose, in UK, Japan, France and Spain.

September 6 London. An important day. Hanno Huth, the boss of Senator, the second largest investor in *The Hollow Reed*, is to screen the film for the very first time together with his head of sales, Edward Noeltner. Jennie Casarotto and a couple of others also attend. I nervously seat them in the screening room and after the film has started return to the office to draft an important letter to Trimark. I return to see the last part of the film, having bought takeaway coffees for Hanno and Edward. The film is very powerful and never fails to move me. Hanno and Edward like it a lot.

September 18 I rang Timothy Burrill, the UK's Eurimages board member, for a last-minute chat about our *Vicious Circles* application. Apparently there are still 'technical problems' with our application. We had 'licensed' our rights to our Spanish co-producers (even though we had a co-production agreement with them). It was suggested I ring their lawyer directly. After a long discussion, I think I understand the changes she requires. I ask Frank to have a go at drafting a letter for our co-producers to sign with the necessary amendments and to send it to Elizabeth at Eurimages for her approval. I also call our director who wants an extra rewrite fee and agree to meet him at the end of the week at Dinard to resolve this and many other major issues.

September 28 At Twickenham studios for a screening of *The Hollow Reed* to check the final dub. It is not a success. The score is not working at all in the first two reels. Angela is crestfallen and depressed. We quickly agree a new plan of action, to strip off much of the score in the first twenty-five minutes and to take out another five minutes or more. We also decide to try some other types of music or radio and to invite Preisner (the composer) over to see the film to get his suggestions. We decide to rescreen it the following Monday.

October 2 We rescreen *The Hollow Reed* with David Aukin and Sarah Geater from Channel Four at the screening room at Planet Hollywood. Again there are problems – the mix and the score are still not working. We decide to rescreen it in a different screening room to see whether the mix really is too busy and to give ourselves time to think about it. However, the five minutes that are cut are a big improvement and we all agree that this cut works brilliantly. It is only a matter of time before we sort out both score and mix to our satisfaction.

Mark Shivas

A major figure in British television and cinema for the past twenty-five years, Mark Shivas is currently Head of Films at the BBC. The following extracts give a flavour of a producer/commissioner's frenetic working life. General aspects of the Corporation's financial situation also (inevitably) intrude into Shivas' account.

April 2   In the evening I leave messages for the MacKinnon brothers to wish them luck with *Easterhouse* which they are starting to shoot for us tomorrow morning. This is largely financed by BBC Films, with the Glasgow Film Fund. Andrea Calderwood, Head of Drama BBC Scotland, and I are executive producers. Gillies and Billy wrote it together. It's loosely based on their lives in 1968 and if it resembles anything it's *My Life as a Dog*.

April 5   Meeting to update Alan Yentob [Controller, BBC1] and Michael Jackson [Controller, BBC2] on plans for BBC Films over the coming months. George Faber [Head of Single Dramas] usually comes to these routine meetings but he's tried to cancel the meeting because it now seems as though the budgets for five of my ten features may come out of his budget, thus reducing his spend and numbers horribly. It goes well. It's quite jokey and Alan and Michael play a game of saying, 'You have that film on your channel, I want this one on mine.' I tell them that this is embarrassing for me and to please stop it. They seem to like all the projects this time. Sometimes I get less than enthusiastic responses.

April 7   Watch rushes of *Easterhouse* which are arriving daily on cassette. Gillies MacKinnon really has a great eye. The performances are terrific, though the Scots accents are occasionally a problem. But the work is delightful.

April 10   A very early morning in the office. Many calls. Proof-read brochure for BBC Films that must be ready for Cannes. Sally Hibbin [Executive Producer] says that *Land and Freedom*, Ken Loach's film about the Spanish Civil War, has been well received in Spain on its opening there. *El Pais* raved!

   6 pm – Charles Denton [Head of Drama Group, BBC] has called a pre-meeting about something wished on the whole of Network Television by Broadcasting House called Performance Review. It will happen tomorrow at 8.30 in front of Will Wyatt [Managing Director, Network Television, BBC], Alan Yentob and Michael Jackson and the object is to review Drama's performance over the past year. A vast document has been written on the subject, taking weeks of one person's time.

April 11   So we assemble – all the heads of Drama, including Regional Drama. There's no criticism, or praise either, of BBC Films there. A certain amount of retilling of old ground over series that didn't work and why. The question of funding my films comes up. It still seems to be coming out of George Faber's budget in the midst of all the cuts he's suffering.

April 12   Flight to Glasgow for the shooting of *Easterhouse*. It's warm and sunny there and therefore hard to recognise! Steve Clark Hall, the admirable and pleasant co-producer of the film, meets me at the airport. Scott Thomas is the editor – he was assistant editor on *A Private Function* in 1984 – and we see twenty minutes of cut footage on the screen. It's hot in the edit suite but it's very pleasing stuff and Gillies is doing a great job as we all knew he would – he and I had worked together on *The Grass Arena* a few years earlier.

We go out to the set – it's the ninth day of shooting – in Bishopbriggs. They're on their lunch hour. Billy MacKinnon, Gillies' brother, is there with a Leica camera round his neck, more relaxed than I've ever seen him. I meet John de Borman, the cameraman, and some of the cast. Watch a bit of shooting with thirteen-year-old 'Lex' being pulled through a window. Steve and I are on our mobile phones talking to London. 'What did we do without them?' asks Steve. We managed happily enough. It was nice to be out of touch sometimes.

My visit was just a go-and-smile-at-them/tell-them-what-a-good-job-they're-doing sort of visit. The best thing an executive producer can do. Unless, of course, they aren't.

April 21   There have been calls from Nick Hellen of *The Sunday Times* and Richard Brooks of *The Observer* on the BBC's cash crisis and how it bites into drama. I speak to Philippa Giles who's already been called by Nick Hellen because Rodney Baker Bates, the BBC's chief accountant, is apparently saying that some of this is caused by there being too many programmes and films 'on the shelf' untransmitted, including two of our films. It's true that *Great Moments in Aviation* hasn't found theatrical distribution in this country and it will be aired later this year, but *Two Deaths* only finished post-production two months earlier. Why did I come back a day earlier? I could have missed all this if I'd returned Monday. I call Nick in the evening and manage to squash the idea of *Two Deaths* languishing in stock.

April 22   I unwisely pick up the phone when it rings at home instead of listening to the machine first. It's Richard Brooks. He's writing a piece for tomorrow's *Observer*. He's got lots of off-the-record stuff from other BBC producers. I say I don't mind being quoted as saying that I don't understand why a deal to reduce borrowing agreed with the government more than a year ago has taken so long to reach programme-makers, in the form of a sudden crisis in April (though I knew of it in February).

April 23   My script executive, Stephanie Guerrasio, arrives in a taxi at 5.15 to take us to the Palladium for the BAFTA awards. Crowds line both sides of Panton Street as we walk from the cab. Screams break out, though not for us. Joan Collins is jiggling along behind us in clinging beige and full warpaint. The Alexander Korda Award for Best British Film goes to *Shallow Grave* and not *Priest*, alas. *Skallagrigg*, which I put into production for Screen Two, wins best television film. Gratifying.

April 24 Meeting with Charles Denton. We discuss the 'cash crisis' in Network Television. Nick Hellen's piece ran in *The Sunday Times* yesterday but was short and not really to the point. Richard Brooks had used the quote in *The Observer*. Always dangerous in terms of BBC politics, but there are always so many cowardly unattributable remarks in pieces about the BBC. But everyone who works there signs a contract which forbids talking to the press direct. Charles tells me he's losing the argument that BBC Films budget doesn't come out of the Single Drama budget. The BBC's commitment to feature films has been stated by Will Wyatt to Parliament and the Governors. I've always assumed that will be impossible to go back on.

I have been summoned to a meeting at Will Wyatt's office at 3pm. Undoubtedly for bad news. Charles and Michael Jackson are there. Will tells us that after production of *The Van* everything is frozen in terms of my spend for the rest of the year.

April 25 Meeting to discuss setting up BBC Films as a separate commercial arm. Afterwards Charles Denton tells George and me that Nick Elliott, the present Head of Series, is leaving the BBC to run drama at the ITV Network Centre. He's only been here a few months, brought in to 'reverse' the BBC's drama series from its so called slump. Who can blame him for leaving an organisation where decisions are subject to so many conflicting interests?

April 27 George Faber sends a memo to Will Wyatt suggesting from now on that 'all theatric commitments should have his editorial and financial approval in the same way Screen One and Screen Two propositions currently do'. Oh no they mustn't. This will need more fighting back than I thought.

May 1 At dawn I pen a long memo to Will Wyatt underlining the potentially destructive results of going back on the £5 million commitment to features.

May 2 I pick up *Variety* early in the morning to read that *An Awfully Big Adventure* has been chosen for the Directors' Fortnight at Cannes. Why has no one told me? I call Hilary Heath who says they were only told on Friday and that it was the last film Pierre-Henri Deleau, organiser of the Fortnight, chose. Good news, though.

May 4 At the Drama Board Charles describes my funds as 'frozen' to the others. Afterwards, Andrea Calderwood, Robert Cooper [Head of Drama, BBC Northern Ireland], George Faber and Tessa Ross [Independent

Commissioning Executive, BBC] agree to meet in my office on Tuesday to plan a fight back.

May 10   8.30 breakfast with Michael Jackson. I've asked for this meeting to explain what a bargain the feature films are for him – an average budget of £500,000 and almost unlimited runs. He seems persuaded, but there's more work to be done with him in this area. I've got somewhere.

May 11   At 20th Century-Fox in Soho Square for the start of the pre-Cannes press show of *Land and Freedom*. Important that the critics realise BBC Films is a part of this film.

May 12   Fly to Glasgow for the last day of shooting of the MacKinnons' *Easterhouse*. There's snow on the ground. The runner drives me to meet Colin Cameron, head of BBC Scotland, in their offices. Colin would like to do a party for *Easterhouse* at the Edinburgh Festival. Fine by me. I visit the location in the Exhibition Hall where they're doing several interiors, notably the art gallery at night. That evening a party is laid out in Henry Wood Hall, a converted church. It fills up slowly and I find myself dancing 'Strip the Willow' and the 'Dashing White Sergeant' which I haven't done in ages. It's a cheerful, happy night and the film's going to be really good.

May 14   Back in London. In the evening, I go to the end of the cast and crew screening at BAFTA of *Two Deaths* which most people say they like. Some are really taken with it. Mind you cast and crew should be, if anyone is to be. But they stay a long time after.

May 15   Andrew Eaton, the producer of *Jude*, comes in the afternoon to discuss the £4.3 million budget.

May 17   Tom Rothman [President of Production, 20th Century-Fox] calls to say that *Variety* have asked him whether he denies Fox Searchlight is in *The Van* with us. He says he can't do that, so the story is out. He has drafted a press release which he faxes through. I alter a little of it and add my own statement.

May 21   Cannes. At 11 am, on the Carlton terrace, Andrew Eaton, Michael Winterbottom and Sheila Fraser Milne [Producer, Director and Associate Producer respectively of *Jude*] are already with Claudia Lewis and Bob Aaronson from Fox Searchlight to discuss *Jude*. Tom Rothman arrives late, pale and, he says, drugged out of his mind with some sleeping pills Claudia gave him that he didn't take till 3 am. But the upshot is that he finds the script too depressing to be sure he wants to come in on it. Do people want this sort of thing when there's just been the Oklahoma City bombing? he asks rhetorically.
  At 1 pm Steph, Michael, Andrew, Sheila Fraser Milne and I are at UGC

[Union Générale Cinématographie – French distributor, exhibitor and production company] on their roof terrace opposite the Palais for lunch with Louisa Dent and Patrick Binet of UGC. The upshot is that they like *Jude* enormously but they couldn't finance it without a major partner like Fox. And Tom is less than enthused as we know. We tell them that we're seeing PolyGram next, who do seem keen to do the lot.

Our next meeting is indeed at PolyGram's office along the Croisette. Stewart Till and Aline Perry are mighty keen and, subject to board approval, Stewart says, would like to be our only partners. The movie's budgeted at £4.3 million. This seems as good a result as we could get. Does Andrew know that it isn't usually this easy?! Michael Winterbottom has a number of projects and his name's mentioned in connection with many. And Hoss's [Hossein Amini's] script is wonderful, as most people who read it recognise.

May 22 Meetings in the office with Sally Hibbin and Carole Myer about tickets for *Land and Freedom* and the party. The business of tickets for events and parties here assumes absurd importance and brings out the worst in people. Sometimes it's not that you want to go, just that you want to be invited!

Steph and I are in our evening finery on our way to the *Land and Freedom* screening for a talk with Joni Sighvatsson and his lawyer Nigel Sinclair at the Majestic Business Centre, which is appallingly hot. We're sitting dangerously close to the Miramax offices. I particularly don't want to see Harvey Weinstein because he may be difficult about the Fox deal on *The Van*.

At 6.30 Geoffrey, Steph, Sarah, Michael Jackson and I forgather in the Majestic bar. Two glasses of champagne cost £20. Steph, Jackson and I are in the group that will go up the red carpeted steps in the Palais with Loach, the producer Rebecca O'Brien, Sally Hibbin, some of the co-producers – Spanish, German – and the cast. It's great for Jackson's first Cannes visit. Surely he'll catch the bug? As we go up the steps, cameras popping, some of the cast sing the Internationale. A wonderful sight and sound, when we're all wearing dinner jackets, surrounded by people who've spent a fortune on tickets, on the red carpet, in a France that has just elected Chirac.

The film plays wonderfully. The applause at the end starts with the end credits, continues throughout them and last for minutes as the lights go up and Ken and the cast stand up. It's incredibly moving. And a triumph. The party for *Land and Freedom* is in Vieux Cannes on the hill overlooking the town. It's in a tent, which isn't needed because the weather is warm and fine. But nothing too posh and fancy, as befits the film. We introduce Michael Jackson to as many people as possible.

May 23 Meeting at 9 am, again on the Grand Hotel terrace below our offices, with Lynda [Myles, Producer of *The Van*], Billy Hinshelwood (her lawyer) and Gretta Finer (our lawyer), to discuss further points on *The Van*/Fox deal. And we've now received a letter from Harvey Weinstein's lawyers, so that needs discussion too. At 9.45 Gretta and I visit Stewart Till again and he outlines a potential structure for a deal on *Jude*. I assume his board will come good, as does he. We now have to stop talking to UGC and anyone else.

Michael Jackson, who was to leave this morning, has been finally persuaded to stay for the BBC lunch. Charles Denton is arriving from London this morning to host the lunch as planned. I discuss with Carole the way to present this to the world. If Charles was coming on the understanding that he's to give a speech then he must. My solution is that Charles talks, introduces Jackson, who talks and 'points out' George and me. Anyway, when Charles arrives I tell him the plan, he tells us what he's to say and Jackson writes a little speech. Jackson has already told me later that he'll want to come next year.

At 5 pm, the William Morris party at the Carlton. On the way up in the elevator Lew Grade gives me advice: 'Mark, make some pictures that make money.'

May 27 *Land and Freedom* mightily tipped for a major award by the critics – the front runners being the Kusturica [*Underground*], the Angelopoulos [*Ulysses' Gaze*], *La Haine* and the Loach. *Land and Freedom* has won the International Critics' Prize and some kind of Ecumenical Award. Sally interprets this as a bad sign – likely consolation prizes for not getting anything bigger.

May 28 I've decided to stay till Monday. If *Land and Freedom* wins something from the main jury, I want to be there as the BBC Films rep. As we arrive on the beach, Carole Myer says she's heard we have no major prizes. I'm disbelieving, but it turns out to be true.

June 9 London. Andrea Calderwood and I join the MacKinnons, Steph and Scott Thomas, the editor, for a screening on video of *Easterhouse* at Columbia Tri-Star in Wells Street. The image is a little squashed, the sound isn't good and the picture quality less than wonderful. Even so the film is really splendid with great performances from everyone. Afterwards we discuss a very few things that need clarifying or seem over long. Then the vexed question of the title that can't be *Easterhouse* because it no longer takes place there. I go home at 11 pm leaving Gillies, Andrea and Stephanie. Billy goes too. The only title seems now to be *Let It Come Down*, a line from the film. I don't like it much and say so, but five of us will never agree on one title, so I say OK.

June 15 Screening of *Easterhouse*, on which Gillies has now done the work we discussed before. Those pieces now work better and the film is very satisfying. Also, it's better to be alert in the morning rather than see it at 5 pm on a Friday.

June 16–26 In tropical climes for a break. Very therapeutic.

Sarah Atkinson, my PA, faxed on Tuesday the 20th, the first day the office let them know where I was staying, to ask me to call Tom Rothman in LA. I did. Miramax has filed a suit in LA against Fox, the BBC and Roddy Doyle. Tom describes it as 'plain vanilla'. Bert Fields, the lawyer, Tom says, laughed and is unruffled. It'll take Harvey [Weinstein, Head of Miramax] three years to get a date. He hadn't moved for an injunction which shows how unserious he is.

On the 22nd comes this fax from Stephanie:

Dear Mark

I'm glad your arms are not long enough to reach me – because you might feel the impulse to violence: Carole, Alison, Jane Wright and Sue B-S are very, very unhappy and unconfident about the title *Let It Come Down*. Gillies and Billy's confidence has been somewhat shaken by this reaction from the sales and marketing fronts and all of this has again raised the issue of the only other title acceptable to both brothers. I am sorry to have to tell you that at the meeting which Carole called today at the Sales Co. for all of us plus Andrea, Sales Company and Worldwide people have urged us to agree to call the film *Small Faces*. Andrea – whilst still preferring *Let It Come Down* – will accept it if you will. As far as my two cents go, I think you know I've always felt that the film is so full of extraordinary faces – both living and in works of art – that the right campaign would really make this work; and I guess you know that the brothers have always marginally preferred it. We here in the Smoke eagerly, nay anxiously, await word from on high.
Jane pp SG

I agree to it reluctantly. I've never thought you should use the word 'small' in a film title.

July 11 BBC Drama autumn launch at the Barbican, which Charles Denton presents. It gives a taste of the goodies to come over the next year, and it's primarily for the press. We've rewritten and remade the piece on *Small Faces*. That and *Land and Freedom* are our only two features in the launch. Rebecca O'Brien from the latter and Gillies and Billy MacKinnon from the former are present.

July 14 I get to the Edinburgh Film Festival launch at BAFTA before 11 am to make sure, by talking to Mark Cousins and Ginnie Atkinson, that Gillies and *Small Faces* get a good mention in Mark's presentation. We have far more films in Edinburgh than Channel Four this year, with both our features and the TV films. I'm concerned they don't all seem to be TV films. And while we want publicity for *Small Faces* as a Scots screening on its, nearly, home turf, that screening must not put off the Venice and Toronto festivals from playing it. A delicate balance. Mark Cousins asks me to host scriptwriter Suso Cecchi D'Amico's scene-by-scene there – I'm delighted.

July 24 *Jude* begins official pre-production today. Chris Eccleston is the only one cast so far.

August 4 During the last days I've been phoning and discussing the flyer for *Small Faces* with Gillies, Billy, Jane Wright [BBC Worldwide] and Carole Myer [Head of the Sales Company]. I'm convinced the shot solely of Lex with a plaster on his nose gives the impression of a film I wouldn't want to see. So discussion has gone back and forth on this. At about 4.30 I go over to the Barlby Road studios where Gillies is in the last hours of dubbing *Small Faces* and tell him my opinion. He reluctantly says, well, it's the marketing people who know about marketing. So he'll roll over. But he still likes the Lex picture! The last couple of reels look/sound great with the music I've never heard on them before. I really like this film and pray that others will, too.

August 22 At lunch time I take a flight to Dublin where I'm met by one of the drivers on *The Van* who takes me to the Westbury Hotel to leave my bags and then on to Ardmore Studios. Lynda Myles is there. Almost the minute I arrive we go on set just at the moment they're having tea. Stephen looks happy. The next scene is with Colm Meaney mooning so the producer will sit that one out. Roddy Doyle is there in the office involved in a little proofreading. He, like Lynda, is on set most of the time. After a couple of hours I go back to the hotel to do some reading. At 6 pm Lynda picks me up and we go off to see rushes, which are funny and vital and rather beautiful.

August 23 A walk and then to the airport for a plane to Edinburgh. In the evening Stephanie and I see Gillies MacKinnon's film *A Simple Twist of Fate* which Gillies introduces and then appears with its star Steve Martin afterwards. Martin does a brilliant half-hour of supposed question-and-answer about the film but which is really a comic turn.

August 25 Gillies' scene-by-scene on *The Grass Arena* takes us through the film almost moment by moment, spinning forward, and is riveting. I know that Suso's approach to her scene-by-scene on *Rocco* is to be very different. She has chosen six clips only. At 6.15 Suso, Caterina and I are on stage. Suso has the audience in the palm of her hand in minutes. We go for ninety minutes and Caterina is excellent when Suso slightly tires (she's eighty-one). We could probably have run much longer. At 8.15, the screening of *Small Faces* is packed. We're all tense. Allowing for one sound problem, the film plays wonderfully. It seems to triumph, but if it doesn't here in Edinburgh, where will it?

September 18 Screening of *Small Faces* to check sound problems at Fox in Soho Square at 10 am. Lunch with Gillies, Billy and Stephanie. I have a meeting I requested with Will Wyatt in the afternoon to tell him news on BBC Films progress, to keep him up to date.

September 29   Guild have made an offer for the UK rights to *Small Faces*, a surprise because it's the first 'small' movie they've bought. They're more known for Carolco fare.

October 20   Train via York to Edinburgh where the sun is beating down. I'm there to visit *Jude* on location in the Royal Mile tomorrow.

October 21   Early to Parliament Square. The skies are overcast today. The square is crowded with extras in costume, cows and sheep in pens. Any modern give-aways on the buildings have been covered up. I find Andrew Eaton and am introduced to Eduardo Serra, the taciturn though excellent cameraman (the rushes have been great), and Chris Eccleston. They're doing scenes with Chris and Kate Winslet walking through crowds. I spend the morning and some of the afternoon there. It's good to be with a film unit again and one working really well together.

November 13   Charles Denton comes with a car to pick me up to go on to the Department of National Heritage to see them about the scheme voiced by Stephen Dorrell when he was Films Minister to start a cinema for showing British films in the centre of London. Both Charles and I are firmly against this proposal for ghettoising (surely the result?) small pictures.

November 17   At Twickenham to see an hour of material from *Jude* projected. Stewart Till is there too. It's wonderful, different-looking stuff and Chris Eccleston is definitely a star. It's immensely cheering. Discussions of Aline Perry [Polygram Film International] showing it to Gilles Jacob [Director of the Cannes Film Festival] for Cannes.
    Lynda Myles meets me at 4 pm at the Groucho for an update on *The Van*. The last nine days of shooting begin Sunday.

November 27   There's a piece by Derek Malcolm in the *Guardian* 'Provocations' column which, among other things, says the BBC has no film policy. Annoying. I see Howard Schuman's film *Nervous Energy* at a lunchtime screening in Wells Street. It has many virtues. As I leave I talk to Ann Scott, the producer. Howard is still inside the screening room, so I'll call him later. I'm at home in the afternoon reading. I call Derek Malcolm to propose a reply in the *Guardian*.

November 28   *The Van* finishes shooting today. Lynda calls in the afternoon and sounds mightily relieved.

Simon Relph

The third generation of his family to be involved in cinema, Simon Relph began his own career as an assistant director before becoming a producer. Between 1985 and 1991 he was the first chief executive of British Screen Finance, and he continues to be highly active in the industry and among other things is a Governor of the BFI and Vice-Chairman (Film) at BAFTA. These extracts find Relph in the process of completing Blue Juice, *his thirteenth film as producer.*

April 3 We began the mix of *Blue Juice* today. Danny Hambrook, a star graduate of the National Film and Television School, is in charge of the sound and this is his third film for me. Quite unusually though and very sensibly in my view, he was our sound recordist on the shoot and is now supervising all the post-production sound editing, particularly the effects.

The big business of the day is to show of the final cut to our French financiers and foreign sales agents Pandora. There is also a contingent from DDA who will be helping Pandora with international publicity. After apologies for the soundtrack, which is very rough, the screening begins. Happily the first graded print is excellent. All enjoy the movie (thank goodness) and we adjourn to join David Aukin and Bill Stephens for lunch to discuss the marketing and screening strategy for Cannes where the film will be launched. We have no intention to enter the film for any of the official sections in Cannes. It is intended as a mainstream, commercial, popular-appeal film for the youth market and the idea is to withhold access to the film until Cannes and then screen it late night on the first Monday in a two-hundred-seat cinema. Both sales agents want to follow that with a really good party but there is concern expressed that we shouldn't overdo the hype.

Channel Four and Pandora have been expecting us to come back with a price for the additional source music. Ever since *Four Weddings and a Funeral* made $250 million worldwide it has almost been impossible to persuade music publishers and record companies that there is any such thing as a low-budget British movie. Standard fees for record tracks start from £3,000 for publishing rights and £3,000 for recording per thirty seconds of music. On that basis ours would have cost £300,000 against a music budget of £50,000 and that was to include the score for the film as well. We have got it all down to £70,000 and we have £25,000 in the budget to set against that figure. We spent months trying to get a record company to agree to put up the extra cash and at the last moment we failed to do so. So we are relying on our financiers to come up with the balance. Luckily they feel good about the film and they know that it needs a really good track. We leave the meeting hopeful that they will support us.

April 11 Meeting of the jury which decides the winner of the David Lean Director's Award for BAFTA. There are four directors nominated: Mike Newell for *Four Weddings and a Funeral*; Robert Zemeckis for *Forrest Gump*; Krzysztof Kieslowski for *Three Colours Red*; and Quentin Tarantino for *Pulp*

Fiction – not an easy decision. The discussion lasts for two hours and the result is somewhat unexpected. As one of those who would have thought *Three Colours Red* was a masterpiece, I am surprised by how many people think it is not Kieslowski's best work. Despite Robert Zemeckis' skill, no one goes for *Forrest Gump*, *Pulp Fiction* is admired, but Tarantino's skill as director is rated second to the script, so it looks like Mike Newell will win for *Four Weddings* . . . The vote is secret and placed in a sealed envelope for the scrutineer but since the jury came to a kind of consensus before they voted, most people can guess what is in the envelope.

April 18   Final mixes are beginning today. It is good to spend as much time as possible in the mix or at least to be available to hear reels as they come together. The conflict here is between the music, which Peter Salmi and Carl Prechezer (director and writer of *Blue Juice*) want to dominate the film, and the effects, which Danny Hambrook and Paul Hamblin (mixer) don't want to lose. In the end we manage to have both.

April 23   The weekend is cut short because I have to be in London for the BAFTA Awards. The evening goes very well. Billy Connolly – very funny – keeps the whole thing going. I sat next to Chris Smith, the Shadow Heritage Minister, who is very frank about Labour's support for the film industry. A pleasure to meet him after so many years being represented by him in Parliament.

April 28   The first married print of *Blue Juice* screened at the Odeon West End. It looks very good but sounds a bit less so. We take the print back to De Lane Lea and find out that with some relief that there must be some fault in the Odeon sound system. Several principal cast come along and all seem to like the film.

May 20   Cannes. Organised a dinner that evening prior to the screening of *Blue Juice* for most of Channel Four's team and Sean Pertwee (the male lead), who has arrived from London. The screening at the Olympia went extremely well. Very full house and everybody seemed to enjoy it very much. It was followed by the 'Wave Rave' party at the beach which was fairly universally agreed to be the best party in Cannes this year. The only problem was getting in, even if you had a ticket.

May 21   Generally the reaction to the screening is good and Pandora and Film Four are pleased. Dropped in briefly to Kodak's Pavilion to find the National Heritage minister, Stephen Dorrell, there. Ann Skinner [British producer] and I were introduced to him and we chatted for a moment. I was requested by Wilf Stevenson [Director of the BFI] to attend a meeting with Stephen Dorrell at the European Pavilion just to reassure him that the BFI was using government money in a good way. Lynda Myles and I, as fellow Governors, have a very short but seemingly constructive discussion with him.

May 22 I pick up the *Daily Variety* to find an absolutely glowing review of *Blue Juice* which is very exciting. I carried it back to the flat and woke up Carl, who was understandably thrilled.

May 23 We have another market screening at 10 am. It was reasonably well attended. Although there are a few of the usual comings and goings, most people stay the course which is pleasing.

May 30 Back home. A rather frantic day trying to sort out problems to do with the all-important videotapes for *Blue Juice* which never seem to come out right. This is holding up delivery of the vital letter of approval from Technicolor, which when presented to the bank, achieves drawdown on the funds due from Pandora with which we can pay off our loan. The main problem has to do with the music and effects track which Pandora at the last minute has required to lay alongside the normal video transfer of the film itself. The issue is complicated by the fact that the usual transfers are being done at Channel Four but they don't have facilities for editing American standard NTSC tapes.

June 7 Afternoon meeting with Gail Pattinson and Sara Geater at Channel Four to reveal that we have spent £10,000 more on *Blue Juice* than our funding permitted. Also to discuss exploitation of music and a deal proposed by Jonathan Channon of EMI on behalf of his composers. Peter Salmi has done a brilliant job persuading EMI and Sony to let us have music tracks for use in the film at a fraction of the normal cost. Jonathan wants to see that he will get paid at the full rate if the film is a hit. Also some of our fees for producing and directing are deferred if we go over budget, but Channel Four, Pandora and ourselves have agreed to extend post-production and to increase the music budget for the film – and this, rather than any inefficiency on our part, is the explanation for our overspend. Everybody is very constructive and we leave the meeting feeling that Channel Four will be helpful.

July 4 Meeting with Carl Prechezer and Pete Salmi before we go to Channel Four to meet the new team at Channel Four distributors headed by Mick Southworth. It's clear that their enthusiasm for *Blue Juice* is considerable and that they are very pleased that it's going to be their first project. They have a date for the release of the film – 15 September, which is somewhat worrying given that the summer holidays are in between and nothing yet has been done about the preparation of artwork, trailers, etc.

July 14 Pete, Carl and I travel up to Cambridge for a festival screening. We were pleased to find, despite very little advanced publicity, a full house, which clapped loudly at the end. Cards were taken at the exit with marks: 5 for excellent, 4 for very good, 3 for good and so on. We were happy to discover that we had scored an average of 4.3.

August 14 *Blue Juice* posters are somewhat disappointing, it's hard to read the title and they're not hip enough for Pete and Carl, plus they're just that bit late. The intention was to have them in the cinemas five or six weeks before the opening. We obviously didn't allow quite enough time for the design and manufacturing process. The trailer is excellent but also late into the cinemas and the standee of Sean and Catherine [Zeta Jones, the female lead], which is being placed in cinema foyers, is also late but it does look good.

September 12 Early-morning meeting with Mick Southworth and the Channel Four Distribution team. I had expressed a lot of dissatisfaction the week before about the lack of advertising for *Blue Juice*'s opening this week and we are particularly concerned about the fact that we had been kept so much in the dark by Channel Four Distribution. The truth is they are run off their feet. This meeting is for Mick to tell us exactly what is going on. We are opening in thirty-five cinemas. The coverage is good. Fingers crossed that we do well.

September 19 A morning meeting with Sara Geater at Channel Four to discuss the final cost of the film and particularly about entitlement to remaining fees. Part of our fees were to be paid out of unspent contingency but in the end the contingency was used to extend post-production by mutual agreement. Channel Four generously offer to meet these payments out of the rebate on the completion guarantee fee. Frankly a relief.

September 20 An early-evening drink with Mick Southworth. We discuss how things are going on *Blue Juice*. The first week is certainly not great and much depends on how things go the following weekend. Peter and Carl are full of imaginative ideas about how to sell the film and to reach the audience we feel we are missing but frankly there's not much response from Mick. We realise that there is no more money to spend on the film but propose some fairly cheap ideas for stunts which might attract interest in the film. He seems unwilling to consider anything beyond the conventional approach, which is already in hand. Very disappointing.

September 21 The Dinard Festival is one of the high points of the British film producer's year, something to look forward to. In my case it is more interesting and unusual in that I am invited to be part of the jury.

September 22 On Friday morning we have a conference with French producers – this has become an annual event and has encouraged a great deal more co-production between France and Britain than there was before. I am whisked away a little early, before the meeting closes, for a lunch at the Talassa Hotel with the rest of the jury, all of whom, except for one Lithuanian, are French. None of us has seen any films yet so this is really just an opportunity to say hello. Among the films I see are *Funny Bones*, *Three Steps to Heaven* and *The Englishman Who Went up a Hill but Came down a Mountain*. Back to the hotel to change for the Gala Dinner,

29

after which the jury retire to the Grand Hotel for a preliminary session. It becomes clear that there is considerable accord between us all about which films should be given prizes.

September 24 There is a general feeling that none of the films is outstanding and that all are flawed. But everybody in the end agrees to give the Golden Hitchcock to *Funny Bones*, which is a highly original and imaginative piece of work. There is a lot of support for *Butterfly Kiss* as well and we decide to give the two actresses [Saskia Reeves and Amanda Plummer] a special prize for that. Normally the Golden Hitchcock carries with it a cash prize to help with the distribution of the film, but since *Funny Bones* is being distributed by Buena Vista and Gaumont, that seems a little absurd, so the Jury decides to switch the money from *Funny Bones* to *Butterfly Kiss*.

Julie Baines

In 1994 Julie Baines set up Dan Films with Sarah Daniel and Cilla Ware. This immediately led to two feature productions: Butterfly Kiss *and* Madagascar Skin. *This diary begins with Baines 'moonlighting' from Dan Films on an opera drama for the BBC. The Sales Company, mentioned in the diary, is owned by British Screen, BBC Worldwide and Zenith Productions and handles foreign sales of all rights for their films. PACT (Producers Alliance for Cinema and Television) is the trade association for the UK independent television and feature film production sector.*

April 3   The director, Peter Manuira, and I went on a recce to Hampton Court Palace which is to be the location for the film of Purcell's opera *Dido and Aeneas*. I am doing the project because it's very unusual to have the opportunity to work on an opera that isn't straightforward multi-camera shooting of an existing stage performance. I normally find TV opera very dull and unimaginative. We have created our own performance to playback of a CD over which we have also had control in casting and recording. It's on Super 16mm – single camera – and it's going to be very beautiful.

April 4   Met Carole Myer of the Sales Company. Discussed where we go from here with regard to selling *Butterfly Kiss*. We have already sold it to all the main European territories (excluding Spain), to Australia, Hong Kong and a few others, but the problem seems to be the US. They're scared of it. It's too tough. We decided that it wasn't sensible to take it to Cannes as there are going to be too many new films opening and all the buyers likely to be there have already had the opportunity to see it in Berlin or at the AFM (American Film Market). We're going to wait until the film opens in London and hope that US interest will be rekindled.

April 7   Meeting with press and publicity people at the BBC. I get the feeling that the press office really doesn't have a clue about the kind of film we are making – it's virtually a feature film, but with a music and arts budget.

April 11   I have been trying to get a soundtrack release for *Butterfly Kiss*. From the pre-production stage on, I have been working with Island Records who publish the Cranberries with a view to putting together a commercial soundtrack that could be released on CD at the time of the film's release. The managing director of Island asked us to get a P J Harvey track into the film, which we achieved, albeit with some difficulty in terms of clearing the master rights in the recording. Then after the film was locked off, the company turned around and said that they were no longer interested in releasing a soundtrack album. This came as a complete surprise as they claimed they liked the film.

Today's screening was for various record company representatives to see who would pick it up. They were all late – at one point I thought no one was going to turn up at all and then the managing director of London Records arrived, saying that there was no point him watching the film as he had learned this morning that Island would not let any other record company use either the Cranberries or P J Harvey's numbers (these having the biggest commercial potential of course). It was very embarrassing, and particularly weird as he relayed this publicly to an unwitting Island representative also at the screening. The whole thing was a waste of time and money. I don't think we are going to get an album release at all now – I don't understand it as PolyGram are releasing the film in the UK and Benelux and most of the fifteen tracks in the film are at least PolyGram published or mastered and in some cases both. I would not have put as many tracks in the film if I had foreseen this situation. A big lesson!

April 28   Serious budget problems with the opera. The BBC have to write off £80 million and seem to be trying to take it all from our budget. The other producer – Nick de Grunwald of Isis Productions – is about to have a nervous breakdown!

May 8   First day of principal photography. Very impressed with all the crew and cast. It's very nice to be filming to lovely music. We've had so many problems in pre-production, what with the original director, Nigel Finch, dying in February and innumerable budgetary problems with the BBC. I hope we are going to have a smooth-running filming period. We deserve it, don't we?

May 9   Spoke too soon . . . The second lead, Sally Burgess, arrived on set feeling unwell. Apparently her six-year-old is just recovering from chicken-pox. I took her to a local doctor who confirmed she has it too. Spent most of the day talking to insurers, loss adjusters and doctors. Sent Sally home without working. Made a public announcement on set about the chicken-pox and everyone has become a bit nervous – the men especially seem to be mixing it up with the mumps! Got the assistant directors to make a list of who has had it, who hasn't and who doesn't know. The camera crew are the most unsure – the director of photography is Polish and his parents are dead, so he can't ask his mum, and the operator is Colombian . . .

May 10   Visit from the loss adjuster from Gaebel Watkins and Taylor. We have a very serious situation because it is virtually impossible to reschedule for when Sally recovers as it may take up to three weeks for her to be uncontagious. Our shoot is only that length and some of the cast aren't available after. Make more public announcements – it's very important to continue to keep people informed.

May 11   The situation gets worse. We have managed to shoot around Sally so far but we are running out of time. It is possible that we may have to abandon the production. I am now the world expert on chicken-pox. Sally is required for a night shoot. She feels fine, although she has a lot of spots and wants to come back to work. Those people who have not had chicken-pox are prepared to work with her providing they are insured if they catch it and as a result can't work on this job or the next. The insurers are being difficult – only people who have had cast medicals are covered they say, and only for this job. Time to give the loss adjuster the facts – either they agree to cover the people at risk (there are only twelve after all), we try to reschedule on Sundays which is difficult and costly and may not even be possible, or we pull the production and they pay for costs we have incurred so far. It's got to be the best bet to take the risk and cover the twelve. You would think I was asking for their blood.

May 12   At the eleventh hour the insurers and I came to a deal which allows us to continue. We're not out of trouble yet, because Sally could still get worse and is needed again next week. Is someone telling me to get out of film production?

May 13   Finally, the end of the first week of shooting. What a week! But we are on schedule and all still alive, and the rushes look great.

May 15–20   Second week of shooting and all is going well. The BBC now understands the quality of the film and suddenly there is a lot of press interest. The head of music who commissioned the film is delighted. There are potential budgetary problems ahead because the BBC took away all of our contingency before we started filming and on this scale you can't live without some spare. The production manager and I are keeping them informed on a regular basis. Nothing is being wasted and the production value is immense.

May 21–23   Flew to Nice with the director Chris Newby and actor John Hannah for the Cannes Film Festival. Our film *Madagascar Skin* is in the Critics' Week section there. The press screening followed by a question-and-answer session seemed to go very well. We were joined by the other main actor, Bernard Hill. The director and I sat in the screening to try to gauge audience reaction and to check out the French subtitles. It is very disappointing that only about a third of the total dialogue actually gets translated and sadly the French missed a lot of the humour. It's hard to know whether this is as a result of the subtitles or because of our cultural differences.

May 24   Flew back to London and went to the shoot – I was in time for the call as it was a late start with a 1 am finish. Peter made me feel guilty about being away on 'the worst two days possible'. I thought it should have been the best two days possible as all the shooting was confined to one room and I had left strict instructions before I left about wrapping times and how much overtime was permissible if needed. Nevertheless they are behind schedule which didn't surprise me because they had eleven minutes to shoot in two days and lip-sync is crucial in a tight environment. That's the most difficult thing with shooting opera to playback.

May 25 Did some rescheduling to enable us to finish on the due date. Spent much of the afternoon on the phone with Equity and the special effects supervisor ready for the night shoot ahead as there had been a complaint from one of the chorus. We were shooting a major effects burning sequence and the chorus member in question had claimed during the rehearsal period that she could blow fire. Of course, this had excited the director enormously and he was planning a shot of her doing this. Yesterday, the second assistant director had come to me because he felt that she was now becoming very nervous about doing this. I had therefore cancelled this shot and told the director, but she had panicked and got a stunt man friend involved, then her agent, then Equity. I was able to clarify that all necessary precautions were being taken with the fire sequence, fire tender standing by etc. We shot the burning (without the fire blowing of course) and it looked marvellous, but we did sustain one injury. The director sprained his ankle when one of the firemen tripped him up with a hosepipe, but the St John's ambulanceman standing by came to the rescue with an ice pack from the caterers.

May 26 Last day – or I should say night – of shooting. In order to finish on schedule, we brought in a second unit which I directed outside the house, while the main unit filmed inside. A manic night, but it worked and everyone was marvellous and in very self-congratulatory mood (quite rightly).

May 31 The rushes are great. We made it, but the art department have a lot of clearing up and reinstating to do at the location. The loss adjuster is delighted that there is no insurance claim because no one caught the dreaded pox. I need a holiday . . .

June 12 Viewed rough cut of *Dido and Aeneas*. Very pleased. Not much to do to the picture, as the director had planned his shots very well to the soundtrack.

June 13 Went to Electric Pictures, the UK distributors of *Butterfly Kiss*, to look at the proofs for the poster. Liked them a lot. Great news that the Cranberries are releasing the song in our film as a new single on July 31. Island Records, after all my problems with them over a soundtrack album, have agreed to allow us to mention the single on the film poster. At least something worthwhile has come out of a year of hitting my head up against a brick wall with record companies.

July 17 Conversation with Carole Myer about an offer for *Butterfly Kiss* she has received from the US. It's not a great deal. Should we take it or take the risk of waiting for the UK opening? My guts say, let's wait.

July 21 Meeting at the BBC in Music and Arts Department with the Isis (producers of the opera) lawyer to discuss additional costs to the budget figure. The BBC appeared *en masse* and everyone looked suicidal at the end. We all got nowhere.

July 26 Meeting at PACT to fight over a claim Equity are making against the opera production company. The Equity representatives decided that the company had to make an offer to pay extra money. I said there was no extra money. We have seventy-two hours to make a decision to go to arbitration or not.

July 27 Phoned Barry Kim [Senior Industrial Advisor] at PACT to tell her that our decision was to tell Equity to sue the production company. We all know Equity does not have a leg to stand on in this particular instance and they even agreed that the company had been open and honest.

August 2 Heard from the agent who brought the case with Equity against the opera production company that they have accepted that they will receive no extra monies. I'm glad it's over but what a total waste of a lot of people's time. Met the director of photography of *Dido* at the NFT where we viewed part of the answerprint on the big screen to check the grading when projected in a cinema. We were both very impressed.

August 16 Travelled to Liverpool for *Butterfly Kiss* charity premiere. It's the first time I've made a speech to 850 people. The film was very well received and everyone had a great evening. A VIP reception was followed by the screening and then a party at a nightclub.

September 7–15 Went to the Toronto Film Festival. *Butterfly Kiss* and *Madagascar Skin* had both been invited there and the screenings went down very well with the Canadian audiences. Saw a few films, made some new Canadian and US contacts and remet some existing ones. As a result of the festival we now have North American and Canadian distribution deals on both films. I was particularly impressed with one of the companies who have a very energetic and enthusiastic approach to our films and our marketing of them. Possibly the most enjoyable film festival I've been to.

September 21 Travelled to the Dinard Film Festival in Brittany. The plane was full of producers. What would happen if it crashed? Shouldn't some of the big cheeses travel separately like the Royal Family?

September 22 The day started depressingly with a seminar on Anglo-French co-production where we were informed that basically the only access to French money would be through a reciprocity deal, i.e. package two films at once, one to be shot in French and the other in the English language. I introduced our first competition screening of *Butterfly Kiss* to the French audience.

September 24 It's been a very\ valuable and fun festival but I feel as though I'm just about talked out. Won our first award though – two in fact. A distribution prize – a Silver Hitchcock and a cheque for 20,000 f. for our French distributor Diaphana, to spend on the release in France in January 1996 – and a Bronze Hitchcock to Saskia Reeves for best actress. Plus some champagne of course, which we had to drink because I couldn't carry it along with the portly Mr Hitchcock . . .

October 16 Day spent at Isis Productions working on our case against the BBC with regard to the financing of *Dido and Aeneas*.

October 18 The BBC dispute is becoming very boring and extremely time consuming. We have to continue with it – apart from the fact that the future of Isis is seriously in jeopardy, the Beeb is becoming much too fond of trying to screw independents into the ground on the basis of their own appalling cash-flow crisis. I can't feel sorry for such a large dinosaur that's brought it all on itself.

October 31 A horrific and depressing meeting about the *Dido* budget across a large table at the BBC with a so-called impartial arbitrator (the fact that he was a BBC employee didn't seem to be considered peculiar . . .). Four of us opposite four of them. We failed miserably to present our case satisfactorily, partly because we were being too 'nice' and partly because Isis are in the very difficult position of having signed a contract for a new series with exactly the same people we were staring at.

November 10 London Film Festival screenings of *Madagascar Skin* at the Odeon West End. Arrived for the end of the evening screening and Chris Newby and I went on stage for a questions-and-answers. It was a very friendly audience and the cinema was packed.

November 11–12 Went to Berlin for the European Film Awards. *Butterfly Kiss* was in the last three of 'Young European Film of the Year'. We didn't win. As I expected, *La Haine* took the prize. Saskia Reeves also came and made a very good job of introducing herself to European directors like Wim Wenders and Jaco von Dormael.

November 20 News of three awards at the Stockholm Film Festival this weekend – Best Screenplay (Chris Newby) and Best Actor (John Hannah) for *Madagascar Skin* and Best Debut Film for Michael Winterbottom for *Butterfly Kiss*.

November 21 Sarah and I went to the ICA to discuss marketing and distribution in the UK for *Madagascar Skin* which ICA Projects is distributing. The film is now opening on 26 January.

Keith Griffiths

A leading independent producer, Keith Griffiths has been associated with such innovative art-house film-makers as Chris Petit, Jan Svankmajer, Patrick Keiller and the Brothers Quay. The following extracts concentrate on Institute Benjamenta, *the Quays' first foray into live-action film-making.*

March 18 We (the Brothers Quay and myself) initially took our first feature film proposal to David Rose in 1987. After some years of haggling with the Carl-Seelig-Stiftung, script development, fundraising, and the excitement of finally shooting and realising this project in March 1994, the screening at the Lumière cinema is an emotional moment.

The film looks spectacular on the large screen, though the soundtrack is clearly distorting and will need further attention. Nic Knowland has done a truly spectacular job photographing the movie and Ben Gibson [Head of BFI Production] amuses me by saying that it was the first film to make an artist out of the focus-puller. Reactions all round are pleasing and reservations are understandable and coherent. The problem is now how to distribute and exhibit such an 'art-cinema' product in the present marketplace. Anyone old enough to see, let alone fall in love with, a Dreyer film or experience the pleasure of light, shade, texture and abstraction in a Brakhage film will love *Institute Benjamenta*. But I sense that the younger generation, whose movie world starts with Tarantino, will be completely lost. However, this is a day to celebrate, not brood, and tomorrow the print goes to Paris for the Cannes selectors to view.

April 11–13 The film is rejected by 'Un Certain Regard' and 'Directors' Fortnight'. This takes everyone by surprise, but surprise is the name of the game in this business. To say I am not disappointed would be untrue, but once the initial shock has passed I begin to think that it might turn out to be for the best. In the past we built up both the critical reputation and the audience for the short films by starting small and showing them in feature-length programmes in small art-movie houses in Europe and the USA. We should clearly do a rethink and use the same approach for *Benjamenta*. The problem may be whether this approach will make the equity investors nervous; on the whole they prefer the safer and more prestigious routes to promoting and exploiting a movie.

April 26 My accountant arrives to do a pile of cost reports. Every week I examine the figures closely and am amazed that we are still in business after sixteen years. The reality is that while we produce modest films and television programmes that are on the margins of the industry as a whole, we keep in work because we produce high-quality, imaginative work on schedule and on budget. What frightens me is the thought of yet another thirty BBC Arts directors, producers and researchers, with terminated short-term contracts, all scrabbling around for the crumbs.

Meeting with Film Four International to discuss strategy with the sales and promotion team. *Benjamenta* also failed to get into Critics' Week, though this was of no consequence to me. I'm convinced that the film should go to Locarno. It is a first feature and based on the work of a major Swiss writer (Robert Walser). If it is accepted, we should then go on to Toronto and, I hope, New York. We will not show anything in Cannes at all and instead start talking to those distributors who would kill to show a film by the Brothers. I would like the film released this autumn and not have to wait in an Artificial Eye/Miramax queue until next year. Film Four are very supportive but I fear British Screen will be tougher to crack. My German co-producers (Pandora) are behind my new strategy but an ominous silence has descended from Japan (Image Forum) – I fear they were very disappointed by the Cannes rejection and I will have to try and pull off something to stimulate their confidence.

May 19–27 Cannes. Not having a film to present or an immediate co-production to hustle into life, I'm determined to use the opportunity to see some films, meet some friends and learn something about the current nervous marketplace into which we are about to launch *Benjamenta*.

I meet with my German co-producer from Pandora, Karl Baumgartner, who feels that Locarno and Toronto are the best launches for *Benjamenta*, with Hamburg for Germany. Locarno would make a lot of sense, taking Robert Walser home to Switzerland, but I have never been and I have only met Marco Müller once in Berlin. Toronto is easier as I know Kay Armitage and my colleagues from Zeitgeist in New York, who hope to handle the film in the USA, will also talk to the organisers.

The UK and USA deals are settled. We all celebrate and I know that with the ICA and Zeitgeist behind us we have got a really committed team. I am also starting to recognise what a lot of work has yet to be done. I leave Cannes feeling that this year I have spent two days too long at the fairground. On my return I sleep for two days.

May 31 View an internegative print of *Benjamenta* that leaves us completely depressed. There is some improvement but the stock can't seem to take both the tonal range of soft greys and the high-contrast sequences. We feel Nic Knowland [cinematographer of *Institute Benjamenta* and *Nervous Energy*] needs to see the print – his name is on the screen. The laboratory is very frustrated and is obviously spending far more money and time than they will ever make out of final print orders. They are trying really hard but are also totally confused.

June 6–7 We get the stereo tracks organised for the Channel Four Telecine, which takes a whole day. We are surprised how good the print looks on the TV screen. We imagined that the image would disappear but I am impressed by the Channel Four grading and confident that the video will work well. We have a crisis meeting about the internegative. The Japanese have started to get very aggressive and now distribution deals have been settled for the UK and USA we urgently need to resolve the problems.

Apparently there is only one grade of Kodak stock and it doesn't appear that it can hold the contrast changes. More tests are required.

Supper with the Brothers Quay and the ICA team so that they know who they will be working with during the long promotional campaign for the film. We discuss release dates and start to look at October, just prior to the London Film Festival. This means that the refurbished cinema at the ICA would open with two potentially strong films – *Chungking Express* and *Benjamenta* – each very different but both ideal for the cinema. I stress to Simon Field that I want a second screen as well, possibly the Everyman, so that we can capture some North London audiences that won't travel to The Mall.

June 16 Marco Müller is flying in to see the film. I feel very tense. If he doesn't like it we will have to rethink the whole festival launch. The Brothers come to meet him before the screening. His response is absolutely positive and he immediately talks about the film in a way that few have done to date. He understands clearly what the Brothers were trying to do cinematically and he also understands their interpretation of Walser. He is also very pragmatic about the exhibition difficulties we will experience with the movie. He invites the film on the spot. A good end to the week and I immediately inform the financiers and hope the good news will placate my very angry Japanese co-producers.

June 30 Have discussions with Locarno, Channel Four and Pandora about the print of *Benjamenta* to be shown in August. Are we going to subtitle it in French and German for Switzerland or ask the festival to screen the film in the original language? Pandora want to show a print to some Swiss distributors before deciding. My anxiety is that at this rate we won't have an internegative or any prints if our on-going saga can't be resolved soon. I decide to order at great cost another print from the original negative in case we run out of time and I have yet another conversation with the laboratory. They are hopeful that the tests currently being done will resolve the issue. We should know next week.

July 3 The internegative situation is reaching a crisis. The laboratory has discovered that the black-and-white stock from the ex-GDR called Orvo has a range of seven grades still available. Tests are being made on this stock and they look very encouraging; they even seem an improvement on the Kodak stock.

July 13 The Brothers call me to say the Orvo tests are brilliant and in some respects the film looks better on this stock than off the original negative. At last we can deliver our first internegative to Channel Four.

July 17 The first of a number of proposed magazine press shows of *Benjamenta*. A good range of people attend including critics Sheila Johnson, Kevin Jackson, Geoff Andrew, the arts editor of the *Observer* and Terry

Gilliam. Afterwards we have supper along with Brothers at the Union Club. It is a really enjoyable evening and Terry in particular keeps us all amused with tales of his latest production along with earlier disaster stories. He has really watched the film closely and tackles the Brothers on a whole range of technical questions. I feel optimistic that the press reaction might not be too negative.

July 27 Catch up with the office backlog of work, with more press materials for Locarno and a really nasty letter from my Japanese co-producers blaming me personally for late delivery of *Benjamenta*. I talk to the laboratory and explain that I absolutely must have an internegative and print ready to be in Tokyo by 14 August. They are convinced that this is possible. Bad news from Pandora: neither of the two Swiss distributors want to take on the film. They all admire it, but it's too difficult for the current climate. This means we will have to screen an original language print. We get together the dialogue lists for simultaneous translation.

A stinking review in *Screen International* which clearly upsets Film Four. I'm not too concerned as I'm expecting a rough ride from the daily hacks anyway. What remains important is the magazine press and specialist articles.

August 4–9 Clear decks at the office, load myself down with promotional materials and leave for Locarno. This is my first visit and the first live-action feature festival that the Brothers have attended. It is a fantastic location situated on a lake surrounded by mountains. It is midnight before I arrive, just in time for a thunderstorm, and I find the Brothers sheltering from the rain in a bar near the town square. The next morning we register and meet the festival staff. Kate Hughes from Film Four has come down to help organise the press, but everything seems to roll without much effort. The festival paper is full of articles on Godard and speculation about whether he will turn up to receive his special award.

The press show brings rumours of a very divided reaction to the film. Marco is very gung ho about it all; he loves a scrap. The second day brings the first press interviews, mainly for radio and television. The Brothers take it on board and are impressed by the intelligence and seriousness of the reporters. The competition screening is held in a converted ice-rink on the edge of the town. We are staggered that everyone makes the short journey and are completely taken aback by the size of the auditorium. It seats 3,000 and at least 2,500 are in the cinema to see the film. I've seen a lot of my own productions at festivals but never have I been so nervous. The projection and sound is astonishingly good, though I'm worried that the film really requires a more intimate presentation. We sit in the bar outside during the projection. The Brothers seem relaxed, though later they admit to their tension. I'm chain smoking like an idiot and very wound up by the apparently continuous stream of people leaving. In reality, we probably lose about two hundred which considering the size of the hall is not too bad, but I find the experience truly cruel. After the screening the Brothers stand on stage and answer questions from the audience. They are nervous but handle the situation extremely well. It is impossible to gauge the true reaction, though we appear to have split people down the middle. At least there's a reaction.

The first German reviews to appear are pretty rough, they find the film boring, though evocative. As ever there is lots of silly shorthand talk about 'Kafka'. When in doubt, wheel in Kafka. To our surprise the Italian press are quite enthusiastic and so are the French. We thought that with Walser's being a Swiss German the reaction would be different. The Brothers are asked to do more French-speaking radio and I get a very positive reaction from Canal+, who think the Brothers are truly talented and that we should take the next project to them for consideration. I'm warned that the *Variety* review won't be encouraging but again this doesn't surprise me. The film will find its audience, we've just got to keep calm.

August 11 I try to clear my desk as I'm going off to Wales and hope to get a bit of a break. I am completely exhausted. The screening at Locarno is in one sense the end of the first phase of *Benjamenta* which started in 1987. It has been a long haul. The Japanese internegative and print arrives on time and is dispatched to Tokyo. I hope that they will put these post-production problems behind us so that we can draw a line and start helping them promote the film in the Far East. Now the second phase – the exhibition and distribution of the film commences.

August 12–20 The Brothers call me in Wales from a phone box in Locarno, the film has won the second prize of the Youth Jury and a Special Mention from the International Jury.

September 11–15 Leave for Toronto ahead of the Brothers Quay. I sort out my accreditation at the festival office and bump straight into Simon Field [Director of ICA Cinemas]. We decided to have a few quiet drinks before the arrival of Nancy Gerstman and Emily Russo from Zeitgeist, Koninck's US distributors. We have a late-night supper with the Zeitgeist team and brief them on all the pre-release tactics we are preparing for *Benjamenta*. They are looking after the Brothers in Toronto and are anxious that the film be well received. They are now planning to open in New York in March, so they have plenty of time to prepare press materials.

The next day I bump into Atom Egoyan. We talk about the Brothers and he says something I haven't really taken in fully before. He says that he was able to evolve his feature-length work very gradually and in many respects anonymously. Slowly his work came to be known to the critics and the film-making world. The Brothers Quay, on the other hand, have developed a cult status with their animation and everyone has been anticipating this first feature for years – it is like releasing a movie of one's first footsteps under the glare of an arc light. He wishes us well but he has made me nervous. Word from the press screening is mixed but good enough to ensure the film is sold out that night.

October 30 I'm exhausted and need some time off. The LFF screening of *Benjamenta* looms even nearer. The Quays have been working hard on the poster design and related publicity materials. We can't do much more now and have to wait for the critics to crucify us.

November 7 The *Time Out* article on the Brothers is first class, and at last a new photograph appears. It took gentle persuasion but looks great. I'm much relieved. Simon rings to say the LFF screenings are almost sold out so he is a happy bunny too.

November 10 The LFF screenings of *Benjamenta*. One of the Brothers fails to turn up to introduce the movie, apparently he has his nose stuck in a wine bottle in some club. However, luckily he does turn up for the question-and-answer session. We have some walk-outs but not as many as I feared after the Locarno experience. Simon Field hosts a magnificent party and I suddenly feel really weary. After all these years of work a film finally flickers into a new life on screen. Whether the film, which opens for its run at the Everyman and the ICA in seven days, will hold its own is impossible to prejudge. Surely the next one can't take as long to develop and produce?

Christopher Wicking

Christopher Wicking is better known as a screenwriter specialising in horror films. His diary concentrates on his efforts to launch himself as a writer/director with a contemporary romantic film noir set entirely on and around the River Thames, On the Jade River. *It was written with actors Liam Neeson and Gong Li in mind, and casting subsequently proves to be a fundamental issue in getting a first feature off the ground.*

Section 35, discussed in this diary, is a special Irish system of tax relief which allows individuals to claim full tax relief on investments in film production of up to Ir£25,000. A special clause allows investments of up to Ir£1 million if the funds are going to a single qualifying production to make one film.

January–March Virtually all of my time so far this year has been spent functioning as a producer, trying to find a 'home' for myself and my project within a financially viable framework. Among various other initiatives, the project has recently been introduced into the Section 35 framework within the Irish film industry, whereby a notional 60 per cent of a film's budget can be raised provided 75 per cent of the total budget is spent within the Irish state. By shooting locations on the Thames, but using studio interiors in Ireland, the film can be made to fit the necessary requirements. I have had preliminary meetings in Dublin, and the first stages of paperwork have been presented to the Department.

Having written it 'for' Liam Neeson – who, as the British Gerard Depardieu, is just about the only one of our actors who could convince as a working man, I have spoken at regular intervals over the last eighteen or so months to his agent, Anne Hutton. Each time she has updated me as to his availability and price, and has not said no to the prospect of his saying yes in the right circumstances.

But now, because of Section 35, I need a firm decision one way or the other – a firm budget and schedule has to be prepared as soon as possible. At this point it is the end of March, and I would really like to be able to get the production underway in the autumn. Accordingly I have met with Anne, who is due to go to New York to meet with him next week. She promises to read it and introduce the project to him, although after *Schindler's List* in particular his price is $4 million.

Via Andi Engel of Artificial Eye (which distributed *Farewell My Concubine* and other Gong Li movies here) I have made contact with Shu Kei (of Shu Kei's Creative Workshop in Hong Kong) who in turn has given me a contact number for Gong Li in Shanghai. A fax has been sent, but so far nothing has come back. I have been told that she speaks no English, and that she is not allowed by the authorities to film outside China. But she has recently broken up her relationship with director Zhang Yimou and has become involved with 'a foreign businessman', so I presume that she might also be thinking about spreading her wings into international production. Certainly, it would be wonderful if I could 'snare' her. Together with Liam Neeson, I imagine she would give the project the required pre-sales value it will require, and which I, as a first-time director, am not likely to command.

April 1 (And what better day than April Fool's Day to officially begin a diary of one's activities in the British film industry.) Other ideas for the *Jade River* lead, should Liam Neeson decline, have been Patrick Bergin and Jean-Marc Barr. But John and Roz Hubbard have come on board as casting directors, and John has another suggestion, another Liam, Liam Cunningham, who is rapidly on his way to stardom. He was in *War of the Buttons*, but more importantly is in two upcoming movies, as Sean Connery's sidekick in *First Knight* and the lead in *The Little Princess*. The script has been sent to him, and word has come back from his agent that he loves it, and so we are having lunch today. He turns out to be a dream. He's Irish, in his early thirties, has only been acting for five years (previously an electrician) and wants to be the new Robert Mitchum, in terms of being a movie actor. I feel like Scorsese must have done when he first met De Niro.

April 10 Liam Neeson's *Rob Roy* has been fast-forwarded from August to beat *Braveheart* and *First Knight* and opens this week in the USA on 139 screens. Obviously, the premiere party was one reason why Anne Hutton was heading for New York. But *Variety* today declares that 'it could define whether Neeson is superstar material'. Steven Spielberg got the credit for *Schindler's List*, but *Rob Roy* rests squarely on Neeson's broad shoulders, and Hollywood will shortly know if he's a bankable leading man. It follows that I will therefore know shortly whether I've got him for *Jade River*, or if Hollywood will indeed claim him.

April 12 No word back from Gong Li, but sending a fax is the modern equivalent of the message in a bottle and who knows for sure if they actually arrive, especially in China. So we send a follow-up, via the production manager of the Hong Kong based company making the film and hope this will have a better reception.

April 13 A fax comes in from Hong Kong, confirming arrival of yesterday's fax to Gong Li, but not the original fax describing my intentions about the film. I am now given two further fax numbers, in Shanghai where Gong Li will be over the weekend, and in Suzhou, where she will be on location next week, along with her hotel room number.

April 18 'Rob is royal,' says *Variety*. 'The season's most audacious gamble looks like it will pay off. No one in the industry believed debuting with 133 playdates and going wide five days later made much sense in the light of lukewarm reviews. When the weekend dust settled, it had a per-screen number of $15,213.' So *Rob Roy*'s off to a good start at least; whether or not it will hold up, it looks as if Liam's going to be okay – which is marvellous of course, but probably bad news for me. No news at all from

Gong Li, but given the original length of time for the message in the bottle to be picked up I needn't worry yet.

April 27   Bad news from Anne Hutton. Neeson rang her last night from New York to say no to *Jade River*. Hardly surprising, and in a way something of a relief, especially as I have Liam Cunningham as a back-up, who I really think I would prefer anyway. But a blow nevertheless – and I have to figure out a graceful way to break the news to whom it may concern, such as the Section 35 finance.

May 4   Lunch with Marina Martin, Liam Cunningham's agent, and one of her colleagues in the agency. They are of course both very pleased by the good reviews of *The Little Princess* – Liam is flying out to LA at the weekend to be handy if anything breaks as a result of the reviews and the opening next week. But they are both now very cautious about Liam being able to commit to anything and are anxious that I secure a producer to help solidify my efforts. Without actually throwing a bucket of water in my face, they flick a few drops to bring me to my senses – and they are of course right; I really have very little in place. I'm determined to put a deadline on the project – to try to get into production by mid-September.

May 7–9   My second trip to Dublin on *Jade River*, this time with a greater range of contacts, understanding about the elements involved, and a certain sense of urgency; in order to capitalise on and maximise the situation which has been developing I can now put a start date on the film and work backwards from it. If I don't make it, I will at least have given it my best shot.

Meeting with David Beattie, a solicitor whose company works in association with Pannell, Kerr & Forster, the accountancy firm who are my contact for the Section 35 initiative. He very clearly elucidates his understanding of Section 35, explains about the various company structures that need to be in place and outlines his desired role in things. A trip out to Ardmore Studios. There's a perfect set for the hall and stairs I need in the Old House that's used as office accommodation and a tank where we can do the small amount of underwater stuff the script calls for. We later look around Dublin docks and realise that we can double up the London locations here, and maybe even build some, even all, of the 'Chinatown East' set there which might not be possible at Ardmore as they had to sell their backlot a few years back due to thin times.

A long meeting with Suzanne Kelly. She tells me that one of the important ministers here is particularly concerned to promote the water-ways, so if we run into problems of a ministerial nature, this 'interest' might be capitalised on. Most importantly, we agree on a deadline date, of 30 June, for me to get back to her with confirmation of other financial interest in *Jade River*, in order for her to be able to activate her investors in time for a production start of mid-September.

Most important of all is my final meeting before getting back on the plane with Kieran Corrigan of John Boorman's Merlin Films and his assistant/ reader Elaine Lennon. After a certain amount of verbal skirmishing, it transpires that Elaine thinks it is a wonderful project and has a few different, but good, ideas about how some of the characters could be. Generally then it seems that *Jade River* could very well be a project that Merlin might want to go ahead with, though they have their own sources of Section 35 investment, which would probably mean that Suzanne's company would be superfluous.

I fly back to London very excited. I feel that all the current bases have been covered and that the project is in a very healthy state.

May 11 Into the office first thing and I'm talking randomly around the coffee machine when a colleague passes by to say, with a little smile, have I seen the fax on my desk? I look and it's a fax from Gong Li, apologising for not having got back sooner but of course she's been busy making her film. She says she'll be finished in June and will want to have a break but is interested to hear more about the project.

May 17 A very busy day as we try to unite various strands going to Cannes. We fax Shu Kei in Hong Kong, who is the fixer for Gong Li, and he instantly faxes back to say he will be in Cannes and looks forward to a meet. It almost would be the best reason to go as he has been so helpful thus far, and it would be great to actually meet.

May 23 Message on the office answer-machine from my colleague Kevin Fraser saying his friend with the villa in Nice is occupied this week but would next week be okay? – which, of course, is too late for Cannes. I guess in his mind that means I won't go, so there's no further mention about any immediate investment in terms of travel finance. This seems to put the final clincher on my trip.

May 25 Shock, horror when I first glance at the back page of the *Herald Tribune* – Gong Li has been in Cannes to help launch the new Zhang Yimou film. I'm really angry with myself, as she's the one person I really didn't think would be there – she is supposedly filming in Shanghai till June and has broken up with Zhang. She is the one person I really would have gone there to meet.

June 7 Robin Hillyard has come up with an interesting thought: as there's theoretically more money floating around in TV at the moment, at least for development, why not make *Jade River* as part of a series, i.e., as a pilot. At some time in the past, the vague idea of thinking about it for television occurred to me, but not really as a series in the way that I can now envisage one. Maybe Bob Barry, the detective character who plays a relatively minor role, could be a common denominator to five other stories. And this might be a way to get into my 'prequel', set in the real Limehouse of the 1910s and 20s and involving the character of Johnny Limehouse's father, based on the events of Brilliant Chang and Billie Carlisle, the showgirl. We could also get into the idea of the political exiles coming over from China. There could be lots of interesting ways of extending it, certainly into another five parts, or, like *Cracker*, as a series of three-hour projects.

June 15   Half-way through the month and my deadline for getting back to Suzanne Kelly with other deals in prospect to allow her to trigger off her Section 35 paperwork, but I don't seem to be any closer to having any other deals.

July 1   My deadline has passed and now it's physically getting more and more unlikely that I would be able to gear things up quickly enough for an August/September start, so it seems that all the efforts of this year, and last, are going to count for nothing.

September 15   Dublin. An early meeting with Suzanne Kelly, who has now left the accountants PKF and gone solo as a 'tax practitioner', putting people together, acting as a sounding board, consultant and so on. She says she doesn't think the Section 35 initiative will be renewed next April, at least not in its present form, in the main because of several unfortunate scandals: among them, the loss of investors' money in the *Space Truckers* project and the Brando fiasco which, while not a Section 35 foul-up, is perceived to be related. Also, with an Irish election just a year away, and with the Exchequer required to fund a new social programme, there's unlikely to be anyone to fight for it.

But in the short term, although March is still the cut-off point for the initiative, Suzanne says there is still plenty of funding yet to be placed. She knows of at least one fund with £10 million waiting to be used, and there's still a hunger in the community to spend the money. Thus a *Jade River* start date could still be on for next spring, using this year's funds. The feeling is, indeed, that *Jade River*, because of it's scale, could be a sort of lifeline for investors who have yet to find any guaranteed 'relief' (as it is charmingly known). And I also have another lifeline – providing I can get confirmation of a facility with a bank (which may already be in principle available via Steve Robbins at Berliner Bank), a draft completion bond, a management plan (cash flow for pre-production, the actual spend itself etc.). The completion documentation would need to be drawn down in March, with 31 March the date for expiration of relief, meaning a start date in April, which would be perfect.

The Director

Gillies MacKinnon

A graduate of the National Film School, Gillies Mackinnon's films include Passing Glory, The Conquest of the South Pole, Needle, The Grass Arena, The Playboys, *and* A Simple Twist of Fate. *The following extracts concentrate on the production of his most personal film to date.*

April 1 Two days from now shooting commences in Glasgow on a new film, *Easterhouse*, which I co-wrote with my brother Billy over a three-year period. He will co-produce it with Steve Clark-Hall and I will direct it. Initially we aimed at a budget of £2.7 million but in the end decided to go ahead on a much smaller budget of £1.2 million, allowing us to make the film we want without interference. The main investment comes from BBC Films, with additional funding from the Glasgow Film Fund. This low budget requires a six-week prep, six-week shoot and a six-week cut. We will shoot on super 16, to be blown up to 35mm for a cinema release. We know the film is ambitious within this framework, but the feeling exists within the cast and crew to make it work. We also know our financiers, Mark Shivas, Andrea Calderwood and Eddie Dick, are right behind us and we are all out to make the same movie. This is a great comfort.

The film tells the story of three brothers growing up in 1968 among the gangs that dominated the lives of teenagers in the city at that time. The drama is driven by violent events, but we want to tell a human story. There is also a lot of art in the movie, and the designer, Zoe Macleod, is busy commissioning the many drawings and paintings described in the script.

At this point I am always fascinated by the gap that exists between the film in my head and the eventual celluloid fact that will one day be a finished movie – absolute, complete, beyond my influence to alter for better or for worse. The read-through gave us a big boost, hearing the story spoken from start to finish. Listening to it, I was pleased to hear a lot of humour coming through what, on the surface, looks like a harrowing story.

In 1968 the Glasgow tenements were black from decades of soot and industrial smoke. Since then they have been cleaned, which causes us real problems. Some dark tenements exist, often between cleaned walls – a strip of black in a shiny yellow sandstone terrace. This limits camera angles and restricts the actors' movements to usable spaces. Also, in 1968 the streets were empty and this is a look we want for the film. We won't be wheeling on a display of period cars and extras. Empty streets suit the atmosphere and the budget!

April 3   The first day went well. I was amazed how small the circus was compared to the convoy of trailers etc. we had in Atlanta, Georgia, on *A Simple Twist of Fate*.

April 4   No more nerves. Everything takes on a familiar atmosphere, people squeezing into narrow corridors to shoot scenes with elbows up one another's nostrils. All trying to live and work together. This is the reality of film-making: trying to adapt all the wonderful possibilities to the fact of a limited number of hours and limited resources. The laugh of the day was provided by one of the popular newspapers: 'Knife Threat to Film Crew!' We are told that knife-wielding thugs have threatened us and trashed a film set. We were amused by the bold lies, but it does seem pathetic that a reporter should invent this trash. In fact, the local residents of Darnley were amazingly tolerant. There is a tendency in the popular press to describe the film as a 'Razor Gang' film. In fact, I believe the film is quite complex, even exotic in its own way.

April 5   We are up against the clock! I mentioned to John De Borman, our director of photography, that we should remember the Scottish football team who always seem to do best when they're losing. Right now, the schedule is eating us up. I am constantly reappraising how scenes should be shot. It hurts, but often a crisis creates the chance to invent something new, even better. This is fundamental: to turn problems to your advantage, to reinvent everything where necessary. When the clock has you on the run, turn around and start beating the hell out of it. You can't make a movie if you don't like a good fight and if you can't be flexible and enjoy it. Bresson once wrote: 'Put oneself into a state of intense ignorance and curiosity, and yet see things in advance.' The contradiction he proposes is something I have found useful.

April 6   Seems the lab damaged the negatives of yesterday's shoot. The film was broken and scratched. A horrible feeling. Iain Robertson (who plays thirteen-year-old Lex) tells me he plays trombone. Must work that into the film somewhere.

April 14   A hell of a week. Every day is a struggle against the clock and failing daylight. An actor, Gary Sweeney (the gang leader, Sloane), twisted an ankle at skating practice and had to hobble around in very physical scenes, but I have to hand it to Gary, who overcame the problem. This is a film full of young actors who can't wait to get in front of the camera. We staged a gang fight in a lane, but daylight beat us and we had to lose a scene. This was disappointing for a minute and a half, but, like all hard decisions, you have to let go of what you can't get done and go with what you can. Tonight we were filming on a roof when someone put an elbow through a pane of glass which shattered and fell down into the void where Iain and the stunt organisers were settled on top of a scaffold tower. Luckily nobody was hurt.

April 22 Half-way through the shoot my family visited Glasgow, which was great for me. This feels so much better than being in North America, thousands of miles away. Last year I was commuting between LA and London over the weekend. Jet lag became the norm. I called home from LA everyday. When I finished shooting the film with Steve Martin, I had to walk away from other American projects. I had to be home. There are career decisions and there are life decisions.

I hoped *Easterhouse* would happen straight away, but I had to wait another six months. It was great to be in London with my family. I could take my kids to school, write, cycle, write again, and even pick them up from school again. After six months I was given the possibility of directing a film set in Ireland, starring Marlon Brando. What an opportunity! I told the BBC office about this dilemma and basically blackmailed them into giving the Glasgow film the green light. It worked. I played an ace to get this film going and making this decision shows me how important *Easterhouse* is to me. Mark Shivas found the extra cash we needed, God bless him, and here we are shooting the damn film. We are very lucky as the BBC froze all drama projects right about then.

The plan is to open *Easterhouse* at the Edinburgh Film Festival alongside *A Simple Twist of Fate* and we hope Steve Martin will be there. He called me on his mobile phone last week and said he'd love to come, before the line broke up. I hope he does. That would be a lot of fun, but strange to open two such different films at once. Tomorrow we shoot at the Glasgow School of Art. I studied there from 1966 to 1970 and have happy memories of that time.

April 26 The central family in the film I feel is well cast, all black haired. Clare Higgins plays the mother and I think she is a really strong actress and looks great with the 'sons' who look to me like real brothers.

April 30 Clare (who is English) took a tape of Gaelic singing away to study. Though I think she is a brilliant actress, I had real apprehension about her ability to sing a Gaelic song. But she manages. She sings it as a Southern Scot, a non-Gaelic speaker, just as our mother used to sing these songs, and I feel she did a brilliant job. I want to talk to her between takes, but I feel so churned up that I can't speak. I'm afraid I will burst into tears and everyone will be embarrassed. The most exhausting day yet. We end it with Iain (Lex) playing trombone. All day it has been bugging me – I must beat the schedule, I must get in the trombone!

Meanwhile the editor, Scott Thomas, is working on an assembly. He's doing a great job, but at this early stage, it's always a combination of the reassuring and the frustrating. I miss being able to grab the controls of the Steenbeck [machine used for viewing and editing films] and say, 'We could cut here.' Being unfamiliar with the computer, I can't stop dead at any given moment (not yet) and still feel the machine is a bit of a tyrant. I can see the advantages of cutting on Avid [computer-based editing system], but I'm still suspicious. It doesn't have that touchy-feely thing you get with the

Steenbeck – grabbing the handle, pushing things back and forth. I try to keep an open mind. I did one of George Lucas's *Young Indiana Jones Chronicles* episodes (Ireland 1916) and that taught me a lot about the advantages of electronic technology, painting in and out whatever you want. But can one use this technology and still make soulful films? The problem is that it's so seductive on the level of 'effect' that it's easy to forget why we want to make films in the first place.

May 1   We still have no composer for the film. I'm starting to feel anxious about this. I have listened to endless tapes. Somehow Billy and I are in not only a director–producer relationship, but also a brother relationship, and we both have strong ideas about the music and need to progress it together. But we seem to have got stuck on this one. Meanwhile, I have been developing a sense of what the music could be: a strong melody, emotional but not sentimental, and a countertheme that might be like tribal drums, maybe African or Celtic, deep and low and rhythmic; these two musical ideas crossing over at times. All I know is that the music is critical. The problem must be solved soon.

I really love the wee thirteen-year-old actor Iain Robertson who plays Lex. He is full of life and ideas, the camera loves him, he understands direction immediately, he's full of fun. Sometimes he seems too knowing for his young age. In the hotel bar in Edinburgh I found him actually sitting beside me on a barstool, holding forth with a coke. At that point I told him, 'Iain, get to bed!' I mean, it was nearly midnight!

May 2   Today we had to shoot a heart-breaking scene in which Clare Higgins dismantles the bed of her murdered son. I knew this could be very powerful. It was a fairly simple track, and we brought Clare in at the last moment, or so I thought. Somehow I have been here before. The actor is there in a corner nursing all this scintillating emotion while the crew inevitably finds more and more last touches – the wall's too hot, the wrong picture is on the wall etc. Nobody is to blame, it's the stupidity of film-making, especially on an impossible schedule.

Over the past few days, Billy has been doing second-unit shots for us. This is a situation which normally makes me nervous. In this case, I don't feel worried at all. Last year in the States, our producer, Ric Kidney, took charge of second unit. I really liked this guy. He was very aware and I trusted him. I could have had any number of lunatic producers in Hollywood. He had to shoot some general polo-playing shots. Maybe in his anxiety to give me everything I needed, he seemed to have made a polo documentary for what amounted to thirty seconds on screen. It's the difference between a Hollywood budget and a BBC budget, I suppose.

May 4   On the last day of shooting in the house of the McLean family it was a desperate struggle. Anything we didn't manage to shoot wouldn't be in the film. Everyone seemed tired and we were all crammed together in an airless room. We started doing complicated sequences in one and two takes and I resorted to resetting cameras to get a second go at separate moments and talking the actors through things as the camera was running. I think we came through this all right, but I made several mistakes that annoy me, details that maybe nobody will ever notice. If a scene is dramatic enough, most mistakes are invisible. It's the feeling that something is wrong when you are doing a scene, some important detail, but it won't click into your consciousness, there are so many other things going on, all in a rush. You finish the scene, the lights are down, then you realise: 'Damn! Why was Joe wearing these silly pyjama tops – he's meant to be wearing a white vest.'

Steven Duffy, who plays Bobby, has brought a wonderful touch to the character. He is the son who is murdered by the Garaside Tongs, his rival gang. The character could have been played on one note, but scene by scene he has found ways to make this very limited character really interesting, even sympathetic. One of the funniest moments of the week – wee Lex has to bite Bobby's ear during a fight between the brothers. It turns out to be an impossible close-up to light. The only way to do it is to get Lex to hold the moment where he is biting Bobby's ear while we light it. This takes five minutes, five hysterical minutes during which time many gross jokes are made as Iain (Lex) lies with Steven's (Bobby's) ear in his mouth, dribbling into his ear!

May 9 Shot a scene where a period bus rounds a corner, only the bus mounts the pavement. I have my back to the bus and my eyes glued to the monitor, so I see none of this. Suddenly there's a chorus of shouts and somebody pushes me off my chair. I still don't get it. I'm trying to keep my eyes glued to the monitor, but I'm sailing through space. In slow motion, a cup of tea floats through my eyeline, then I hit the pavement with a thud. The cup of tea hits the ground close by. I look up. My briefcase lies under the wheel of the bus. My mobile phone and my camera are goners and a bottle of white-out fluid has burst over everything in the bag. Worst of all, my peppermints are crushed! It was amazing – in the second take the driver hit the bus stop and we had to replace him.

May 23 We finished shooting over a week ago. I feel we did very well on this thirty-day schedule. We cut scenes but not many. The last day we were on-stage cramming in pick-ups. Billy was shooting second unit in the room next door. Things normally get a bit loony at this point. Actors are climbing down ropes, running about with tilly lamps, shouting into phones for all those fragmented shots.

Then came the 'wrap' (the wind, roll and print) party. The best bit was the Highland dancing and there was Mark Shivas hurling around a mad eightsome reel. His assistant, Stephanie Guerrasio, couldn't get the hang of one reel where a man was grouped with two women. Being Italian-American, she kept saying, 'What? One man and two women? It would never happen in Italy!'

June 3   With a six-week cut we project the film at the end of each week in a preview theatre. This weekly event feels essential, to get a little distance, sit back and then try to reflect over the weekend. Today I invited about fifteen friends and gave them a questionnaire and 'executive' sandwiches after the film. This was not a high-powered event, as in LA, though it felt important to sit with an audience, to get a basic reaction and comments. I felt I was seeing the film with fresh eyes. It was suddenly obvious where things were getting bogged down and some surprising and helpful observations were made. We got a great response, though it's important not to forget that it was an audience of friends. The confusing instruction 'It's too long, but don't lose anything!' came through on several questionnaires.

June 4   Billy and I got our heads together to crack the ending of the film once and for all. This led to us sitting in silent bewilderment in a cafe. We would record the voice-over for the ending tomorrow, but there was nothing on paper. We had been trying to crack this for months and now the deadline was here. Billy suddenly told me about a dream he had. Oor Wullie (a Scottish boy cartoon character) had a terrible nightmare in which he grew hair all over his body. He had turned into a man. He woke up and was so happy to find he was still a boy he danced down the street. I listened to this amazed, and said, 'That's it.' So Billy went home and wrote the ending from there. We cut it into the film and everything seems to have fallen into place. I now love the ending!

Working with BBC Films has been great, but there has been one problem – finding a new title for the film. The title *Easterhouse* is no good to us because it is a reference to an idea no longer in the film; nothing in the film resembles the real Easterhouse area and we have promised the people who live there that we won't use the name of their community. The problem is that the BBC have been unable to accept any new titles we have suggested and it's now very late in the day. We need a title, now. In the meantime, the Sales Company went ahead and produced a poster for the film which went to Cannes with the BBC. Billy and I were not consulted. The first I knew was when I saw this poster for *Easterhouse* (no mention of 'working title') on the BBC table, featured in *Film '95*. Also, the poster called the three brothers in the story at one point McLean and at another McGrath, a name we changed long ago. I created a bit of a stink, but the whole thing seems to have been put down to a misunderstanding.

There seems to be a last-minute botch-up in the post-production budget with some bills coming in late and squeezing us hard and restricting us. At this stage it seems so strange to be scraping around for a couple of thousand quid here and there to save our bacon – I'm not used to things being so very dire. I can hear the piggy bank rattling dully – only a few coins left. I fear the use of 60s music will be the element to suffer from this.

Spent a day with John Keane, the composer. Still at a playing-around stage, but it looks hopeful. John came up with a nice, light and quirky theme to go with the character of Lex, the boy at the centre of the story.

Working on Lex's imaginary map of Glasgow for the title sequence. My daughter, Carla, is doing the cartoon characters for Lex, mainly teenage gangsters with hatchets in their heads, populating the gang territories. Pushing hard now to get a decent cut for the first screening with the BBC on Friday. We started losing scenes and seriously putting things in a new order.

June 10   Screened the film for Mark Shivas, Andrea Calderwood and Stephanie Guerrasio. It went down well. Everyone seemed in a jolly mood and pleased with progress, especially Stephanie who always wears her heart on her sleeve (an Italian-American trait?). She seems our greatest ally. We all went to a hotel around 7.30 pm and we were still there at 11. Some interesting suggestions were made and we will try some restructuring on Monday. The frustration over the title of the film continues. I went through my little black book where maybe hundreds of titles are recorded, dating back six months. We still couldn't agree to one title. The issue is serious. We shoot the titles this week and Mark Cousins at the Edinburgh Film Festival needs to make up his programme.

June 14   I had a dream last night, the title of the film in a song – 'Little by Little'; I have wanted the title to reflect the idea of littleness, or childhood.

June 16   We all seem interested in *Let it Come Down* for a title, a quote from Macbeth. (Not being a luvvie I really can't go around calling it 'the Scottish play'.)
 We had a day of shooting pick-ups. Clare Higgins turned up looking tanned and relaxed. We shot a grim scene where her character, 'Lorna', views her son's body at the mortuary. Steve Clark-Hall, the co-producer, volunteered his services as a mortuary attendant. Another frustrated actor! We spent the rest of the day shooting the titles of the film, superimposed over fragments of a map showing cartoons of gangland characters.

June 23   There are quite a few projects circulating that I should be interested in, but I'm trying to postpone discussions as my head is still in cutting this film. One more day of cutting the film and then lock-off, no more picture cut. Though there was one director in Hollywood who maintained 'There's no such thing as lock-off!' and went on to prove it by continuing to make cuts until the last moment.
 Last week we narrowed down the film's title to *Let it Come Down*. Most people liked it. Then some negative reactions started to seep through, mainly from the sales agent. Meanwhile, general opinion has swung back to a title Billy and I have wanted for ages – *Small Faces*. But my daughter has just told me that the band the Small Faces have just been asked to do a Levi ad! I can't believe it. Will this prevent us from using the title? Will this title problem ever end? Sadly, Steve Marriott is now dead. How can there be a Small Faces without him? I just hope we can afford to use one of his songs in the film.

June 24 We have finished the picture cut. I had a last-minute brainwave and went over the material one last time with the editor, Scott Thomas. We finished chopping about 8.30pm and I went home feeling nervous, in case we had changed things too fast. We get a last chance to review the cuts on Monday morning.

June 29 BBC Drama sent us a trailer to screen at the BBC Drama launch. Mark Shivas and I both felt it stressed only the violence in the film, no reference to humour or art, just people biffing one another! He asked me to cut a trailer with our editor, but it has to be done in two days and Scott is under pressure. So I'll sit down and chart exactly which shots to use for exactly how long and hopefully Scott will manage to fit it in to a one-and-a-half-minute cut.

July 5 ADR session in Glasgow. Brought in mostly young people who were supporting artists in the film to fill out the soundtrack. They were great and spent all day shouting into a microphone. I wish I could have given them bigger parts in the film. Those playing main roles were very curious to see some cut scenes and seemed very excited. Kevin McKidd, who plays gang leader Malky, confessed to feeling very uncomfortable watching himself in this role.

A sudden rush to find a few words to describe the movie on a poster. Billy came up with:

SMALL FACES
Pure Genius, Pure Nerve, Pure Hell.

We also decided to dedicate the film to our mother and father. Everyone I've spoken to seems to be going to Edinburgh for the film festival and the film's opening. It's beginning to sound quite exciting. Meanwhile we have no money to use two 60s songs we want, so we may have to approach the Glasgow Film Fund and BBC to plead our case. We want to use Georgie Fame's 'Sonny' over the art school sequence and the Small Faces song 'All or Nothing' over another scene. If we don't get these bits of music I'll never feel the film is quite complete. One is optimistic, the other so totally part of that aggressive mod era. Together I feel they would give the film a certain authenticity.

July 8 Finished recording and mixing the music today. I'm very happy with John Keane's contribution to the film, sometimes light and humorous, sometimes incredibly dramatic. Sadly, we can't get the rights to the Small Faces song 'All or Nothing', though we are still considering a couple of other 60s tracks if the BBC will cough up the extra dosh. Our session musicians improvised a mod-ish arrangement for the fight in the lane scene. Later I sneaked in a couple of screams/shouts of my own, hopefully in the style of a 60s group, which John mixed into the instrumental. Also my daughter, Ivana, came in to sing one of the songs. This is such great fun; it's turning out to be a real family affair, and why not, since it's such a totally personal film. DIY, so to speak.

July 26 Visited designer to see ideas for posters and publicity for *Small Faces*. I prefer simple image of boy's face with a sticking plaster over his nose. Otherwise, checking dialogue tracks before final mix etc.

July 30 *Divine Rapture* has folded. I sat in the dubbing theatre shaking my head and muttering, 'My God, what a close shave.' Just before starting *Small Faces* I discussed directing that movie. But I didn't and I now have a small and (I hope) good personal film, instead of a large nightmare.

August 4 Finished mixing *Small Faces* in a mad day with an STV [Scottish Television] camera crew in attendance.

August 29 An incredibly dense six days at the Edinburgh Film Festival. First, Ginnie Atkinson and I picked up Steve Martin at the airport. He was as I remember him, down to the baseball hat and sunglasses. He seemed more relaxed than us. We were worried about protecting him from the press etc. We slipped into an Italian restaurant and ordered food. The place was empty, dead to the world. Steve suddenly said he wished he was in a cafe because this restaurant reminded him of a place he knew in Ohio. We left Ginnie paying the bill for food that still hadn't arrived and went to find a cafe. He obviously liked the thought of mingling with the crowds. Instead we had brought him to an empty place that made him think of Ohio! In the end I wandered up and down Princes Street with him for hours, browsing through stalls, past buskers, looking in shop windows. Not many people seemed to recognise him. I suppose you don't expect to see Steve Martin in Edinburgh. At one point I turned around and saw a stout man in a white shirt and black suit following us. He swung away to look in a shop window just as I spotted him. I nudged Steve. He looked back and said, 'Oh, God!' There were two of them, not-too-subtle bodyguards appointed to tail us. Every market corner we turned, there was one, leaning against a pillar examining his fingernails or whatever.

Steve and I went to open *A Simple Twist of Fate*. We went on to the stage and I was astonished to find Steve did a stand-up routine (more or less) for about fifteen minutes. He had the audience eating out of his hand. They loved him. I actually cried with laughter, or maybe it was relief that everything was going so well. The next night Steve and I did a scene-by-scene together on *A Simple Twist of Fate*. I felt like the straight man in a comedy act, but it seemed to be what the audience wanted, Steve being quick-witted and throwing everything humorously back at them.

Mark Cousins [Director of the Edinburgh Film Festival] and Ginnie Atkinson [Producer of the Festival] laid on an impressive formal dinner for him, Suso Cecchi D'Amico and some others in some kind of stately home. It was great to talk to Suso, who co-wrote *Bicycle Thieves* and other masterpieces! She is over eighty, but she came to see *Small Faces* and I had the chance to announce that this film would probably never have been made had Billy and I not seen *Rocco and his Brothers* years ago; which prompted us to make a film about brothers. She worked with Visconti, she knew Pasolini and has worked with other heroes of the cinema. I couldn't stop talking to her.

The actors started turning up for the *Small Faces*. Steve Clark-Hall and Marie Betts [Co-ordinator] turned up, as did John De Borman [Cinematographer]. I had to do about two days solid press. I kept saying the same things over and over again. Now and then I got so sick of listening to my own voice I would sort of explode on some issue and rant and rave a bit, then fall back into the same old pattern again. Billy was only there for one of these press conference days and I felt that when he wasn't physically with me I wasn't getting the message across that this was a film we made together.

I felt very nervous about the first screening of *Small Faces*. There were a few sound-level problems. I don't know how this happened. Either a computer fault during recording, or maybe we were all just too tired on our very short post-production schedule that didn't allow for even an afternoon to review what we had done. Despite our anxiety, the film went down really well. People cheered.

We went to a party for the film. Stephen Baldwin turned up. I haven't seen him since *A Simple Twist of Fate*. He was in town to publicise *The Usual Suspects*. It was great to see him. He's an up-for-anything kind of guy! Sounds like he and Gabriel Byrne had a great time on this film. Both Gabriel and Steve Martin were quite unhappy when we started to shoot *A Simple Twist of Fate*, having both broken up with their wives. They both seem so much better now. The party seemed good, with a music tent, though I don't recall much about it. It took me an hour to travel the distance of about twenty feet to get a drink. I suppose I was in demand, people wanted to talk to me so. Best enjoy it while it lasts!

Next day we received the Critics' Award and word started filtering through that the international jury were keen on *Small Faces*. In the end we were given a unanimous vote. Simon Perry introduced Billy and me. We got up on stage to receive the Michael Powell Award, a great feeling as it was an acknowledgment of what we had struggled to do, that it has been of some value. We donated the £2,000 cash element of the prize to the Iain Robertson Trust, which was set up to keep Iain at drama school. I do think Mark Cousins and Ginnie Atkinson did a great job and created a lot of excitement and really raised the festival's profile. They also created a happy atmosphere and made us all feel welcome.

September 23 The week started with a summit meeting after a screening of *Small Faces* to determine what exactly are the sound problems we are experiencing. The sound level for Dolby is seven in the projection room, but the level sounds right at five. A long section of black before the funeral scene is not true black, which disturbs us. Black seems to need white to truly set it off, otherwise it looks muddy. Good news is that the film has

57

been sold to October Films in the USA and to Germany (unseen they tell me!), so if France buys it, we will already have come close in sales to the production cost of the film, even before a UK sale.

Small Faces has generally been very well reviewed. Better than the much bigger-budget *A Simple Twist of Fate*. It's something for me to think hard about. I make a Hollywood movie with Steve Martin and the film people like is the one I write with my brother and which we make in Glasgow for a fraction of the other's budget. The reviews of *A Simple Twist of Fate* were quite good but lacked wholehearted enthusiasm. I was genuinely impressed by the critics' understanding of my position as a British director making a Hollywood movie.

September 28   I believe the Sales Company is showing *Small Faces* to UK distributors today. Fingers crossed. Carole Myer seems confident.

Postscript (December)   It's December. *Small Faces* was accepted for Sundance, but we didn't take up the offer. Instead we waited for the result on Berlin, but they only took two films for competition and ours wasn't one of them. So, I understand, we crawled back to Sundance, but by then it was too late. We have to hope someone drops out and lets us back in. Folly I fear. You work so hard to get a movie made, then it goes out of your hands. I would have loved to have gone to Sundance and I'm sure it could only have helped the North American campaign. It is so frustrating. In fact, we were advised by the sales agent not to go to Edinburgh originally and only went after Billy and I absolutely insisted. Thank God we did, as it has now been bought by almost every territory worldwide. I'm beginning to have a sense of apprehension about the film's release. I love this film so much, please let it work out alright!

Billy, my brother, has gone to Australia to work on his next film. I want us to write another film together. *Small Faces* is perhaps the most satisfying film I've ever made, because it is so personal. Meanwhile we had an encouraging meeting with Guild, who are responsible for UK distribution. They seem very enthusiastic and have an optimistic plan to open *Small Faces* in the West End on 5 April. Thank God it isn't April the first.

Michael Apted

A director working in movies, documentary, television and commercials, Michael Apted trained at Granada TV in the mid-60s but has lived and worked mainly in America since 1980. His feature films include Coal Miner's Daughter, Gorky Park, Gorillas in the Mist, Thunderheart *and* Nell. *Extracts from his diary for 1995 give a flavour of the excitements and problems of living and working as a film-maker in Hollywood.*

April 1 I fly back from New York where I've spent the last five weeks preparing and shooting a pilot for Warner Bros. Television and CBS. It was a brutal schedule: twelve days photography for a one-hour film, which works out at roughly six pages a day come rain or shine. So why do it? I like the energy of it all; there's a lot of downtime with movies, a lot of waiting around; but it's not so much a question of boredom as of a fear that unless I keep working I'll forget how to do the job. Set at a New York tabloid, it needed energetic storytelling in a documentary style, the sort of thing I think I do well. So, I put together a good cast (Mary Tyler Moore, Madeleine Kahn, etc.) and a willing crew, rolled up my sleeves and got on with the job.

On top of that I was depressed by the reception of *Nell*, my movie with Jodie Foster. It had performed reasonably well in the USA ($33 million), but the critical response was very mixed, with some of it so vehement that it made me wonder whether the whole enterprise had been a horrible mistake, that my judgment had somehow deserted me.

April 2 Los Angeles. I do the first of a series of press interviews on a documentary I made last year about the students of Tiananmen Square. It's called *Moving the Mountain* and was part-financed by the BBC. It opens in New York later this month, and any success will depend first on good reviews and then on word-of-mouth. But without the reviews there may be no word-of-mouth as the distributor may fall over dead if there isn't any good press to work with. It's a tough business selling documentaries with very little chance to make any money, so if things don't go swimmingly from the start people tend to bail out.

April 3 On the movie front, I have my first script meeting on a project at Fox for Laura Ziskin [Head of Fox 2000] called *The Piece*. It's a tough, contemporary story of a black woman detective set in LA. I get sent quite a lot of scripts, and it's hard making decisions about one I'm going to have to live with for the next eighteen months. I don't write my own stuff so I'm at the mercy of whatever's out there. This turns out to be a typical first meeting; everybody a bit cautious, feeling each other out, no one giving much away, but all of us aware that the real business of the day is to find out whether we all want to make the same film. But it went well and I felt a good rapport with the writer, John Ridley. We agreed to move ahead and start work on a new draft.

April 4 Tuesday is the day for the weekend returns on *Nell* and although the selling was tough, I must have done a pretty good job, because the film is a great success in Europe, fast approaching $100 million.

April 6 I see the editor's cut of the TV pilot knowing I have four days to get it ready for the producers, who in turn have three days before it's screened to the studio. We're cutting on video – the Avid system – which I love, as it's so quick and flexible, easy to change things, and compare different versions; everything at your fingertips. I could never go back to editing on film, it feels almost medieval in comparison.

April 11 Attend a meeting of the Documentary Branch of the Academy. I've been at war with them for years over their insane nominating process for Best Documentary. They always manage to get it wrong, but never more spectacularly than this year when they overlooked *Hoop Dreams*, one of the best films of this or any year. The committee has become an embarrassment not just to the Academy but to the whole documentary world. Rather than attack from outside, I've decided to infiltrate and see whether I can storm the citadel from within. These are early days, so the meeting was uneventful. There will be rockier times ahead.

April 12 Have lunch with Jodie Foster on the set of the film she is directing. One of the few attractions for me of living in LA is the sense of being in the centre of an industry. There's so much going on, so much energy, so much enthusiasm for making movies. In the end that's what got me down about England – it was so hard to get anything done. Here you just pop down the road and have a taco with Miss Foster. I've got all my directing jobs by being on the spot, able to develop relationships and pursue material.

April 18 We screen the TV pilot for Warners and they like it. However big or small the project, whatever's at stake, these showings are always stressful. You try and pretend it doesn't matter but of course it does; you build up a defence mechanism but it's easily punctured. You vow not to be defensive, but you always are. Today, mercifully, I don't have to worry, but TV has many masters and this is only the first sortie.

April 19 In New York for the glitzy premiere of the Tiananmen Square documentary. It was produced by Trudie Styler who is married to Sting so there's no shortage of celebrities on hand. The irony is not lost on me that the Beautiful People are celebrating an event that ended in bloodshed and despair, an event created out of a desire for the most basic human dignity – freedom of speech, and here we are rocking and rolling in all our finery. But the occasion is a success, we raise money for good causes and people are moved by the film, so why rain on the parade? I do a lot of press and the responses seem positive, so far.

April 23 Mike Newell [British director] wins the David Lean award at

BAFTA. What a thrill! We were at Cambridge together and started at Granada TV on the same day. My delight is slightly tinged with envy as I've never got anywhere near something like that; but at least it's in the family.

April 26 My worst nightmare – Janet Maslin in the *New York Times* hates the Tiananmen Square film. She creams it, so there goes my audience. The review is particularly annoying as she doesn't criticise the film for what it is, but for what she thinks it should be. She wants a film that has scale and scope, I wanted something intimate and emotional. God knows it's hard enough making movies without having people in influential positions second-guessing you. I seriously doubt the film will survive such a hostile review in such an important paper. Do critics ever think of this, or is that considered outside their terms of reference? The subject matter of my film is serious and well intentioned, it isn't a piece of Hollywood trash, so why kill it? The rest of the reviews are excellent, but they are meaningless – my target audience reads the *Times*.

April 28 Off to London for my mother's ninetieth birthday. No chance of emulating that in this job!

May 8 Disturbing meeting at Fox on *The Piece*. I sense panic in the air. The producers start throwing insane casting ideas around as though the material needs a strong acting package to push it through. I know when a film is driven by cast and when it's driven by material, and of course sometimes it's both, but this subject will only succeed on its script and vision, and for the producers to be grasping at casting straws this early is a little off-putting. Don't they trust it now? After all they did buy the script and ask me to direct it, so what's up all of a sudden? It's pretty clear that the writer, who's never had a film made, is traumatised by the confusing signals flying around the room, and it's important for me to keep him on track and energised. So I arrange to meet him alone the next day, out of the studio, so we can establish our priorities. The script still needs work, but we mustn't confuse studio nervousness with the real issues of what has to be done.

May 15 Another meeting at Fox, this time to discuss a preliminary budget. My vision for *The Piece* has to be translated into dollars and cents. I have to figure out how many days shooting I need; what the film should look like; what sets need to be built and what can be done on location; what special equipment we might need; how much stock I'll use. The studio calls this first budget a 'flash' but it gives them a good idea whether their notion of what they want to spend bears any relation to my appetite for what they should spend. Many a project can get terminally unstuck at this point so I have to be wary. I know that if I can keep my budget in the mid-teens the project will be attractive to them and give me freedom to operate. In some ways these meetings are as important as script sessions – the 'big picture' begins to emerge, the bottom line is defined.

May 19 I have another meeting with the Documentary Branch of the Academy. We're planning a big International Congress in October/November to bring in film-makers from all over the world to LA and I'm entrusted with recruiting from England. I make the case that the UK is one of the few places where documentaries flourish largely through the patronage of TV, so it would be informative to explain how the system works. I write to some old friends back home setting them up for a freebie to Hollywood. I'm enjoying the work, so what started off as subterfuge to get the Academy nominating process changed has become more positive, but I'm not, however, forgetting my real agenda.

May 23 I learned today that CBS has passed on my *New York News* pilot. After three weeks of testing and analysis, of rumour and anticipation, the project is dead. I'm angry and upset. All that work is in the toilet, part of the bizarre wastage of the Network Pilot System where ideas are developed, written and produced and a large majority abandoned. I know it's hard sometimes to picture what a treatment or script will look like on film, but it seems so crass and indulgent to spend that much money ($2.3 million in my case) on so many projects with few of them ever likely to make it to the screen. I made a decent film and it's never going to be seen.

May 25 *Nell* finally broke the $100 million barrier.

May 26 John Ridley – the writer of *The Piece* – has persuaded Oliver Stone to produce and let him direct one of his own scripts, so it'll be his first time out. John comes round to pick my brains. I enjoy talking about the job – it is a craft that has to be learned, and it's fun to analyse it and pass on what you think is valuable. I tell him to surround himself with the best talent he can buy and put himself in their hands, but to hang on for dear life to whatever vision he has carved out for his movie. That's the hardest thing – to know when to take advice and when to politely ignore it, what to delegate and what you have to do yourself.

June 8 There is justice in entertainment heaven! The management team at CBS, who rejected my TV pilot, have all been fired. They're being replaced by Leslie Moonves, Head of Warners TV, who commissioned the show in the first place. So maybe there's life in the project yet. What goes around comes around.

June 12 Dismal news from Fox. They've decided they don't like the rewrites of *The Piece*. I've had this feeling for over a month that the studio got me involved because it seemed like a good idea at the time and not because of any great passion for the subject. It's a reality of life in Hollywood that different branches of the body politic march to different drumbeats – a corporation controls literally hundreds of projects, but the individual can only focus on a handful at most, and the bottom line is 'time'. They can dick around asking for rewrite after rewrite and not pay attention until they feel they have to, whereas the rest of us invest our life's blood in the work, watching the weeks and months slip by. It takes time to figure this out, but once you do it's a useful part of your Hollywood survival kit. Know when to jump ship. So Fox and I agree to meet at the end of the week to discuss the script, but it seems beside the point because I'm sure it's over. I'm angry but must keep my head so I can winkle the project out of them and take it somewhere else. If they get too pissed off with me, they'll just sit tight and let it die on the vine.

June 15 The Fox meeting went well – we cut through all the bullshit and I told them I wanted a real statement of intent, that I wasn't going to develop the script any further without a production commitment and that I wasn't interested in overtures about changing writers – always a good studio ruse to buy time. I agreed it might be worth making the film non-union and putting it through another company so we could remove the studio overhead and reduce the budget by 25 per cent at a stroke. They promised me a decision in a few days.

June 17 I heard today that one of my movies, *Thunderheart* (1992) – a hard look at the political mistreatment of Native Americans by the US government in the 70s – is to be broadcast on Fox TV, but with 28 minutes of its 118-minute running time deleted! That's 24 per cent of the film. I'm having a nervous breakdown and ring the Network, the production company (Tri-Star) and the Directors Guild of America [DGA] to see if there's anything I can do to stop it. Apparently there isn't, as the DGA has a poorly negotiated position over syndication, and Fox, although clearly a Network, is still anomalously regarded as a syndicate. All that's left is to insist on taking my name off the film and hope it creates a ripple of attention. This is 'Artists' Rights' at its most basic and urgent – the right to preserve the identity of your work. No one minds making small adjustments to accommodate the needs of different outlets because it increases the visibility of the film, but this sort of massacre is something else.

June 23 The new management at CBS is already sniffing around *New York News* and have asked for six scripts. It is not a full-blown commitment by any means, but it could be the beginning of something.

July 5 Suddenly the *Thunderheart* issue has blown into huge proportions. I get calls from the DGA and Artists Rights Foundation people in LA and Washington asking me how far I'm prepared to push the matter of fighting Tri-Star and Fox over the recutting of the movie. They like the case and see it as an opportunity to push the issues of moral rights and film labelling. There's also some real urgency as the film is being broadcast on 18 July. I agree to go to Washington to join with lobbyists and lawyers to talk to members of Congress about backing the Film Disclosure Act. This would make it compulsory to tell audiences what changes have been made from the original film. Fair enough you might think, but the studios oppose it vehemently and claim the right to do whatever they want with what they own, without tarnishing it with untidy and unappealing labels. Moreover, by allowing film-makers to have any sort of disclaimer on the film, the studios fear they are opening the door, however slightly, on the treacherous area of authorship. European directors have a version of this, but the American industry lives in terror that these artistic rights may one day turn into economic rights and where would that end? With the DGA lawyers, I set in motion one arbitration claim against Tri-Star to label the film and another to allow me to take a pseudonym if no label is forthcoming.

July 11   As expected, CBS announce they are picking up *New York News* and make a full order of thirteen episodes. They schedule it for Thursdays at 9 pm against *Seinfeld* so it's going to be tough – not only the competition but, as it got picked up six weeks later than everything else, there's much less time to get good scripts, directors, cast, crew and locations and all the other elements that feed the weekly TV juggernaut. The show goes on the air in ten weeks!

July 12   Today I leave for Washington and frankly the whole thing has gotten a little scary. I imagine I'll be getting a fairly hostile reception because the Hollywood studios, through the MPAA [Motion Picture Association of America], donate lots of money to re-election campaigns so most of the politicians will be primed to be unsympathetic to anything that threatens the status quo. The DGA has warned me not to expect much and I wonder whether there will be any career fall-out in taking on the studios. Tri-Star are playing hardball by refusing to grant me a pseudonym although the DGA had approved it. They also gleefully announce that a well-known local film critic had viewed the TV cut and thought it acceptable. I'm furious and call him up and wonder how he could have got himself into the middle of a dispute between the legal department of a major studio and the creative community. He's apologetic, but the damage is done. I am looking forward to meeting Fred Thompson, the Republican Senator for Tennessee, who plays the head of the FBI in *Thunderheart*, one of his last roles before he gave up acting and went into politics. If I can't get his support I'll be in a sorry state.

July 13   We start with a briefing from the lawyer and lobbyist who will shepherd us through the day. It helps that the film has serious political content – it's not a piece of Hollywood froth edited down for sex and violence – so we can put the mistreatment of the movie into the context of the abuse of the Native American. We visit twelve senators and congressmen and no one rejects us. Some, like Fred, are cautious, on the lookout for any downside, others supportive while warning us that Film Disclosure is not a 'hot button issue'; only Pat Shroeder, the congresswoman from Colorado, is indifferent. Our advisors tell us we did well but there's no time for 'pats on the back' as I have to fly back to LA tonight for tomorrow's arbitration hearings.

July 14 I'm happily rehearsing a statement in my mind when suddenly I'm asked to go and sit by the arbitrator to be sworn in, examined and cross-examined. I had no idea there would be such formality and that the proceedings would have the weight of legal process. I stagger through my testimony with my heart in my mouth, wondering why I have precipitated these monstrous events. I'm sure it isn't going well; our arguments of 'good faith' and 'moral rights', although persuasively expressed, seem wishy-washy when compared with the slick 'letter of the law' studio case. We are operating in grey areas, whereas they throw my signed contract at me. I waived my rights, they say, for the crock of gold. It takes until lunchtime, and we're promised a decision by late afternoon. In the meantime we scurry across town for the next hearing – my request for a pseudonym.

This session is something of an oddity as I am appearing in front of a panel of two directors and two studio representatives and have to win a majority to succeed. The mechanism was negotiated in 1981 and has never been used, so all previous claims for a pseudonym have either been cut off at the pass by the DGA or agreed by the studio. Although less formal than the arbitration, it is just as depressing. Our case seems hopelessly fragile, and sure enough the studio guys quote the agreement and ask how exactly we think it has been abused. We can only answer with talk of principle and artistic integrity and speak of our fears for a future where our work is unprotected from the purely commercial needs of the big entertainment corporations. One of the most chilling moments of the whole day is the pride with which a studio post-production head catalogues the number of films that have been re-edited, some more brutally than mine. It's obvious that we are dead in the water, and sure enough the panel is divided and the claim lost. But then comes the startling news that we have won the earlier arbitration in spectacular fashion. The arbitrator has decided that the studio has indeed acted in bad faith and that a mechanism exists for recourse – the pseudonym – but if that fails I will be entitled to a disclaimer on the film. The language of the disclaimer is stronger than we have dared hope for; it says exactly how much has been cut out and that I, the director, am therefore disassociating myself from it.

But the studio has one last trick up its sleeve; when they hear the arbitrator's ruling they do a quick 180° turn and give me a pseudonym. So there will be no label. Never mind, a ruling now exists that might make studios think twice before they ride roughshod through our work!

July 18 So *Thunderheart* goes out on TV directed by Alan Smithee, the DGA's standard pseudonym. It's weird and I wonder whether anybody notices. I can't even bear to watch the mangled version.

July 20 The bubble of good feeling about *New York News* suddenly bursts when I'm told that CBS wants to recast the three male leads. That means I'll have to redo at least 70 per cent of the show. They're crazy, but that's the decision, so I have to face seven days of shooting while I repeat myself; same script, same locations but different actors. It's not an appetising prospect and feels more like an exercise than a real job, grafting new performances on to something already established. 'We love the pilot,' they all say, 'so don't change a thing' – just the faces! What kind of double-think is that?

August 1   New York. Back in the saddle – the comforting regime of preparing for a film; scouting, casting and answering, or trying to answer, the endless stream of questions. It's empowering to be back in a familiar routine, even if it is redoing old work. We are doing make-up tests with Mary Tyler Moore, one of the leads in *New York News*, and I sense her pain and anxiety. She's one of the truly great stars in the television firmament and this is her series comeback. We're all trying to pretend she hasn't grown old, that she's still Mary Richards, the liberated, self-reliant young woman my generation grew up with. Filters, gauzes and even pantyhose over the lens to turn back the years and stop the clock. She handles it all with grace and skill, but it's not easy for her.

August 17   Major earth tremors in Tinsletown as Mike Ovitz leaves CAA to join Disney, and in so doing redraws the map of Hollywood. CAA are my agents so I wonder how this will effect me. Not in the short term, as I hardly know Ovitz; but in the long term the agency might be seriously weakened. I like the people who look after me and can't imagine leaving unless everything falls apart. But already I've had a couple of calls from other agencies about nothing in particular; clearly they're feeling me out. It's a tough town.

August 18   Today I finish shooting the pilot and tomorrow start post-production on that and the pre-production on the next episode. I have only seven days to prepare the next film, and three to cut the old. It's a military operation and hardly the stuff of intelligent film-making, but as long as you accept it for what it is, there's a satisfaction in meeting the challenge and solving the problems.

August 23   We screen the pilot and it's way over length and needs major surgery, but as I'm about to start shooting the next show, I have to hand it over to the producer to take time out. I hate to do that, but we're under the gun and can't stand on ceremony. In any event, it's a producer's medium and once the director has delivered his cut, he's gone.

August 28   We've submitted *The Piece* to a couple of places and the early returns are in. A pass at Interscope [US production company] – too dark and depressing, but cautious interest from New Line, although they are hinting at some restructuring. Hardly what we'd hoped for, but it's alive and we'll push it out to some other places. I'm not bothering with the major studios – I know it's not commercial enough for them, so why beat myself up?

August 29   The producer's cut of the pilot turned out well, thank God.

They made the trims and with a bit more finessing we'll get the best out of the material. Dodged a bullet this time. It's been fun working the last month in New York – the city is much more user-friendly than LA. Its energy informs the work, and it has a magnificent pool of actors.

September 7 I finish my stint on *New York News*.

September 12 LA. I meet at New Line to follow up on *The Piece*. They're very respectful but make worrying noises about how hard the film might be to sell. I know their decisions are almost exclusively determined by foreign pre-sales, so the tail wags the dog. As this story is built around a black female character, it doesn't add up to big foreign bucks, so that could be my downfall here.

September 22 Bad news as New Line pass on *The Piece*. They say what I thought they'd say, that it is too difficult to sell in the foreign markets. Big surprise!

September 24 Everything is brought dramatically into perspective by the news of my mother's death. I head for England. But before I leave I have to start to sort out arrangements for next month's International Documentary Congress. I have agreed to moderate two seminars at the Congress: one on the UK scene with representatives from the BBC, ITV and the Independents; and the other a complicated and high-profile event on directors who move between fiction and non-fiction. There will be a number of panellists all showing clips to illustrate their work, plus the prospect of a volatile discussion on the ethics involved in the mixing of documentary and drama.

September 29 A glimmer of hope from Hollywood as I get a script from Castle Rock – one of the largest and most successful independents, with Hugh Grant producing and starring. I like it and they want the film to go immediately. It's out to a couple of other directors but I'm asked if I'll go to Paris in a few days and talk to Hugh. You bet I will!

October 3 I'm running around London in a flurry of meetings. But I'm only sort of half there because what I really want is a crack at the Hugh Grant project. A big movie with a bona fide male star. It's strange having detailed script meetings on films I hope I'm not going to be free to do. I feel guilty but that's absurd since they all know what's going on. I haven't hidden anything from anybody.

October 6 I take the train to meet Hugh Grant in Paris. My audition lunch with Hugh and his partner Elizabeth Hurley goes as well as can be expected. It's a beautiful autumn day so everybody is in good humour. I make my script points and survive a fairly rigorous questioning without putting my foot in my mouth. Hugh has certainly done his homework and I sense this is a big decision for him, as the film is a significant leap for him, and, if he pulls it off, it will consolidate him as a major player. It's challenging material, tricky too, and if he's not believable or can't find the proper tone, he'll come unstuck. The director decision is crucial and he seems nervous about it, and I imagine it will take time. I'm sympathetic, but I don't want to be kept dangling for long – it's going to be a tough few days waiting for an answer.

October 11 I'm behaving a bit like a headless chicken. Over the last two days I've had three meetings on different scripts but these other projects may not be still around if I lose the Grant film. I've been involved on the periphery of one of them for nearly three years, and at last it's come my way with a real chance of getting made. But the producers are making it clear that they won't wait for me, although they don't have a star or a half-decent script. It would be perfect for me to develop as I have a vision of how to do it and how the writer could pull it off. But no, that's not enough and unless I commit to them and blow off Hugh Grant, they're going to find another director. For me there's no decision to make; I have to wait for Hugh, but I'm sad and annoyed at losing such good material.

October 13 A red-letter day for me as I hear I've nailed the Hugh Grant/ Castle Rock movie. It's thrilling and I'm delighted, but friends and colleagues wonder why I don't seem more excited. In truth I'm scared to death and full of doubt whether I can pull it off. I love to work and once I start and get settled, I'll be fine, but for the moment I'm daunted by the challenge.

October 14 Hugh and Elizabeth come over for lunch to talk about script and crew issues. I decide against meeting in a restaurant as they are still prey to LA paparazzi after the events of last summer, and I don't want our first session to degenerate into a circus. They're both smart and very committed and we seem to agree on a style and tone.

October 16 A roller-coaster of a day with a fruitful meeting at Castle Rock to look at the big production picture; when to start, who to hire and what our priorities should be. They have a reputation of being a good home for film-makers – supportive, knowledgeable and non-intrusive. The director Rob Reiner is one of their principals, so already we have a common language.

October 25 Back in LA, this is my big week with the International Documentary Congress. I have to introduce, moderate and participate in the first big event: a panel of directors discussing their work in both fiction and documentary. I get through the introduction, but the first speaker begins to seriously waffle. I realise that, whether I like it or not, this is my show, so I interrupt him and generate a flood of nervous giggles, and move him along. The next guy introduces his first clip and it's the wrong one, so he dances around the stage until the projectionist stops the film, then he fills in with a couple of stories until we're ready to start again. The lights go down, the clip comes up and its still wrong. He leaps off the stage, rushes out of the auditorium and up to the projection booth leaving me alone with an audience of 350, and more nervous giggling. I survive until the lights go down again and mercifully the right clip comes up. Things could only get better, which they did, and next day I'm on again with some Brits discussing the documentary scene at home. This is a joy, as the panel is articulate and concise and has something significant to say. I'm not sure, all the same, that this moderating game is a good career move.

November 8 I'm in the midst of a good-natured but rather difficult disagreement over crewing with Hugh Grant and Elizabeth Hurley, the producers on *Extreme Measures*. It's awkward because we're all trying to protect and position ourselves – they're ambitious to have an input into how the film is made and have been developing the material for over a year and don't want to back off now. I respect that but want to feel free to use the people I think are most appropriate, so I can do the best job I can. We'll sort it out but it's taking too long and makes us look a little foolish in the eyes of the studio.

November 20 We're back on course with *Extreme Measures*, having carefully defined our areas of responsibility. Today we do a reading of the film with a group of recruited actors, each playing about ten parts, and it gives us all – studio included – a chance to see how the text is working. We've been doing such a lot of rewriting that I need to make sure we're going forward, not sideways, and have to figure out what needs more work. There's a section in the middle that sags pretty badly and will have to be restructured, but we're three months away from shooting so there's no reason to panic. Hugh is very good which is enormously encouraging. He seems very focused and energetic, playing for reality rather than just for laughs. He did an excellent job rewriting his own role to give it his distinctive humour, yet without disrupting the dynamic of the story. It's a serious part but has enough of him in it not to disappoint his fans. This is a fine line to walk and I remember failing in a similar situation with John Belushi in *Continental Divide*, when I asked too much of John's fans in making him a romantic lead. They were used to his broad slapstick and couldn't cope with such a radical change of tone. Audiences have expectations of movie stars and if you want to push the envelope you have to be very cautious – it's hard to think of a star who could take on any part in any genre and still pull in a big crowd. Hugh seems to know who he is, what is expected, and how far he can push it.

November 24 The crew issue has become tricky again, but for different reasons. It looks as though a lot of my trusted collaborators – directors of photography and editors – aren't going to be free, so I'll have to find some new best friends. It's hard to move from the comfort and familiarity of continuing relationships to the uncertainty of new ones, but I'm told it's good to be challenged and to re-evaluate the way you work. I'm not so sure.

November 28 We begin the first round of casting. It's unproductive and frustrating. I make it difficult for casting directors because I never really know what I'm looking for until I start to audition actors and hear them read. I tend to change my mind mid-stream, about how I see roles and who we should bring in. Although I don't find anybody I like today, I begin to get a sense of what I'm going to need. It's a long process and I like to keep going until a decision has to be made. Casting is as important a job as any I do on the film, so I'd better get it right.

November 29 I leave LA and go East to start work on the locations for *Extreme Measures*. The film is set in New York but we're thinking of doing studio work in Toronto plus some other bits and pieces, so that's my first stop. I close up the office, put my affairs in order, pack my woollies and hit the road. It's a nomadic life, unpredictable and exciting, but sometimes so full of anxiety that I wonder why I do it. On reflection that's easy to answer – I don't know how to do anything else.

December 1 I'm scouting in Toronto and it's as cold as hell. It's down to minus thirty, and there's months of this ahead. The work is dispiriting as we're pretending Toronto is New York. It's cheaper to shoot here, but I'm wondering why I even agreed to contemplate this fiction let alone try to make it work. On top of that most of the exteriors will have to be shot in New York, so I'll be shooting in two countries with different union jurisdictions and will have to change a chunk of the crew half-way through, which is unsettling and time consuming. Toronto brings good things of course: plenty of excellent studio space, a fine crew, and most importantly, an unjaded attitude towards film. As long as I can keep my spirits up and stay focused, I'm sure we'll do fine.

December 4 New York. I visit the emergency room at Bellevue Hospital where much of the action is supposed to take place, and its night and day compared to what's in Toronto. We're building a set so that'll be fine, but where do I find the characters to people it? From my early days at Granada I learned that if you put a place on film you shouldn't just shoot the geography, but use the people too. The emergency room scenes are at the beginning of the film and will set a tone, an atmosphere, and if I don't get that right, what price the rest?

Hugh Grant, who plays a physician, seemed excited by what he saw and found a sympathetic doctor to give him the inside scoop. I always insist on actors researching their roles as much as possible, but it can be a double-edged sword when they come back from a successful day in the field reporting that the story doesn't work and real people don't speak like the script. It's at moments like these you need an iron nerve because reason will prevail, but first you have to let the enthusiasm and discovery play out, gratefully use what's helpful and politely junk the babble.

December 6   I visit the set of *New York News*, but if I was looking for a happy reunion, my timing could hardly have been worse – the show was cancelled yesterday! Everyone's depressed and annoyed that CBS never really gave it a fair shot – they put it against *Seinfeld* and just let it die. A sad end to all the promise of a new show.

December 12   We've sent *Extreme Measures* to Paul Newman to co-star with Hugh Grant. He would be the perfect foil – he would bring dignity and credibility to a villain who must be seen to be both rational and charming. So far the auspices are good – we've chatted on the phone and he says he likes what he's read but wants more time to mull it over. He asks when, where, how much and for how long, so it's encouraging. All I can do now is prepare for the Chinese water torture and stand by my bed and wait.

December 25   I'm home for the holidays and Christmas gets off to a rollicking start with the news that Paul Newman has passed on the film. He sends me a charming note explaining his decision and I write back in a vain attempt to get him to change his mind but I think it's a lost cause. Now we're in a quandary about what to do next, and the producers, studio head and I spend a chunk of Christmas morning on a four-way conference-call linking London, LA and New York, arguing over the candidates. There's not much we can do until the New Year so we all have plenty of time to brood and worry. Confidence is fragile and turn-downs can be very dispiriting, so we need to move quickly and hope we get lucky.

Postscript   I've spent January moving between Toronto and New York, casting and scouting locations and working with Hugh on the script. The spilt production base has been very stressful, even the travel is a drama with the bad weather. I have to deal with two of everything – assistant directors, scouts, propmen, co-ordinators, special effects, etc. – and it's both confusing and wasteful. But the film's fortunes took a giant leap when Gene Hackman and Sarah Jessica Parker signed on, so with them and Hugh it feels like a big movie. The studio wants to open it on 4 October, so I've got a busy year ahead. It's scary having a date when you haven't shot a frame of film, but exciting that Castle Rock have enough confidence to make that decision this early. But who knows where I'll be this time next year. That's the fun of this job – you never know.

Gary Sinyor

A National Film and Television School graduate, Gary Sinyor burst on to the scene in 1993 with the no-budget comedy Leon the Pig Farmer *which picked up awards at Edinburgh and Venice. His second feature* Solitaire for Two *was released in 1995. He has a development deal with Chrysalis and is currently raising interest in a new feature,* Period!*, described as 'Monty Python meets Merchant Ivory'.*

April *Period!* has been turned down by Sony. Is this the beginning of a familiar treadmill?

The screenplay is being read by actors, that is, once their agents have 'approved' it. Peter Ustinov is apparently thinking of playing Horace. Superb if he does. I can't get a letter of intent from Brian Glover's agent because Equity have blacklisted me and all my projects. When I found out I arranged to see them. I'm advised that I can sue but if I sued Equity everytime I could do, I'd never make any films. Maybe that's their plan.

May *Period!* is now with Buena Vista. Emma Clarke at Fine Line London office is also very keen. Apparently she wants script changes. Fine, if that means they pay for the movie.

I've decided to go to Cannes. Although I loathe and detest it, there are legitimate reasons to go: *Solitaire for Two* is screening twice, plus Chrysalis are launching their sales arm, plus I could be talking to people about *Period!*. In the next week, I hope, I'll have a clearer idea of who my cast will be. I'd like to get Alan Cumming for Cedric. And I'm still awaiting news on Peter Ustinov.

May 24 Back from Cannes. Who said it was horrible? I love it. *Solitaire for Two* sold really well. The Germans actually got into a bidding war – which is a first for me. What was most surprising was how much I felt more at home with the film crowd. Partly I guess because the young turks in the UK are definitely taking over, or at least moving up. We're now accepted more, and this feels good. The worst place to feel like an outsider is Cannes. In addition to meeting *Solitaire* distributors, I had a meeting – set up by Lyndsey Posner at Chrysalis – with Ruth Vitale at Fine Line, and I pitched *Period!* to her. Irrespective of what she thinks, it was the most relaxed meeting I'd ever had with a US distributor which speaks volumes about her. Anyone who can make a paranoid film-maker feel at ease when looking for money is surely destined for greatness.

The only downside was that I heard that Eric Idle has also written a film parodying British period drama, and which Miramax are keen on. That's a bummer. But a comedy is a comedy – we'll have different jokes and different humour in ours. Plus, if I'm quick, I might get in first. Thought of Minnie Driver [British actress] for Emily. Emily Lloyd is very keen too. Oh, and British Screen turned down *Period!*. Surprise me!

July Sometime in June, Ruth Vitale passed. It's now 21 July. I forget the date when she passed but it was a moment of classic rejection after a positive build-up. And I reacted to it by moving up seventeen gears. The result of which appears to be that I now have a cast, a start date, and all the pieces of financing coming together quicker than I could ever have dreamed. At a budget of £3.6 million. Frightening.

Much of this is due to the money that the National Lottery is setting aside for film production. If this works the way it's meant to, the British film industry could seriously be boosted into the stratosphere. All you need is 50 per cent of your money in place and UK distribution assured, and you can then get a grant of up to £1 million. It's remarkable – if it happens. I've brought in Nigel Savage to be executive producer. He was studying in Jerusalem after raising the finance for *Solitaire for Two*. He is now living in my flat with a remit to raise £1.6 million in three weeks. A doddle.

I found a great house on the Isle of Man to shoot the English bits of the script. In return, we're hoping (expecting?) that the Manx will give us half a million in grants and tax-relief thingies. My cast is looking excellent with letters of intent from Emily Lloyd, Sean Pertwee and Brian Glover and by next week Peter Ustinov and Prunella Scales.

I've spent most of this week working on a new draft. The humour has gone a little down-market. But at least it's my view of down-market. And I've moved into the new Chrysalis offices. What a month! It has been the most amazing turnaround. Everything is looking so rosy, I can't understand it. And its all due to the Lottery. Without that the private investors wouldn't come in. It's a miracle. They'd better give us the money. Or quite simply, it won't happen.

And *Period!* is not going to be called *Period!* The title is now *Stiff Upper Lips*.

August In search of a producer . . .

September Jeremy Bolt and Ricky Posner have now come on board to produce the film and until last Friday everything was going swimmingly. We had 1.8 million in private investment, another million from the Isle of Man and UK rights, and all we needed was the million from the National Lottery and we were there, shooting in nine weeks. The Lottery has taken up most of the last two months. We geared the whole production around the idea that if we passed the various thresholds, ticked the right boxes, the money would be forthcoming. Then we started to hear rumours (well, not so much rumours, as certain powerful people directly telling me) that we had no chance. The Establishment, one way or another, vetoed the Lottery application.

October I sent a version of the following article to *Time Out*. They wanted to print it. Jeremy and Ricky went bananas and insisted I pulled it. I've agreed, temporarily at least.

The papers are full of the Lottery giving £30 million to Sadlers Wells. Virginia Bottomley says 'There is a misunderstanding that it goes to ballet dancers and bassoon players. It goes to brickies and electricians . . .' People aren't annoyed that it's going into ballet dancers' tights. They're annoyed that its going to something they don't give a hoot about. The charge of elitism sticks like superglue. How many people go to the ballet, compared say to cinemas and bingo halls? What's obvious is that the Lottery is scared of publicity, but it patently isn't scared of publicity that offends the majority. Almost every day they make a controversial decision and it's always controversial because it's always biased against the vast majority of people up and down the country. The Arts Council just doesn't care how many Sun exposés there are. The publicity they do want to avoid is a whiff in the *Hampstead Gazette* about Lottery money going to a film that takes the piss out of the slice-your-cucumber-thinly brigade who get the *Hampstead Gazette* delivered to their holiday homes in the Tuscany.

And taking the piss out of this elitism is what my next film *Stiff Upper Lips* is about to do – despite the fact that the Lottery turned me down for finance. But hey, maybe they turned me down because it's a crap project? Not according to Emily Lloyd, Peter Ustinov, Brian Glover and my mother who are all keen to play in it. Not according to the private investors who have put £1.8 million of their own money on the table.

Since they turned me down, I've tried to avoid getting het up. But the danger is now too apparent. Everyone is running scared of Bottomley and Gowrie. Which means British audiences will get more of the same, rather than as the Lottery Film Guidelines explicitly state 'a wider range of British Cinema'. More Shakespeare, more Henry James, more Thomas Hardy, more adaptations. Less original work by writers, directors and producers trying to balance things out a bit.

The only reason I've been given by the Lottery for not funding part of my film, despite the fact that we had approval from at least two of the three advisory panels, was that they were unsure about a comedy that was a parody of British period drama. In principle, that is. Because they didn't actually read the script. Someone else has told me that at least one doyen of cinema (and sadly an old hero of mine) didn't like the idea of private investors. Despite their own guidelines which state that they are actively seeking alternative forms of finance to the standard film ones. Such as?

The Lottery's Film Guidelines are workable and are a real boost to the British film industry. But they are being made unworkable, not by too many cooks spoiling the populist broth but by a few cooks wanting to make *consommé royale*. I'm lucky. I can continue to make my film. But I pray that the people involved at the top level start to listen to the people (and there are many within the Lottery funding procedure) who want to make commercial films for a multiplex audience and who are creatively bringing new finance into films. If they don't, the Arts Council will continue to masturbate into the handkerchief of British Cinema.

And now? I hereby issue a decree: this film will get made and it will. It's time to baton down the hatches. Miramax are talking about dropping their rival project because ours is better. We will have to trim the budget one way or another. But it will get made.

Since I last wrote up this diary, we've had more major interest from the Americans: New Line are very keen, Miramax are offering us money to go away as they have a rival project (how sweet), and we've had meetings with private investors. We've sold Italy and Spain for good money. Nigel ('Genius') Savage suggested I contact Yorkshire TV. We did, at a very high level, and we got an immediate positive response. Fingers crossed, they could really play an important role. The cast is holding. Geoffrey Palmer, my original first choice for Hudson, is now free and rang to say he loved the script and would play the role. We may yet make January.

November   After some swift and painless discussions with Yorkshire TV, the money is in place and we're green lit!

I've just come back from the Isle of Man where we're shooting the main British section of the film. There's a fantastic house there, The Nunnery, a huge, sprawling castle of a mansion owned by Robert Sangster, and it's going to be our location. I went out there with my newly appointed production designer, Mike Grant, and my astonishing line producers Simon Scotland and Simon Hardy. Mike and I came up with a brilliant idea for Eric's cottage, using a set of existing exterior walls and making them the interior of the cottage, effectively turning it inside out. If all goes according to plan, the cottage will have a tree growing in the middle of it. Simon Archer is going to be my director of photography. John Gordon Sinclair has agreed to play Bumbletwist. Reading this, it looks like the money has actually come through quite easily!

A recce trip to Italy proved worthwhile, if wet and a little too shellfish oriented for me. We found one excellent location for the *pensione*, and some specific shots in Rome itself. Next week we're off to India, where apparently I stand an 87 per cent chance of getting ill within an hour. It's very, exciting and very, very frightening at the same time. John and David send me a reworking of the Italian song which is amazingly catchy and very funny. Actors are starting to be tied down. I'd like to tie down some of the agents too, but Ricky and Jeremy are on the case. I'm now starting to focus on nothing except directing the film. G–d help us!

Incidentally, we were scheduled to shoot over Passover. Not any more. We're now celebrating the Seder night in India. Oh, and *Leon and the Pig Farmer* sold to Russia.

The Writer

Peter Capaldi

*For Scottish actor and writer Peter Capaldi, 1995 was dominated by one project,
the writing of his second feature script (after* Soft Top, Hard Shoulder*), a career
move spurred on by an unexpected Oscar triumph.*

Preamble On 27 March *Franz Kafka's It's A Wonderful Life*, a twenty-
five-minute film I wrote and directed, and funded by the Scottish Film
Fund and BBC Scotland, won an Oscar for best short film. I spent the week
in Hollywood with, among others, my wife Elaine, my daughter Cicely and
Ruth Kenley-Letts who produced the film. My American agent Robert
Newman of ICM set up dozens of meetings with studios to try and sell
Moon Man, the second draft of which I have just completed. By the end of
the week we have a number of offers and finally we all decide to go with
Miramax who seem really to want to make the film.

April 6–7 Fly to Glasgow, and then am driven for two and a half hours to
Fort William to present a prize at the Celtic Film Festival. I talk to a
number of people about the Miramax deal and the general opinion is the
same: 'Your life will be hell.' I want to put a mark by these words in this
diary.

April 8 1 am. I talk to Robert, my agent in America, who tells me
Miramax have rejected his financial proposal for *Moon Man* and come back
with a MUCH lower offer. Elaine and I get very depressed. Having been
fanned into a frenzy of avarice by Hollywood, we have got very tired of our
two-bedroom flat in Crouch End, which, since the arrival of our daughter,
has become the incredible shrinking flat. Our delusions of grandeur have
become so real that we even went into the local estate agents and asked for
details of houses in the £250–300,000 price range. I have to admit this did
feel great, and it will almost be worth the humiliation of telling them to
forget it.

April 12 Ruth rings. Miramax have approved our proposal. We are all
delighted. Then madness sets in again. The estate agent arrives, and we
welcome him enthusiastically. The house we have seen (and fallen in love
with) is also with his company. He is sweating with the effort of suppressing
his natural spiv qualities (in accordance with the fashion of the day), but he
is obviously delighted he's caught us on the up. He suggests we put in an

offer for the house. We don't have the money but what the hell! We're in the movies!

April 13 Bob Weinstein, the president of Miramax, has rung and asks me to come to New York. He wants to talk to me about a book that he's sent me, *A Wrinkle in Time*. It's about a group of kids who get drawn into an alternative universe. I am not keen but suspect Bob is. Bob says he respects my views and then says, 'And it doesn't mean we don't want to do *Moon Man*. That *will* happen.' But just for a moment I feel the possibility of 'switch and bait' which is what big studios do. They talk for twenty minutes about your project (the bait), then show you the script they really want to do (the switch), which has usually already been through just about every director's hands.

April 25 Talk to Bob as I want to tell him that I don't want to develop *A Wrinkle in Time* for him. He accepts this with his usual charm. 'Have we closed the deal yet?' he asks. 'I think we're about to,' I tell him. 'But you haven't signed yet. So I've still got to be nice to you. Once you've signed I'll be like Moon Man! What is this shit? Get outta here!'

April 27 Cary Granite (yes, his real name) phones from Miramax. We are 'seconds' away from closing the deal. Bob wants me to come to New York next week to get my first note session on the script. 'When would suit you?' I ask. 'Thursday,' he says. 'Thursday will be fine,' I reply. Me. In New York. Show business, don't you love it?

April 28 Type up more pages of *Moon Man*. The script is on my mind a lot. The whole middle act is problematic. I don't think there's enough inventiveness in it. And a lot of the characters are performing the same function. There's a hunchbacked woman who tells the heroine much the same as the old man and woman do. But she's funnier. But I don't know if she's right. Maybe she's in the wrong place. The whole second half needs to be more focused. I've got a lot of work to do. Also, Ruth shows me the budget. The actual document that's been prepared has a breakdown of my script with costs. My knees go to jelly. She then makes a criticism of the script. I take it, but it's really hard. And she's absolutely right. But if I find it hard coming from her, how am I going to feel in New York with Miramax?

May 4 New York. Put my dark suit on and wait for the car. Meeting at Miramax with Bob Weinstein, Richard Potter (director of production and development), Deborah Porter and Amy Israel. Bob opens the script. The first scene is a night exterior. He says, 'Does this have to be outside?' I look at him, a little stunned, and I am about to muster a weak 'no' when I realise that he's joking. In the end I am very happy with their reaction. I get a lot of criticisms, but I think these are valid and I am most pleased that we all seem to see the same movie. I also pre-empted them, I think, by launching into my own pile of notes on the script, which I think was a first. The only worry I have is that they seem to want a moral dimension carried by the lead character. In short, she is for me simply a woman who has her child abducted, searches for the child, fights for it and is reunited. They, on the other hand, seem to feel that the script would be more powerful if the woman were somehow responsible for the loss of her child, for example if she were a career woman, she could somehow neglect her child, thus allowing the forces of darkness to enter her life and make off with him. When they are reunited, she would learn that, hey, being a mother is more important than having a career. This I don't agree with, as (a) I think it's saying women's place is in the home and (b) it's too pat. I think we're going to have problems with this.

May 25 Telephone Amanda (ICM London). She's back from Cannes and tells me that Miramax have made an announcement in *The Hollywood Reporter* that they are doing *Moon Man*. She says she has met a lot of their people out there and that they are very serious about the project.

June 8 Getting really stuck trying to pin my lead characters down so I concentrate on one scene. It is the scene where 'the painter' is first shown the room he has to decorate. I spend the whole day on it and discover some interesting things about him. He can be witty in an acerbic way, and his language should be a mix of the archaic and the new. 'Stella' still remains a problem but I feel as if I am inching towards an understanding of her. She is imaginative and should have plenty of good one-liners. A good day. But slow.

The survey on our new house is OK. Looks like we'll be moving. But we haven't signed the contract with Miramax yet and that's where the cash is coming from. One day at a time.

Get out to do a test voice-over for Sainsbury's at 5 pm I'm going to keep doing voice-overs as they are my only source of income at the moment.

June 12 Speak to Amanda and Robert (ICM, LA) both of whom are anxious to close the deal, though not half as anxious as I am. Speak to our buyer and our lawyers who say we could exchange next week, meaning we can move in soon after. So we need the dough!

June 13 Minor breakthrough writing 'Stella'. She's much more interesting if I make her a little bit of a control freak. Her life is spiralling into chaos, and she's trying to keep it in check in a million little ways. But she's got to let go.

June 22 Miramax have been very quiet so now I fear that they don't want to work with me at all and will not be coughing up the fee for the script, which is the shortfall on our house. This is the doomsday scenario and I am beginning to believe it's going to happen. I just keep thinking 'Get into the house, get into the house'; at least then we've got some capital. And if I'm going to be in the shit, I might as well be in the shit for a lot.

June 23 Phone Robert, my agent in LA. 'Have we got a deal,' I ask. 'Of course we have a deal. And if we haven't we'll fuck the bastards and just sell it to someone else.' I phone Michael, my agent in London, and ask the same question. 'Of course we have. And if we haven't, we do two things: we sue the bastards then we set it up somewhere else in three seconds.' Fighting talk, but it makes me feel ill.

The lawyers (for the house move) call. They can't exchange contracts. The two other parties' lawyers have buggered off for the afternoon. It will have to be Monday. We get frantic messages from the woman we're buying from. She sounds like she's just had a hit of helium. Is it all going to collapse? If it does we won't be penniless but we'll have to start all the house shit again and I can't bear it. My calmness is fading.

June 26 We exchange contracts on the house. Weird.

10 pm. Robert phones from LA. Miramax have signed. He's faxing the contracts to us. I am so happy I can barely talk.

June 30 A blip with the contract. They need another document signed. We have to move fast as ICM in LA have a half-day today then are off until Wednesday for their Fourth of July celebrations. Manage it all by 8 pm.

July 6 Talk to Richard Potter at Miramax in New York who says they'd like to see something. I suggest the first fifty-five pages of the new draft. He agrees and I say I'll send it to him Monday.

July 17 Move into the new house. Villa Miramax!

July 20 Miramax ring. Bob Weinstein and Richard Potter. They hate the script. 'What happened?' says Bob. 'Too much information, don't know what's going on or where I am. The first script I couldn't put down, but this one, let me tellya, I put it down. And page twenty. Tell me, please, you did not write page twenty. Tell me you were looking after your kid, or you were sick that day. Tell me you did not write page twenty. Can we still stop the cheque?' They really hate it. But they are hugely enthusiastic, as only the Americans can be, about the bits they like. Bob tells me he wants to go to the line with this. He wants to do this picture. And that if we can make it work it'll be fantastic. I promise them I'll finish this draft by 18 August, in four weeks' time. But I have to admit, my heart's not in it any more.

August 3 Ellie Jason of Miramax UK takes me to lunch at L'Escargot. She is very kind and supportive of the script, then gives me her notes, which do vary from Bob and Richard's in New York but that's OK as I think I can find a way to make it all work. Leave feeling glum about the script as I always do, but cheered up at such support.

August 31 It's the middle of the night. 2 am. I can't sleep. I've spent all day working on the script which is to be presented to Miramax tomorrow.

I've drunk too much coffee and spent too long in front of the word processor. I can't escape *Moon Man*. It keeps playing in my head – over and over again – bits that don't work. What setting for this? What actor for that? Over and over.

The last three months have been devoted to this. I've gone into an office every day and written. I've never done that before. Inevitably August has seen the script invade more and more of my time and thoughts. The script isn't right. I wouldn't want to shoot this version, but it's closer, much closer. One or two drafts should do it. But I'm happy that this phase has drawn to a close and I have fulfilled the terms of my contract.

September 18 Still no news from Miramax. Getting worried about surviving financially. Phone Michael, my London agent, to ask if he can get me a job. Acting or directing commercials.

September 19 Elle Jason from Miramax London rings me at home and says she's been in touch with New York, who like the script, but the co-ordinator has been both ill and away and that's held everything up. But she confirms with me that New York remain very committed and excited about the script. I really appreciate her doing this and thank her for her kindness.

September 29 Richard Potter rings. He enthuses about the script then moves on to some soft criticisms. These are fine and what I expected, but it seems clear to me that the real criticisms will come from Bob Weinstein, as will the real decisions. But Richard is very nice and we talk a lot about the movie without really getting into notes. He arranges for him and Bob to ring me on Monday at 8.30 pm our time.

October 1 According to our contract Miramax have thirty days from the delivery of my script to make up their mind what its fate is. Otherwise the material reverts back to me. Their time is up today.

October 2 8.30 pm. Richard Potter rings without Bob who sends his apologies. He should have been in LA but missed the flight due to some crisis in New York. He arranges to phone me tomorrow at 8 pm. Put briefly, Richard is asking for an extension, maybe a couple of days, maybe into next week.

October 3 8 pm. I sit waiting for Bob Weinstein's call. I wait, and I wait. About 9 pm some off-hand secretary who I've never spoken to rings to say Bob will be ringing tomorrow at 9 am LA time. That's it. No explanation, no apology, nothing.

October 4 I sleep until almost eleven this morning and wake up miserable. I feel completely uncertain about the film's future.

5 pm. Waiting for Bob to ring. Richard Potter rings to say he'll be fifteen minutes late. Waiting for Bob. He rings. Bob sounds like he has just woken up. Asks if I'll be in New York sometime as this kind of conversation would

be better in person. He likes the script but ... 'We have this kind of relationship so I'll just go straight in, I won't pull any punches, we have another writer, George Wang, he's just done something for us, and I think he'd be great on this, what do you think?' I am really hurt and taken by surprise, but say, 'Intellectually I know that may be of great use but emotionally I can't give you an answer right now.' Bob says fine and then gives me an hour and twenty minutes of notes, many of which contradict those given by the story department via Richard. From all of these criticisms it seems to me he is not interested in this film. At he end he says, 'You told me once you'd never direct a script you didn't feel secure with.' (True.) 'Would you direct this?' I say 'No'.

Now we have a problem. The contract allows for Miramax to make a decision about production based on this draft. It does not legislate for another draft. I tell Bob, I'd like to do another draft but I don't have any money. He says he'll get back to me in a couple of days with a proposal.

I try to get in touch with Robert in LA but ICM is closed. It's Yom Kippur today, the Jewish Day of Atonement, and if there ever was a bunch of folks who had a lot of atoning to do it would be agents. I phone Robert at home apologising on his answering machine for ringing on this holy day. I didn't have him down as a religious guy, and I'm proved right as when he finally rings, it's from his gym. Unfortunately for him I just ask him to listen to how I'm feeling which is bad. He says he'll talk to Michael Eisner (not *that* Michael Eisner [Chief Executive, Walt Disney], another one) in legal affairs tomorrow.

October 5 We have a conference-call with Robert and Michael Eisner who tell us they have already said no to Miramax's offer which is not much money and another writer. They want to know how much they should ask for. We all sit around Ruth's kitchen table, can't think of a figure, laugh sickly at our daft inexperience and ineptitude and tell them to think of a number. It's 1.30 am before the calls are finished and I can get to bed.

October 6 Miramax has accepted. I've asked for six weeks: 16 November to 24 November to rewrite and draw. They've committed enough money to it to mean they're serious about the movie. They are being generous. I love them. They are going to make my life hell, but I love them. It's my task now to deliver them a script that I am prepared to direct. Thereafter if they choose to bring on another (mutually acceptable) writer then that's fine as I would have had a crack at it. I think they are being extremely generous.

October 15 Tomorrow I start work. I've got six weeks to pin down the film I want to make. I'm worried. I'm going to spend the first week drawing as I think the visual side of the picture has been neglected. I hope it is going to fire my imagination.

October 20 I've spent a week drawing images from the film, abandoning the word processor, abandoning the words. I've only got six weeks and the script still has lots of problems. Should I be doing this? Yes. The script, the document Miramax is judging, is a literary thing, made of words, structure, logic. It's a map of a route we haven't settled yet, through a landscape we think, or thought, years ago, we were interested in. But the logic is tyrannical. The words constricting. I've got to make the script the best that I can, but at the end of the day, I'm trying to make a film. An experience that happens in a cinema, Butterkist in one hand, Kia Ora in the other. The lights go down, the curtains part and this experience *happens*. You don't read it. So the drawings are important because they are a more direct path to my imagination, and closer in some respects to nature of the final medium itself.

October 25   Have spent the last three days sitting down working on *theme*. Over and over again searching for the theme of the film, largely because Miramax seem to want to discuss it. I don't. But I'll have to. So I better know what it is. Three days of digging deeper and deeper into the script so I can discuss what it's *really* about. But what's the point of articulating in words what is, I hope, a visceral response to a set of moving pictures? I don't know. But I found it. And it was there all the time. Does the fact that I can name it help? Only time will tell.

October 26   A whole day spent actually writing. Concentrating on 'Andy'. Trying to bring him to life. Then it becomes obvious. Although he is not the lead, he must *drive*. His character, his ambition, is what has put 'Stella' into this place. And he must continue to drive. Until he drives into the side of the garbage truck.

October 27   'Stella' and 'Andy'. How do I make them appear married? How do married people talk to each other – all the while saying the things I need them to say? And being sympathetic and interesting and funny? And then I turn a corner. I make that scene work. They fall out. It cuts out two pages of stupid dialogue elsewhere then gives me a scene of them making up. Suddenly they're married. I'm very excited. I've pushed it into somewhere else. Parts of the script are reaching out to each other. For the first time I feel this could be something.

October 28   Yesterday's excitement fades as I try to rewrite the sequence of the 'Painter' meeting 'Jack' and actually painting the mural. At the moment I've got to do this in about two and a half pages and it seems too cramped. Do I have too much going on in the set-up, which is now spreading, with Act One ending on page thirty-five? Can I compress?

November 23   Finish the script. On schedule. Having worked around the clock. Eyes painful from the word processor.
   I've learnt a lot in the past six weeks. I've written faster. Been braver. Worked harder. And I think it's there. I like the script now. And if someone were to say to me 'Would you direct this script?' My answer would be yes. It

has transformed into something else. All the work and criticism have been worth it. It's a movie now.

November 29 To our great surprise Richard Potter from Miramax calls about the script. They only got it yesterday. He says, 'Without giving anything away, we're all smiling.' He asks me to wait in for a call from Bob Weinstein. About half an hour later Bob calls. He seems very happy about the script. 'This is a movie now,' he says. 'I am excited now as I was the first time I read it. We want to do this.' He winds up on a very positive note about the script and congratulates me on my work, 'Way to go.' Richard stays on the line. He says they are all very excited. He says Bob was calling from home! I say 'But what happens now?' The truth is he can't really say, so I suggest that what happens now is we wait for Bob to come to a decision. He says yes.

Contractually they must come back to us by the end of the year and tell us their intent otherwise the rights of the script revert back to us.

December 6 One year ago today I finished the first draft of *Moon Man* which had taken since January '94 to write.

December 14 BAFTA for a screening of Miramax's new film *Restoration*. Harvey Weinstein is there and says to me that he loved the latest draft of *Moon Man*. He then says, 'We're going to make your movie.'

'We're going to make your movie' – I don't know if I believe that or not. I *want* to, but I am frightened to, as I'll be setting myself up for a very long fall if I do. But there is something very nice about seeing those words come out of Harvey Weinstein's mouth. Even if he didn't mean it.

December 19 Phone Robert in LA to ask about getting my money out of Miramax. He says he's on to it. I ask him if he saw Bob Weinstein last week. He says yeah. That's it. I'm disturbed by his tone. And after I've put the phone down I begin to fret over something I'm picking up. Something negative. There's something going on and it doesn't feel good.

Go to bed. Robert rings from LA. I tell him I felt something negative from our exchange. He says, 'You wanna hear somthin' negative? Bob wants to make your movie. He wants to bring you and Ruth out to discuss rewrites at the start of the year but you are not committed to doing anything.'

He knows they are going to make this proposal but haven't yet. So I was correctly picking up on something going on. Miramax are going to make a proposal for me to write some more. This seems to me a delaying tactic to give them more time to come to a decision about the film. I know any work the script needs I could do on the move in pre-production. I want to make my movie. And if Miramax don't want to, I want to know now so we can get the script out of there and into another studio. No more rewrites until we are green lit.

December 27 A fax from Richard Potter at Miramax confirming that they'll be bringing Ruth and me out early in the new year to give us a final decision re *Moon Man*.

December 28   Ruth, Elaine and I discuss the possibilities. We assume Miramax would like to make the picture as flying us out to say no would seem like a waste of money. Therefore there are issues they would like resolved before picking up the option which would commit them to more money. However, their time is up. I am anxious to get into production now, and if they don't want it we have solid evidence that a number of other companies do. We decide to put a ceiling on it and give them two weeks to fly us out there and give us their decision.

Postscript (January 23, 1996)   New York. A limo comes at 2.30 to take us down to Miramax. The driver, Rolf, is a real gentleman. When we get out I give him five dollars. He says, 'I'm with you all day.' 'Well in case I don't see you.'

3 pm Miramax. Tribeca Building. Bob Weinstein's office. As I walk into Bob's tiny office he is on the phone. A cool young American film-maker would have sat down and lit up. I stand. Still on the phone he indicates I should sit. Obviously. He finishes his call. Then, 'Hi good to see you' etc. Uncomfortable silence. Something odd. I hear myself say, 'This is weird.' I instantly feel stupid, gauche, unable to resist the pressure to fill the silence, and so fill it with nonsense. 'Why is it weird?' asks Bob. Something in his voice alerts me.

Uncomfortable silence. Something is wrong. He looks at me and says, 'OK, I'll just get straight to it. I asked my brother Harvey to look at it, he'd read it before but I asked him to apply his mind to it. And as distributors, which is what we are known as, we don't know how to sell this. Is it a kids' film or an adult film? There are parts in there that seem like a kids' film but no kids ever going to see it because it's too scary.'

I'm thinking 'Kids' film'? Where is all this coming from? Nobody has ever mentioned *kids*' film before.

'All the doubts I had originally about the script are still there. The problems with the material have not been resolved.'

WHACK. Where the fuck did that come from? Last time he spoke to me he said 'This is a movie now. I'm as excited now as I was the first time I read it. We want to do this.' But I know it's over. Dead gone buried. He just has to say it. And he does.

'So we don't feel we can do this.'

The whole of last year and the next turn on this moment. It's weightless, quiet and intimate and then it's gone. I relax. Though I think I can feel the word 'SCHMUCK' appearing on my forehead. But Bob's carrying on: 'And at $10 million it's a risk. It's not like *Sex, Lies and Videotape* at one million or *Reservoir Dogs* at two. It's a risk. But I gotta tell you, you're one of the family here. And we love you. We love what you do. It's been great working with you. And I know I'm mad for passing on this and you're gonna see me at the premiere on crutches and laugh but that's the way it is. I know Richard Potter wants to have a word with you.'

I don't cave in. I respect Bob's position and I tell him so. I also tell him I think he's wrong and that the script has been resolved and that I would have no doubts about starting shooting it tomorrow. But it's all academic. I thank him for his support which has been generous and encouraging and if I ever write anything again I'd bring it to him. Then I'm up. He's shaking my hand. Richard Potter has come into the office. As I leave Bob's office I say 'bye' then shout 'NEXT'.

Richard is looking for somewhere for us to talk. What's the point? But I say I've got to see Ruth. I'm not looking forward to this. I step into reception. She's come thousands of miles and she won't even get to see him. I start to laugh. 'They're not doing it,' I say. 'You're joking?' she predictably replies. 'No. They're not going to do it.' I can't describe the expression on her face. She looks stunned. Cary Granite appears looking ghostly. He shakes my hand, says something then vanishes. Richard is floundering, 'We love you, we really want to work with you' etc. Like everyone here, he's really saying nothing. I tell him I want to go.

When we arrive at the hotel Rolf, our driver, opens my door. I've got a couple of bucks and move to give him them. But he grabs my hand and shakes it. In the palm is the five dollars I gave him earlier. 'This one's on me,' he says.

February 7   I take my three-year-old daughter to the supermarket. As we drive out of the car park I am stuffing a bar of chocolate into my face. I don't usually do this. So Cicely says:

'Why are you eating chocolate, Dad?'

'Because I'm fed up.'

'Why are you fed up?'

'Because no one will make my film.'

'I'll make your film,' she says.

Allan Shiach

Allan Shiach is a Governor of the BFI, chairman of the Scottish Film Council and the Film Production Fund. He is a director of Scottish Television. Under the pen name Allan Scott he produces and writes screenplays. His credits include Don't Look Now, Joseph Andrews, D.A.R.Y.L, Castaway, The Witches *and* Two Deaths. *The following extracts recount the hectic life of someone who splits their time between Los Angeles, London and north-east Scotland!*

April An extremely busy month which began in the aftermath of hosting a cocktail party in LA for the British Oscar nominees. Over seventy people came to the house, vivid with expectation, and drank more than fifty bottles of champagne. The Awards ceremony the next evening was a thin affair, the main highlight being an Oscar for *Franz Kafka's It's A Wonderful Life* which the Scottish Film Production Fund developed and funded. The British contingent included Nigel Hawthorne, Nick Hytner, Hugh Grant, Elizabeth Hurley, Helen Mirren and Peter Capaldi (whose new screenplay we are also developing).

In London immediately after this and then four days later flew back to LA. Delivered the second draft of *Hemingway in Love* to New Line with which they are very pleased. The major rewrite now requested is a new title. Apparently 'Hemingway' is a box-office turnoff.

Met with Penny Marshall to discuss *The Preacher's Wife*, a remake of *The Bishop's Wife*, an old Goldwyn film starring Cary Grant, David Niven and Loretta Young. By coincidence, I ran into Judy Lewis two days later – she is Loretta Young's daughter by (she believes) Clark Gable. I liked Penny Marshall a lot; very direct, ridiculously overworked and shrewd on script. The story is entirely set in an urban black community, to star Denzel Washington and Whitney Houston. It's a charming romantic tale – or could be. Disney told me I had thirty days to write a screenplay, which is far too little, but I will face that in due course.

My best writing of the month was the new title for Hemingway. It is now called *Seasons of the Heart*. Jeff Berg read it last week and called the studio to ask if he could submit it to directors. The perfect director for it, whom he represents, is not approved by the producer.

May The culture shock of travelling from LA to the Highlands of Scotland not as great as might be expected. Springtime on Speyside and a dram of the Macallan probably accounts for the cushioning.

We screened *Two Deaths* at BAFTA for cast, crew and friends. The film is, in my non-neutral opinion, really good in the way that all Nic Roeg's best work is good: brilliant acting, fascinating, ambitious, technically accomplished, filled with resonance. It will probably be widely denounced for the first few years of its existence.

Meanwhile, and within the quite impossible time of thirty days, I have completed the (very) rough draft of *The Preacher's Wife*. This was warmly received and I plunged straight into work with Penny Marshall. The main problem is still the structure of the ending; the love story resolves too soon and it will be difficult to push this to the end, although clearly it must be. Penny and I meet almost every day for two weeks. She reads through page by page, often acting out or improvising variations on the dialogue; she gives very detailed notes, working line by line, figuring out how each character works, interrelates, etc. Many alternatives are tested. I go home after lunch and try to implement the changes, often working till late at night so as to give the new pages to her for the next day's session.

It's been difficult trying to weave in enough time to work on the *Samson and Delilah* script I'm doing for Turner. But at least I now have the basic architecture.

Back in London I have set myself ten days to finish *Samson and Delilah*. Shortly thereafter, I'll be heading back to LA by which time script notes on *The Preacher's Wife* will be given by: Penny M, Andrea Asimow (her reader), Elliott (her partner), Sam Goldwyn jr., John Manulis, Donald Deline (president of Touchstone), Christina Steinberg (vice-president of Touchstone), Denzel Washington, Denzel's reader/partner, Whitney Houston and her reader/partner. *Film is a collaborative medium.*

How, in the name of God, did the auteur theory ever arise? The French, who advanced it in the 60s, now have a film industry which, with distinguished exceptions, has no screenwriters. In Britain the main espouser of the auteur theory still seems to be *Sight and Sound* which sprinkles directors' possessive credits around (Zinnemann's *A Man for All Seasons*, Hytner's *The Madness of King George*, as if Robert Bolt and Alan Bennett were figments of the directorial imagination). The editor of *Sight and Sound* will not be surprised if I take into this diary my five-year campaign against their offensive lists of film credits which assign the writer a position somewhere beneath that of location manager or caterer. Robert Riskin, who wrote many of Frank Capra's greatest successes, was so irritated by the way his screenplays were overlooked and the films' success ascribed to the 'Capra touch' that he once flung down 120 bound blank pages and demanded: 'Give that the fucking Capra touch!'

July Finished the *Samson and Delilah* script with a last-minute rush and the early feedback has been favourable. The committee of religious wise-men who sit in Rome and scrutinise each Bible film for the RAI/Turner consortium are, I am warned, going to ask that all the love-making scenes be removed. So perhaps Samson and Delilah should just hold hands.

Penny Marshall came to London and we worked on *The Preacher's Wife*. The deals have now been done with Denzel Washington and Whitney Houston and pre-production has begun.

Dimitri Villard called to say that *Seasons of the Heart* is about to sign a director and they hope to begin shooting at the end of the year. It is no longer called *Seasons of the Heart*. Here is a true Hollywood tale. *Seasons of the Heart* (or as it was once and is perhaps now again called *Hemingway in Love*) was an original screenplay, the story entirely original, inspired by a couple of letters written to Hemingway by a young woman of whom he was fond but with whom he almost certainly did not have an affair. In the movie, he does. I wrote a full story outline. Then a screenplay, plus a second draft based on studio notes. Everyone expressed delight and admiration in fulsome terms. There was no further work to be done until a director came on board. The director is now on board. The studio has now hired another writer to revise the script. I am reminded of a *New Yorker* cartoon: four moguls sit around the swimming-pool, one of them is saying: 'I've just read the best screenplay I've come across in thirty years in the business. It's superb. Who shall we hire for the rewrite?'

Flew back to LA during the last week of the month for meetings and work on *The Preacher's Wife*. Also saw the executive at Turner responsible for *Samson and Delilah*. He is delighted. Unfortunately everything he likes about the script the Italian religious committee dislikes. Writers don't write – they negotiate between the employing parties!

August Los Angeles. The reading of *The Preacher's Wife* took place at Penny's house. Denzel Washington, Whitney Houston, Gregory Hines, Courtney Vance and others sat at a table and read the script aloud to about twenty people, mainly Penny's friends and trusted colleagues. Some of the actors gave a wholehearted reading, others less so. It was a cheery evening. I noted afterwards to Penny that it was the first time I'd sat in a room looking at fifteen people who all believed O.J. was innocent. There was a lot of laughter over dialogue (gratifying) and more over misreadings and mis-understandings (less gratifying). I made a grand total of three notes. But Penny – who does readings on all her projects both potential and actual including one the previous night with Tom Hanks and Eddie Murphy at the acting table – was fuelled by it and we have combed and recombed the script endlessly since. Some of the brightest notes came from Garry Marshall and from James Brooks. I think Penny uses the process not so much to hear what others have to say, as to test their comments against her own feelings, views and uncertainties.

The *Samson and Delilah* saga continues. First with a fulsome apology from Bernabei, the head of LUX, for their response to my first draft. What I wrote was based on a treatment they'd imposed and it turned out that the treatment had not been approved by the religious 'committee'. However, reaction elsewhere has been so favourable that the committee have been backed off gently. Turner (and the Italians) now want me to expand the script to a four-hour mini-series. Allen Sabinson was complimentary and tremen-dously supportive. It'll still be more of a negotiating than a writing job, but shouldn't take long. The religious 'advisor' asks that I revert to the sequence of events as described in the Bible. This will be impossible. Stories from the Bible are difficult enough to dramatise; there is no narrative arc, no character development, just a series of reported incidents that must be strung together with some rising line of plot imposed upon them. What would Robert McKee or the other screenwriting gurus make of an assignment where nothing fits in to their predetermined pigeonholes for screenwriting?

The last weekend of the month I am invited to dinner with the Secretary of State for Scotland in the King's Hall in Edinburgh Castle. Our party of about fifteen includes Mel Gibson who is in Scotland for the premiere of *Braveheart*. At the end of dinner there is a short formal discussion in which the Secretary of State asks how to attract more film-making to Scotland. Mel Gibson says that *Braveheart*'s move to Ireland had less to do with tax incentives – the savings from which were eaten up by the cost of moving from Scotland – than with the Irish army being made available to them; then he advises the Secretary of State to listen to his own countrymen's advice. That's my cue. So I rattle off the needs of our film-makers and watch our host try not to flinch. There are real signs that he wants to help support film. Let me count the ways.

October Flew to New York on the third day of the month to resume work with Penny Marshall on *The Preacher's Wife*. During the week we changed some of the structure. I told her that I don't feel confident of writing 'street' dialogue. At the moment the script hovers around 'neutral' which was what was originally wanted. But I think especially with regard to the role of Dudley (the angel), this needs work.

I met Pliny Porter, who runs Julia Roberts' company, while in New York to discuss a project which they and Paramount are interested in my writing. He told me that she was on the verge of closing a deal to star in my Hemingway project (now called *In Love and War*).

A journalist from *The Hollywood Reporter* called me on a Monday to seek verification of Julia Roberts' interest in my script. I gave nothing away except the phone numbers of the producer and the studio. However, on the following Friday I was called again and this time was read the story which they were running. Again I confirmed nothing – because I knew nothing, that was easy – but corrected their false impression of what the script was about. When the Julia Roberts story appeared in *Variety* and *The Hollywood Reporter*, I was quoted outlining the plot and asserting the script was 'original'. The shit hit the fan, with Dimitri Villard, the producer, and Sara Risher at New Line both certain that I'd leaked the entire thing. In fact, as I discovered, the main source was Ms Roberts' own publicist. ICM told me it was 'all over town' anyway. But guilty is guilty even if innocent.

Penny and Carrie Fisher give a joint birthday party to which we were invited. It was a real Hollywood A-list evening. And a tremendously enjoyable party as well. I had to read *People* magazine the following week to discover the heavy-hitters I hadn't spotted (Penny said she learned about guests this way, too!): Warren Beatty, Gregory Peck, Meg Ryan, Annette Bening, Jim Carrey, Michael Keaton, Danny de Vito, Dennis Quaid, George Lucas, Marvin Davis, David Geffen – and on and on. Early in the proceedings I spotted Courtney Vance, the actor who had just been hired for *The Preacher's Wife*. I had been spending hours watching tapes of Courtney reading with other actors, so when I spotted him I thought I'd congratulate him and tell him of the hours I'd watched him recently on my TV. We shook hands like old friends and I was about to speak when I realised this was not Courtney Vance at all. Another fellow, frequently seen on TV recently, Christopher Darden, the co-prosecutor in the O.J. trial! Narrow squeak avoided, Kathy and I noticed that Darden was head and shoulders the star of the evening. Or, as the lawyers would put it, *primus inter pares*.

Heard on the last day of the month that the Julia Roberts deal is off, but Sandra Bullock is now in negotiations. I know nothing!

November I have this theory about screenplays. Decent scripts usually reach a point at which they become – relatively – invulnerable. Changes can be made that improve them; changes can be made that make no difference to them. With luck, however, their internal dynamic is eventually strong enough to support almost any amendments, except obviously, for rethinking the entire structure. This theory, however, doesn't square with another observation: there is an anodyne feel to a script that has been worked on by several hands and several story people. All the plot points click into place, all the characters are over-drawn, all the backstory delineated. And the scripts are dead.

Another theory: screenwriters either have a natural instinct for dramatic construction or they do not. You can work for a year with a writer and despite changes and 'improvements' the thing still lies there. The danger is that those with the dramatic flair can deploy it to conceal conceptual flaws. Like great actors can make lousy dialogue seem OK. It doesn't make the dialogue better, but their skill deceives during the initial moment of performance. (Roman Polanski made this point about Jack Nicholson's acting. You have to be wary.)

We have got Lottery financing of £1 million for *True Blue*. This, together with Channel Four and Booker plc finance, means the film is now greenlit. David Aukin has been a great support on the project – known in my household as 'Chariots of Water' – and put up a small sum for Ferdy Fairfax to shoot some of the autumnal/boat racing shots on the River Thames which are crucial to the movie. Ferdy left for the USA to cast the several American parts. *True Blue* starts shooting in January. Rupert Walters has worked to great effect on the screenplay and we're confident. Do I seek a writing credit? I wrote three drafts and then proposed hiring Rupert. Or should I just leave it? There is now a serious danger that no less than three projects with which I'm involved will actually be made into movies in the first few months of 1996 (*The Preacher's Wife* and *In Love and War* being the others). But I expect history will take care of that small hope.

I go to Rome for *Samson and Delilah* in the last week of the month. In a fine room overlooking the Piazza Navona, I sit across the table from two charming priests, interpreters and co-producers. We thrash through the religious committee's concerns (a committee consisting, I am told, of all the major religions) on matters theological (but not necessarily any other kind of logical). Then, at the moment he deems appropriate for an entrance, *il presidente*, Mr Ettore Bernabei, wafts silently into the room from a sidedoor

90

like a ghostly presence flanked by attentive *consigliere*. Evidently he approves of the script because he concedes the only important point and the meeting concludes with his inviting me to write another film for them. I will decline in due course.

The month ends on a decent note with the announcement that Sandra Bullock is to be paid over $10 million to star in *In Love and War*, shooting next April. Richard Attenborough talks about the screenplay in the accompanying article. It's weird. We've never met to discuss it, yet he describes my script, devised from my head onto 120 blank pages over painful weeks. The script is a deal now. And it's his.

December   A productive four weeks, for the most part writing *A Very Long Engagement*. A writer's life must seem very dull to those outside. But here I've been re-creating World War One, destroying the Philistine temple and trying to solve the murder of Julie Ward. Inside, it's fascinating.

A cast read-through of *True Blue* bodes well. We sat around a big table, shivering with cold, in the reception room of one of the boat clubs on the banks of the Thames. The actors are wonderfully well cast (by Celestia Fox) and gave a fluent account of the script. I remain unconvinced of the value of these readings other than as a bonding opportunity.

The month ends with Christmas festivities and I remember a conversation with five of our most successful writers, all of whom had in common that they wrote something every day of the year, Christmas included. That puts me in a dilemma. Shall I write on Christmas Day trying to keep up? Or just revert to being the kind of hack who takes holidays?

Richard Curtis

An experienced writer for film and television who struck gold with his script for Four Weddings and a Funeral, *Richard Curtis here gives a brief taster of his latest foray into movie scripting.*

May 1–June 2 I put this time aside to write the first draft of the film version of *Mr Bean*. There was a definite deadline because my girlfriend is due to have a baby on 9 June – so I had to stop, and that's that. From experience I know that I really need three to four months to write the first draft properly.

We've all always thought it would be great to write a *Mr Bean* film, but it's been hard finding the right time. We had our first meetings around two years ago and although we experimented with some very fanciful plots, I kept coming back to a very, very simple one: of just taking Mr Bean to stay with a family on an American campus – and then destroy their lives. I've always liked this for two big reasons: (1) because it has nothing to do with jewels and drug heists, we could go on doing what's best about *Mr Bean* – small, intimate, embarrassing situations, closely observed; and (2) I could actually try to write real characters for the family, and write a little film about a relationship in trouble, which would be interesting per se. This would mean that Mr Bean didn't have to be on screen being stupid all the time, but that we'd have a story we were interested in.

About a year after the first meeting I offered to write a treatment on my plan. I wrote a fifty-page document with Rowan Atkinson and Robin Driscoll, who's been writing most of the *Mr Bean* stuff in recent years, and this was liked – with some reservations. Enough to encourage us all to go on. Which brings us to 1 May, when I first sat down to write the first draft.

It's now finished – horribly long at 132 pages, but I think it's gone pretty well to plan. It's a simple plot about Mr Bean going to stay with a man called David who works in an art gallery. His marriage is having troubles anyway – and Bean absolutely finishes it off. Meanwhile, the gallery is also in trouble and Bean does the most terrible thing, which makes closure a certainty, but it all comes right in the end. Most of my time has been spent trying to get David and his wife – and about five other characters in the gallery – right, and I think where I've failed is in thinking up enough new Mr Bean jokes. I've tended to lean on the memories of things we've done already. However, having Mr Bean in the background – instead of always in the foreground, as in the TV shows – has been a delight. I hope that they'll like it – 'they' being Rowan, Robin and Working Title, who are involved in this film, as they were in my previous films *The Tall Guy* and *Four Weddings*.

June 21 Scarlett is born. Hurray! Doesn't look much like Mr Bean. More like Golda Meir.

July 28 Today was the day for the big meeting, to be held in my garden in

Oxfordshire, with Peter, Rowan, Robin, myself – with Peter, Rowan's agent and my friend, as referee and Scarlett as official distraction.

Rowan wasn't over-happy with the script – but not despairing either, quite a usual result for me and Ro. He's actually happier with the non-Bean story but doesn't feel it gels very well with the Mr Bean stuff. He's also worried that I've given Mr Bean quite a lot to say – which I always said I would and think is right. But Ro can't imagine himself saying it. In fact, it was a very useful meeting, incredibly so. I usually come away from 'creative' meetings with a general sense of what should be done but no specific ideas. However, today, we really tried to dissect the work we'd done and to try to solve some of the problems. I'll now leave the thing for two months, for Robin to do a total rewrite. So far, so good.

August 1 I've just typed out the minutes for Robin and everyone so that we all know what happened at the 'Garden Meeting', what was wrong with the script and remember some of the solutions. I hope it will be useful for Robin and encourage him not to be gentle with my script. There's a lot to do to make Rowan happy – and there is absolutely no point starting on this film unless he is – *very*.

October 9 Robin has delivered his script, and certainly there was no need for me to worry about him being too gentle – as I remember from my *Blackadder* days with Ben Elton, it's always a shock when you get your script back and so much has gone. But on the whole I'm pretty pleased – it's a huge step forward and there are, which is a crucial joy, lots of funny new lines. Robin has added a lot of very good plot, where I was very plot light indeed. There's probably too much of it – but I think all the elements he's used I agree with, and will go with. He's also taken out almost every word of Mr Bean's – and I hardly notice. On the downside, all the plotting means he hasn't just sat around and thought of ten more stupid Mr Bean bits, which is a disappointment because I didn't do that either. He's also taken out masses of my 'character' stuff, but again I've got a feeling he's right, and we should use my old draft as the 'backstory'. However, some of the dialogue he's left is shortened and doesn't seem to work – a horrible amount of what I write depends on repetition and when you try to thin it out, the joke mysteriously disappears.

This is now the plan. Robin and I will meet and work out which 'routines' we want to rehearse with Rowan so when Ro finally reads the script he actually understands the physical jokes   they are stunningly boring to read, as you can imagine: 'Enter Mr Bean – pulls amusing face. Sits down – pulls another amusing face etc.' After that week of rehearsal, I'll do another draft of the film, working in my changes with the new stuff from rehearsals.

November 13–19 An excellent week of rehearsals. Robin and I spent a day together working on some things – as did Emma and I – and we had at least ten sections to work on, half of which were totally new to Rowan. And it was fun. Rather like rehearsing our theatre shows ten or fifteen years ago. Just three people in a room with biscuits, setting up very simple situations and then exaggerating and exaggerating them. Being physical rather than verbal comedy, this is easy and incredibly important – since if the stuff doesn't make us laugh in rehearsal it will never make anyone laugh on film.

Among the highlights: a lot of very foolish stuff for Bean on an aeroplane, a 'mime battle', Bean against an annoying mime artist in the grounds of the gallery he goes to, and, to cheer us up on the final afternoon, a laxative joke. So – good fun and good results!

November 21–December 6   I've reworked the whole film script. All the material we rehearsed is in, and I've been through Robin's scripts and kept, I hope, all his best stuff. But I've simplified things massively – sometimes to include the new physical material – and again, I'm aware of not having quite enough time. Some potential subplots just drift away. But I think many of Ro's original worries are answered – and it could be quite a funny film.

December 7–8   Robin's reaction to my new draft is to be rather alarmed. He's spotted some sloppiness and, as was bound to be the case, noticed the horrid cutting of things he loved. Very unfairly, I'd asked him to try to make corrections within a couple of days – but he wants a bit more time. So the script which was meant to be in on 1 December is now going to be about three weeks late. Not bad really!

December 10   To my surprise I've written my first thriller – this diary. I've been given tomorrow as the deadline and everything hangs in the balance. Robin and I are having a day together tomorrow and with any luck will reach agreement on what needs to/can be done before Friday when the film must be in to Rowan if he's to decide whether to do it by Christmas – which was always the plan. (Damn – shows what a crap thriller writer I'd be – I think that's the first time I've mentioned that crucial fact. We've always been working to Christmas when Rowan, who otherwise might dither forever, has to definitely decide whether he wants to make this film or not. If he does – we'll do lots more work. If he doesn't – we'll never look at it again.)

And who knows what will be the outcome? What makes this an exceptional thriller is that we don't even know if there's been a murder yet! But if about nine months after you read this, there hasn't been a whisper of a *Mr Bean* film – then it was probably killed sometime in late December '95. The suspects: Rowan Atkinson guilty of ruthless indifference to an excellent script; or Richard Curtis and Robin Driscoll guilty of producing a dodgy rushed script. If, on the other hand, you do hear of a *Mr Bean* film, then things have turned out fine – and all we can do is hope that at some point a mature mind was introduced into the proceedings, and the laxative joke was cut out!

The Actor

Alfred Molina

A leading film and television actor (Letter to Brezhnev, Prick up Your Ears, Enchanted April, Hancock), *Alfred Molina now lives in Los Angeles but continues to work on both sides of the Atlantic. The following extracts begin with Molina in Massachusetts on the set of* Before and After, *a thriller directed by Barbet Schroeder.*

April 12   Today we completed the first major scene my character has with Meryl Streep and Liam Neeson, and I was more nervous than I expected to be. Acting with the two of them was a real delight. Generosity between actors always brings out the best work, and by the time we got to the close-ups I was feeling right at home.

April 16   It struck me today that since film-making is essentially a bunch of experts in very narrow fields coming together to create something larger, how come we know so little about each other's skills? I became aware of this as I watched the second assistant directors choreograph the extras in a complicated crowd shot. It made me think twice about ever snapping my fingers for another cappuccino!

April 17   Had lunch today with Nini Rogan, our script supervisor. She said one difference between English and American actors is that in the downtime from one set-up to the next, the yanks disappear to 'trailerville' while the Brits like to hang around the set and socialise. She interprets this as one way that hierarchy manifests itself in the US industry. Nini felt there is a keener sense of us and them over here, and delighted in the way English actors unwittingly subvert it. I'm not so sure. It seems to me we suffer from petty status distinctions just as much. I then added that if trailers were as common on English movies, I wouldn't hang around the set either!

May 1   Los Angeles. Everything here is gearing up for the release of *The Perez Family* on 12 May. We've just done a weekend of press and TV interviews, in English and Spanish. The issue of ethnic casting came up constantly but I think we dealt with it diplomatically. The last thing we need is controversy right now. The veiled question is why are all the major roles being played by non-Cubans? The answer is, simply, that the director, Mira Nair, chose the people she thought to be the most suitable. However, this is such a hot potato in a society hamstrung by political correctness, that one is instantly on the defensive. I gave my stock answer that an actor should not be denied the chance to play Hamlet because he doesn't happen to be Danish. A little glib but the best I could come up with.

May 6   Sat through a screening of *Perez* at the Academy. It was like an opening night in terms of the terror it induces. Hylda, my US agent told me this would be the kindest audience the film will ever have. 'They all want to love it and they will ... until the reviews come out, and then they'll know what to think.' The build-up to the opening has been very exciting. Suddenly, the invitations to functions, talks, other people's openings, etc. start to arrive, and it is hard to fit them all in. Then, as if some almighty power had just discovered a terrible mistake, it stops and moves on to the next project in line.

May 11   Had an interview with Andrew Bergman the other day for his film *Striptease*, starring Demi Moore. The part I'm up for is ... yes, that's right, the Cuban! I walked into his office, sat down and traded some of my small talk for his and was surprised to hear myself stressing my English accent, and rather obviously at that. I don't quite know what I was trying to convey to him but it served only to confuse him. The next five minutes were taken up in explaining my family tree. This just made matters worse. He thought he was meeting with a Latino actor, only to find some geezer going on about his Italian mother and how handy he is at accents. He put me to the test on the script and the whole thing fell apart. I'm still waiting to hear. Thinking about it now, everything is clear. I went to the meeting completely unprepared and, because of the circus surrounding *Perez*, way too cocky. I probably won't get the job and it will serve me right.

May 22   First weekend of the *Perez* run, with very mixed reviews and the suggestion that audience response has been lukewarm. The hyperbole that kept me high for the last two weeks has evaporated like mist. We fell foul of the ethnic casting issue, with Marisa being singled out for specific attack. I've been left alone, largely thanks to my Spanish surname, which only goes to highlight the hypocrisy of the argument.

July 7   I'm back in London working for the BBC. The job is a Screen Two production written by Howard Schumann called *Nervous Energy*. The director is Jean Stewart and it is being produced by Ann Scott. We start a week of rehearsal on Monday, so I have the weekend to recover. London feels like a foreign city to me now. I walked for an hour or so through Soho and finally ended up scrunched in a corner table in the Pâtisserie Valerie, staring at my over-priced cappuccino and feeling like a total outsider. I was not prepared for that.

July 11   First proper day of rehearsal; we sat round a table and began by talking about the larger themes of the script. Howard Schumann took us through the elements of the story that are autobiographical. It is very interesting to be playing a man who is not only sitting in front of you, but who has given you all the words to say. The script is clearly highly personal but Howard has impressed me with his limitless capacity for openness and frankness. We spent the morning talking about the events leading up to where the storyline begins. For an actor, this is priceless material. I play a gay man whose younger lover is dealing with the debilitating effects of AIDS. My lover is played by Cal Macaninch and his instincts about his character are razor-sharp. The issue of AIDS is so emotive, subjective, painful, that a dramatic treatment has to work really hard not to end up as melodrama. The position Howard has taken is to concentrate less on the details of the disease and its horror, and more on the relationship. In other words, he has written a movie about love.

Knocked off work for a late lunch with my agent to celebrate the news from LA about the opening weekend of *Species*. It's number two at the box office and the biggest opener for MGM in a very long time. Nothing like a blockbuster to aid the digestion.

July 13   Fantastic work today on some key scenes with Cal and Jean. I came away feeling very excited about the film. It's a brilliant feeling when the choices you make about how to play a scene turn into moments that really work, and simply feel right! Acting becomes more than craft; something magical occurs.

July 19   Glasgow for the next month. I checked into my hotel, took a walk down Byers Road and along Dumbarton Road to the Museum and Art Gallery. The last time I was here was as a member of the 7:84 Theatre Company in 1980/81. I'm nervous about starting tomorrow. I've been acting for twenty years and every job feels like the first.

July 22   With the first few days under my belt I can begin to relax and enjoy the work. On my very first day, we did the big love scene in the shower. It broke the ice to say the least. Cal and I are still getting to know each other in terms of how we work but given the tight schedule, right off the bat we're into some serious nipple squeezing and various orgasmic grunts. I was making more noise than I did on my wedding night! By the time we wrapped the scene, we were both quite hysterical. It struck me how easy it all was. Doing a love scene with a woman is harder because there is always the danger of actually becoming aroused, or as Kenneth Williams put it, 'getting the half hard'. Cal is cute, but not that cute!

We average about two to four takes per set-up. Our director says the real pressure is the lack of time to explore the possibilities of a scene in terms of how she can shoot it. So getting enough coverage is more important than using the camera to tell the story. Yet within the constraints of time she is dealing with, the shots are very imaginative.

July 27   Well into it now. The pace is fast, perhaps too fast. We've had to drop some grace notes like car sequences and stunts etc. just to keep up. It is a case of kick bollock and scramble! Interestingly, the sex scenes between Cal and I have been the easiest things to do!

August 2   Filming is falling behind schedule rather seriously now. We dropped some shots today and I felt the reason was a lack of time. Jean bounded up to Cal and me saying she didn't need any more coverage as the master was excellent. I wasn't convinced but I lacked the courage to say so. She is resolutely on the side of the actors when it comes to giving us enough time to prepare, so not wanting to seem unsupportive, I kept my mouth shut. Clearly we are collectively responsible for losing momentum. That does not change the fact that none of us have enough time to do our jobs. The BBC is now run by managers and accountants, who don't think creatively. They look at figures and charts and projected timeframes. Making films doesn't fit into preset guidelines. There has to be leeway for hold-ups, changes, an inspired idea for a scene that may add an hour or two to the day's work. You can't itemise that kind of thing. Wouldn't it be great if the people who employ us knew what our job was about?

August 5   More than half-way through and the cast and crew starting to get weary. Small, silly mistakes begin to drain energy and shorten tempers. I find myself getting pissed off by constantly feeling compromised by the lack of time. It's the same old story; every other department gets time to do their job, but if the actors need another take, they have to fight for their corner. This always puts us in a negative light. If the focus-puller wants to go again, he is being perfectionist. The actor asking for 'one more' is simply wasting valuable time.

August 19   We wrapped last night on *Nervous Energy*. The crew and cast like wet rags from the sweat in this very un-British heatwave. I don't think any of us are sorry to see this one end. It was good fun to start with, and the high level of work was maintained, but the killer was this new meanness on the part of the BBC. If they want feature-length films, they will have to put up the money to pay for it. Give us some realistic scheduling, instead of banking on people's goodwill. And if they are going to ask for crews to work overtime, pay for it! I cannot think of any other line of work where the employees are asked on a regular basis to work extra hours with no payment involved.

August 22   On my last night in London, Howard Schuman took Cal, Jean and me to his favourite restaurant. The evening was pleasant, and we managed to avoid the usual, excessive complimenting of each other's work. It was clear from the start we all had respect for each other, and we left it at that. One thing I know; I would work with these guys again in a heartbeat.

August 28   LA. For the last few days there has been no wind. LA feels like it's being choked. The movie side of town is dead, apart from some new films opening. So I go from cinema to cinema, catching up on those I missed first time around. I did have an interview with a very pleasant man called Michael Pressman, who is casting a new film with Michelle Pfieffer and Kathy Baker. They saw me for one role and told me there and then I was the wild card on the list of candidates. I appreciated the candour, and when I thought about it more, I realised they were right. However, they want to see me again. At the first interview, I read the scene with the casting director, Lynn Stalmaster, who, despite the name, is a man. He used to be an actor and consequently gives you a real sense of the other character to play with. It makes such a difference. I left the room, feeling I had been given a good shot at it.

September 22 I've said yes to a Broadway show. Possibly a little prematurely. It means that I won't be free for any film work until the end of March 1996. I have gambled with my luck. But as each film project has bitten the dust, the fear of not working before the end of the year has grown.

September 23 The Oscar Wilde project drew breath again this week. I received the new draft of Julian Mitchell's script. Each draft gets a little better, a little tighter. I can see myself playing the role more and more. The focus is on the love story between Oscar and Bosie, and the cruelty of it. I read the new draft and came away loving Oscar. It is a fab script; please, please let's do it. A message came from Peter and Mark Samuelson (the producers) that eight of the ten million required has been raised, and they plan to begin in the spring of 1996. This business. What a roller-coaster! Last week I doubted I would ever be employed again. Suddenly, after two years of talking about it, one of my chickens might be coming home to roost.

September 27 Excellent news on two projects today. First, there's a phone call from Jean Stewart, director on *Nervous Energy*, telling me how pleased she is with the cut she has and that, furthermore, the film will be getting two screenings at the London Film Festival. The other source of joy, and one closer to home, is that *Scorpion Spring*, the low-budget indie movie we did in '94, has been accepted at the Hamptons Film Festival, and is currently under consideration for Berlin. The festival season has begun, and it is very gratifying to know that the smaller films are getting some breathing space. This is a wonderful way to see the month out.

October 4 Had a meeting with Ron Howard yesterday. He is at a very early stage of casting his new film, *Ransom*, with Mel Gibson in the lead role. There is a part for me in it; a deliciously sleazy villain, who turns out to be a rotten cop. Good script, the director comes trailing glory after a very successful summer with *Apollo 13*, and arguably the biggest contemporary male star attached. The dilemma is one of scheduling. The present dates for shooting clash with the play in New York. However, Ron Howard was aware of the conflict and still thought it worthwhile to meet. He assured me none of the dates were set in stone, so should I hope against hope? This one is a long shot.

A low-budget indie feature, *Mojave Moon*, is now an offer. The money is terrible. Everyone is being offered the same, apart from Danny Aiello, who, as the lead and the best known of us, deserves it. He is the main attraction about this job, for me. I have been a fan of his work for years. One of those classy New York actors who can spin gold out of flax. Even if my agent can't raise the offer, I'll do it. Every penny I earn right now will help to offset the drop in earnings that the Broadway play represents.

October 12 Lou Coulson, my agent in London, informed me of the initial offer on the Oscar Wilde project. There is now a concerted effort to try and improve on it, but the going is getting tougher by the minute. I was surprised at how off the mark the offer was, but however upset or angry or disturbed by that I might be, I have to prepare myself for turning it down. If it comes to that, it will be the toughest thing I have ever done. I went to Brian Gilbert with the original suggestion over three years ago. If I say no, it jeopardises my relationship with Brian and with the Samuelsons as well. On the other hand, why should my loyalty to a project be traded on by the producers in order to get me cheap?

October 26 My first week of work on *Mojave Moon* has gone by. I spent the week in the company of two truly delightful actors Zack Norman and Danny Aiello. Danny, of course, is one of America's best-known actors. For years he was in that character-actor limbo until his Oscar-nominated role in Spike Lee's *Do the Right Thing*. Since that time he has enjoyed a richly varied career. Zack comes from a very different background. He enjoys being vague with details but I squeezed out of him the fact that he was on the bill in cabaret at the Playboy club when it opened in London in the mid-60s. He was a stand-up comic in Las Vegas and has worked in films constantly. His cabaret background really shows in his work to great effect.

The Oscar Wilde saga continues, with each side crawling for advantage. I've become more stoical about the whole thing. When I talk to actors about it, they say I must do it, it is a career-making role, the film of the year, etc. But as I sit here, thinking about it coolly and as dispassionately as I can, I begin to wonder if that is enough. I am in the curious position that my agents on both sides of the Atlantic are less than happy with the deal and, I think, though they have not said so, would love me to turn it down. However, wanting a role badly is probably the worst criterion on which to base a decision.

November 3 I find myself still reeling from the decision to turn down *Oscar*. Strangely, though, now that I'm out of it, I feel extraordinarily relieved. Had I done it, the sense of resentment would have simply grown. Nothing worse than working your arse off and knowing they got you for nothing.

November 13 Back to work in LA after a quick trip to New York for the *Before and After* reshoots. When I arrived at the airport, Matt Salinger, our producer, was there to whisk me straight to the set out in the desert. He filled me in on some dramas that had been occurring while I was away. First of all a whole day's filming had to be redone due to a faulty lens. No one was admitting responsibility, but we were covered by insurance. Then he told me that our first assistant director had been fired and our second assistant director had resigned in protest. Another day lost. At this point, we are still in transit to the location. Matt's car phone starts to ring with that tone that tells you at once you've got trouble. Almost as if he knows what is coming, Matt shouts out, 'Oh fuck, what now?' After he replaced the receiver, he began to laugh. I ventured to ask what was the problem. It appears that the new first assistant director, who took over the day before, had been fired by the director after it had been discovered that he had sexually harassed no less than three different women, including the director's assistant. All in a day and a half on the job! This cost us another half-day's delay.

November 21 The end of a week of night shoots in a gravel quarry in a place called Antelope Valley. Not a bleeding antelope in sight – they clearly have the right idea. This place is possibly the closest I'll ever get to hell. The wind whips up the sand and gravel something fierce. Of course, according to sod's law as applied to film, the more disgusting and unpleasant the location, the better the rushes! The movie looks wonderful, thank God.

I'm wrapped on *Mojave Moon*. We will celebrate Thanksgiving in LA, and the day after I fly to New York for the start of work on *Molly Sweeney*. Effectively, it means the end of my year working in film. I've had a fun year. Worked with some nice people, made some chums, bought a house. The real highlight was the reaction to *Nervous Energy* at the London Film Festival. I haven't been as proud of a film for a long time.

Katrin Cartlidge

After gaining critical attention for her role in Mike Leigh's uncompromising feature Naked, *Katrin Cartlidge has concentrated on similarly hard-hitting low-budget productions, frequently with European directors. Much of the following extracts recount her experiences with the unorthodox Danish film-maker Lars von Trier.*

April 3 Industry. The British film industry. This is supposed to be a diary informing Martians or whoever, what it is like to be involved in the British film industry. Writing this feels very strange – mostly because the word 'industry' doesn't sit very comfortably with me. Nor with many actors I would have thought. Acting is as creative as any other art form. It is about making things – other worlds, six-dimensional sculpture – and this word 'industry' sticks in the gullet. However, it is a fact of life. It has to be negotiated by every creative person wanting to be involved in film-making. Unfortunately.

This time last week, to my shame, I actually stayed up all night and sat through the live transmission of the Oscar ceremony, because it is probably the only time that I will ever be in a film that is nominated. *Before the Rain*, written and directed by Milcho Manchevski, was nominated for best foreign film. It had already picked up a clutch of awards from all over the world. It is Milcho's first feature film and it was funded by three countries: Macedonia, France and Britain. 6 am arrived and with bleary eyes I witnessed Jeremy Irons' mouth uttering the words, *Before the Rain*. However, the words, 'And the winner is', did not precede them. Irrationally, stupidly, I felt a twinge of rejection. The whole thing is like a night out at the Bingo, except less honest, and yet there is still this feeling – albeit momentarily – that the horse didn't jump the hurdle. As if a film were a horse! How can this happen? Could it be something to do with 'industry'?

I saw *Before the Rain* in Belgrade in a 4,000-seat cinema slightly on the outskirts. There was a terrible storm that night and in spite of the lack of fuel in Belgrade, 3,000 people turned up to see it, mostly on foot. For them, the film was not a horse in a race or purely entertainment. It was a film attempting to express something about the fractured state of their country and, to a large extent, of their hearts.

April 24 I am not working currently and financially things are getting difficult. It's ridiculous to think that although I've made two award-winning, internationally acclaimed feature films (*Naked* and *Before the Rain*), have my next one premiering at Cannes (*Three Steps to Heaven*) and another in Finland in post-production, and have done at least four theatre projects in the last three years, I am still broke. Obviously it's because the work I do is all low budget, non mainstream. It is high risk and unknown. *Before the Rain* is only half-way to recouping its costs in under a year of slow releases across Europe and the States. Britain will be the last to get it. I was pretty much bought out in all my film contracts to date. I think there was supposed to be some set payment on *Naked* if it was released in America, but only if the film went into profit. Unfortunately distribution companies are very good at never allowing films to 'officially' go into profit, so I doubt whether I'll see any more money from either *Naked* or *Before the Rain*. Nevertheless it's still the kind of work I'm committed to doing. I am actually very lucky – I know that – but it irks me that equivalent actors in other countries don't seem to be in the same financial rut as actors here.

July 26 Denmark. Most of this month has been spent doing press interviews for the forthcoming opening of *Before the Rain* in London and preparing for going away on a three-month shoot. I'm in Denmark for rehearsals on Lars von Trier's new film *Breaking the Waves* and this is my first evening.

Got picked up from the airport and driven to the house of the producer Vibeke Windeløv. I am the last person to arrive and I'm aware that Emily Watson (the lead actress) and Stellan Skarsgard (the lead actor) have been rehearsing with Lars for three days already. I'm introduced to Bente, Lars' girlfriend, who is a primary school teacher. I have already been told (by Lars in my audition) that Bente not only inspired Lars to leave his wife and children quite recently, but that she also inspired a change in his attitude towards his work. He is now more interested in character and relationship than in the technical wizardry he revealed in his much acclaimed *Europa*. He now wants technique only to serve the freedom of the actor.

July 27 First day of rehearsal. The Danish Film Studios are situated in a leafy residential area a short way along the motorway out of Copenhagen. I am introduced to Morton, the first assistant. He has worked with Lars before and in addition to making films in his own right he is also a senior lecturer at the European Film School in Denmark. Clearly a different breed to the British equivalent!

Emily and I sit outside waiting for Lars. Finally he comes out and sits with us and seems as nervous as I am. I enjoy his repartee. It's amusing and relaxes me. Lars says he wants to talk with me on my own first while Emily has a costume fitting. He is dressed in khaki knee-length shorts and a blue T-shirt. With his cropped dark hair and pointy features, he resembles a rodent in *Dad's Army*. Once we've settled in the room he explains a little about how he wants to work. 'I want us all to feel completely free to make mistakes.' This is music to my ears:

We won't be worrying about the exact script or continuity. I want you to feel free to experiment. We'll be doing lots of long takes and I'd like to try something new in each one. When I cut it together sometimes I'll choose a reaction which doesn't quite fit the delivery that caused it. I like the idea of a scene not having continuity except in the characters, in who they are. The camera will be hand held and the format CinemaScope. This means the movements will be amplified. A lot will be close-ups. The camera will follow you, it will cross the line, break the rules.

103

All this is sounding more and more incredible. To have that much freedom thrills and terrifies me. There was a wonderful freedom working with Mike Leigh who spends four months with you before any camera comes anywhere near you, finding the character and the situation in which he/she will be in. Filming starts in seven days and I have today and tomorrow to rehearse! The character of 'Dodo' is far from myself – will I find her in time? I loathe worrying about continuity in filming, and to have the opportunity not only to forget about it, but positively to court discontinuity sounds beautifully liberating to me. When Emily returns we spend a little more time talking before Stellan arrives. Then we read through the relevant scenes with all three of us in, and once we've read through a scene a couple of times we disregard it and improvise around the script. I am definitely not as warmed up as Emily and Stellan and I feel everything I contribute is unimaginative and basic. Improvising is so much about knowing who you are and trusting your acting comrades.

July 28 It's late and I'm back in England after another day's rehearsal where I felt more released and adventurous. We carried on in much the same vein as yesterday and 'Dodo' is beginning to emerge. So far, I've decided she should be from York. It's a place I know reasonably well and Dodo's actions in the story have something of the strength and straightforwardness of the 'northern spirit'. The rest is instinctive. Being a nurse gives her a natural authority (she is a ward sister), and being a widow (Sam has died before the film starts) gives her an inherent sadness. A submerged feeling of loss and abandonment, and I have to ask myself with what has Dodo replaced that loss? Lars feels it is definitely in her relationship to Bess that she finds most satisfaction. Bess is Sam's sister and in Dodo's view needs looking after. She thinks she isn't right in the head and is therefore vulnerable. Lars is very willing to discuss these questions and is trusting that we as actors will find the answers. Filming begins in a week and there is precious little time to ferment any ideas. That is always the way with filming unless you are in Mike Leigh land!

October I'm trying to look back over three months of filming and make some coherent sense out of it. The script of *Breaking the Waves* is a very strong, almost old-fashioned story. It is a love story, a melodrama, set in a small, religiously strict community in 1972. The narrative is clear and chronological. The characters are solid, with quite simple shapes. They are real but only in terms of Lars' fictional world. The geography is recognisably Scotland but Lars deliberately thwarted any conventional approach to the landscape. For example, we would be in a breathtaking valley with a shimmering loch and he'd be using a 50 mm lens with scarcely enough depth of field to capture it. The vistas would be peripheral to faces. In some ways Lars is as interested in opportunities missed as the ones taken, fascinated by those moments others discard and bored by those they would put centre frame. He confessed to me that in one scene he included a shot of Stellan trying to put his watch on before the take had started. Because, he said, there was something about it that no acting could reproduce.

On location, weather inconsistencies, which are usually the plague of other directors and cost thousands of pounds from the budget, delighted Lars. When we filmed the exterior of a wedding ceremony in one take, it began in brilliant sunshine and then suddenly started hailing while the sun was still out. It was amazing – an ice confetti stabbing all the wedding guests, making us run or shield ourselves in the brilliant autumn light. Many directors would have shouted 'cut' for reasons of continuity. But Lars loves that kind of serendipity and the fact that by using those shots he may be breaking a cardinal film-making rule. I cannot but agree with him that such rules are screaming to be broken. To my mind, Lars is basically challenging the technical control of the film-maker. He is inviting himself and his technicians (the actors too, but in a different way) to lose control. Written in large letters everywhere on set and on monitors were the words 'MAKE FAULTS'! If a radio microphone is accidentally showing in an actor's hair, he is thrilled. If the camera operator (Jean Paul Maurice – an exceedingly fit Frenchman, who at sixty is an intrepid rock climber and whose idea of relaxation was to cycle eighty miles on our days off) tripped over some cables and crashed into one of the actors, Lars would be furious if he had stopped filming. It seems to me that most of Lars' battles on set involved him trying to puncture the professionalism of his crew.

For me, filming was in two phases: the first, two summer months in the hermetic studio in Denmark filming all the interiors; the second, a month on the wild west coast of Scotland filming all the exteriors. Working on the studio set was fittingly claustrophobic. The interior world of Western Isle cottages was brilliantly reproduced by Kalli Juliusson. Here we were, in the heat wave of a Copenhagen summer, trying to imagine the chilling damp of a Hebridian autumn. Lars was insistent that nothing be moved from where it would naturally stand. No furniture or props could be altered to accommodate the camera or surrounding crew. The result was extremely cramped and often hilarious. It must, at times, have been excruciating for the cinematographer, Robbie Muller, who has worked with the likes of Wenders, Wajda and Jarmusch.

Stellan, the only actor brave or stupid or experienced enough to watch rushes, expressed a concern to me that Robbie couldn't light for different lenses or shots – the eyes of the actors were getting lost. This worried me because obviously an actor's eyes on film really are 'the messengers of the soul'. If we lose the intimacy of their expression then the other factors have to compensate. 'Trust', I said to myself. Trust that Lars' vision and 'no style' style will carry this deprivation. I certainly didn't feel there was anything I personally could do to compensate for it, as this would have involved a degree of self-consciousness unconducive to the kind of abandon Lars required of the acting.

To all this chaos and claustrophobia you have to add the presence of a Swedish documentary crew which Emily (Watson, playing Bess) and I dubbed the 'rhinoceros on the wall' because a fly it certainly wasn't. They could be heard everywhere crashing around, getting in everyone's way, desperate to film an argument or a prima donna incident. On the first day it was established that the battery for my radio-mic had to be strapped to the top of my thigh because it was noticeable everywhere else. Sure enough, there they were, filming the Dutch soundman's shaking hands fiddling round the top of my suspenders under my nurse's uniform!

But within all this anarchy there was, of course, a great deal of order. The filming day was the most civilised I have ever experienced. Shooting began around 8.30 am and was over between 4 and 6 pm. In part this was due to the 'make mistakes' policy. When so little can technically go wrong then the only thing which matters, as far as retakes are concerned, is the nature of the acting. Lars was meticulous about this. He wanted us to absorb the basic elements in a scripted scene and then discard the literalness of it. He was happy to keep retaking until he had a multitude of versions. The takes themselves were long and not one of them was to be an exact repetition of the last. In this way he can cut together inconsistencies of mood and interpretation. It's quite frightening to think that some combinations will make one sort of scene and another will make a completely different one.

My most difficult and rewarding day in the studio was the reception scene. My character, Dodo, has to give a long speech in honour of the newly-weds, but particularly for her sister-in-law, Bess. It required a lot of conflicting emotion. She is happy and resentful, proud and jealous, generous and harsh, warm but feels deeply abandoned by her friend. I used the basis of the speech in the script but rewrote a lot of it the night before filming. I was very nervous about doing this speech because I knew that in a sense the whole character hung on it. If I didn't get the dynamic right (the scene is early on in the film) then later aspects of her wouldn't work. Lars wanted to do the speech first thing and I showed him what I had written. He approved and said, 'Do you want to rehearse it?' And I heard myself say, 'No'. I have never done that before with such an important moment. But instinctively I felt that since Dodo would not have rehearsed and would be worrying about the impact of her speech, the best preparation I could do would be to feel all those things with her for the first time. Lars was extremely pleased to go for it immediately and the beauty of his method is that one can take risks like that. We ended up filming versions of that moment four or five times. Emotionally I was so released because I had given nothing away in a rehearsal, not even a technical one, and I felt vulnerable in front of all those people at the reception. The camera swung around as usual trying to watch the speech as well as the reception to it. I have no idea what will come across. Whether the 'reportage' of the camera caught details of contrary feelings. But for me it was the most open I have felt after the word, 'action!'.

Towards the end of studio filming we went for about ten days, on location but still in Denmark, to a hospital. This period veered from utter emotional exhaustion to uncontrollable hilarity. The former was due to the strain and pitch of the story at this point. The latter due to the absurd nature of myself and Adrian Rawlins trying to be a nurse and doctor respectively. We'd had very little time to research properly and I had a Danish nurse called Gretta overseeing everything I did. She was aged around forty-five, large with blonde plaits. There were times when she would say, 'Yes – zis is very good but you vould hev killed him like zat because you forgot to take zee air out of zee syringe first.' Equally I will never forget Adrian's face when Lars decided, on the spur of the moment, that it would be better if he performed the brain surgery on Stellan rather than the real brain surgeon that had been booked. Then there was the joy of watching the real brain surgeon's face watching Adrian slipping with the drill, knowing that the prosthetic on Stellan's head was only a 1/4 inch thick. Need I say anything about the expression on Stellan's face!

Filming the exteriors was obviously less intimate and contained. We all had to pit ourselves against the elements, the overwhelming wildness of the landscape we were in. It was a huge adjustment. A different country and season for a start. For the first few days Stellan, Emily and I felt we had lost contact with Lars. He seemed remote and unfocused. Luckily he realised this. By his own admission he's trying to rectify the mistake he feels he made on *Europa*, where he was utterly uncaring and uncommunicative with the actors. Now he is almost overly sensitive to how he treats people; intensely apologetic if he feels he's done wrong. He definitely misjudged my strength in the beginning. I think that he thought I was more experienced than I am and felt I didn't need much encouragement. This couldn't be less true. Unfortunately I am not very secure in my ability and I require a great deal of reassurance. Gradually he began to realise this. Often the character you are playing affects your relationship with a director, especially when they themselves wrote the script. There's no knowing what you represent to that person. Then there's how much your character expresses certain aspects of yourself. Dodo in a way was a practical, rather conservative person whose self-righteousness often blinded her to the truth. It drove me mad to play her, on one level. It was like wearing a straight jacket. If Sophie in *Naked* was like peeling myself then Dodo was like suffocating myself.

Anyway, the mercurial weather in the Highlands provided a great distraction from all the emotional demands. There was an eighty-mile-an-hour gale blowing at Niest Point on Skye when we filmed all the graveside scenes. It is almost impossible to stand in such a force and I loved it! One shot involved me, dressed in black, battling down a steep hill towards Bess's funeral. It is a passionate scene and one of the few where Dodo is allowed to vent her frustrations. I could barely get there and the sight of the community elders – also black clad – their white and grey hair vertical to their heads was incredibly dramatic. Most of the time we were all wet through to the bone.

It is impossible to capture all the fascinating minutiae that occur during filming. It is so intensely personal. I find that my life and work are not wholly divisable. The subtle dynamics between people all go to make the chemistry of a film. There needs to be a lot of love when you make anything as a group. I don't mean the sort people gossip about – although obviously there's that too – I mean the love of vulnerability. This is why the word 'industry' sticks in my throat.

The Cinematographer

Peter Suschitzky

Peter Suschitzky is the acclaimed cinematographer of many features including
Charlie Bubbles, Valentino, The Empire Strikes Back, Falling in Love,
Dead Ringers *and* Naked Lunch – *the last two directed by David Cronenberg,*
someone who figures largely in what was a very exciting year.

April 1   David Cronenberg is in London to interview Salman Rushdie for
a magazine and to talk to Jeremy Thomas, his producer for one of his
projects, *Crash*, adapted from the novel by J. G. Ballard. It will make a
wonderful film, I feel sure, the way I felt about *Dead Ringers* when I first
read it. But it isn't proving easy to raise the money. The feeling of
bleakness, the aberrant behaviour of its protagonists, the violence, the sex,
the violent sex – the mixture seems to frighten a lot of people, but slowly
some fine actors are coming forward and committing to it . . . we shall
see.

April 5   I'm in Barcelona shooting a commercial and thinking about a
meeting which I am supposed to have with Tim Burton next week in the
USA. It seems that I am on a shortlist for his next film *Mars Attacks*. Of
course, I'd love to do it. *Ed Wood* is fresh in my mind, and I loved its
quirkiness and great style but I've become almost superstitious about
mentioning possible projects for the future, as if talking about them will
make them disappear. Years of disappointment over the films that got away
have made many of us feel the same way – hence the maxim, never talk
about it until it is really happening. Writing this diary feels dangerous.
However, considering future projects is part, even an obsessive part, of my
daily life, and my wife never seems to show signs of being bored by my
musings on what might or might not happen.

April 10   Back in London. During this week Spyros Skouras, my agent in
LA continues to tell me that I am on a very restricted shortlist for Tim
Burton's next film, but it seems he is not ready to meet yet. I get a call from
Barcelona later in the week: would I agree to come on Sunday to prepare
and shoot a car commercial which includes some high-speed (1,000 frames
per second) shots of a car window exploding?

April 19   My agent tells me, 'You're top of the list for Tim Burton's
project.'

April 20 Surprise. Tim Burton has met with another cinematographer, Michael Balhaus, and has given the film to him.

April 21 My agent again: 'There are "artistic differences" between Balhaus and Burton, they want you to come over on Monday.'

I spend the next few days waiting for either the production office or the LA travel agent to confirm that the trip is on, but, somewhere over there, someone has forgotten to inform me and I am left in the dark. Perhaps they have changed their minds, which wouldn't in the least surprise me.

April 24 I finally get an answer in the evening. I am to leave in the morning, but as I have now agreed to shoot (a commercial) in Paris on Thursday and Friday, I will have to return to Europe the next day. I get to LA on Tuesday afternoon, drive myself to the hotel, shower, shave and leave immediately for my meeting with Tim Burton. It is a very friendly affair – he couldn't have been kinder about my work, tells me a little about his next film and asks me a few questions. I'm struck by his open face, wild hair and nervous energy. We talk about a mutual friend, Anton Furst, who designed the first *Batman* film and who killed himself two years ago. Twenty-five minutes later, as I come out of the meeting, not even having had the chance to read the script – quite unusual that – I smile as I think of the eleven-hours flight here, and the same awaiting me in the morning.

April 27 I arrive in Paris at 7.30 am, go to my hotel, sleep for an hour and am taken to a small studio in order to shoot part of a commercial which I worked on in Italy in November – the client wants some small changes in the product shots. It may sound ridiculous to travel all the way to LA and then leave again so soon just because of some close-ups of pasta, but in this business, if you break your promise you may never be forgiven.

May 1 Commercial companies continue to book me for jobs that never materialise, but finally one of them does, and on 16 May I travel to Barcelona. A few days before travelling to Spain I had thought of sending Tim Burton a photograph I made many years ago in New York, of a down-and-out man reading a newspaper on 42nd Street, with a cinema behind him showing a film called *Invasion Mars 1000 Years from Now*. When I have made the prints, I notice some unusual staining, the result of the silenium toning process which I have started to use recently. Thinking that perhaps there is something symbolic in the staining, I decide not to send the prints, but to await the final 'no' which I feel must come from the production. Shortly after arriving I receive a short fax from my agent announcing unexpected and great news about Tim Burton's film. I find it difficult to believe and pass a sleepless night.

May 23 Tomorrow will be my brother's birthday. He and I spend an early evening together and open a bottle of champagne which Robert De Niro gave to me at the end of *Falling in Love* in 1984. My agent calls to say that 'the deal has been closed'. I still can't believe my good fortune, and we drink the champagne, long kept for such an occasion.

May 24 I travel to Israel with my wife to visit her parents. David Cronenberg tries to reach me there, and a few days later, I speak with him. It seems that *Crash*, a movie which I really have been wanting to make with him for three years now, will go into production this year and, consequently, I won't be able to shoot it! I feel so sad about that; my elation at the prospect of working with Tim Burton disappears for a moment. David is, after all, very special among all the people with whom I've had the good fortune to work, and we have become fast friends. I've been nursing and nurturing ideas for *Crash* for ages now. Oh the frustration of our business! The thought of working with Tim Burton still excites me though.

June I was to leave for LA on Sunday 18 June. On Friday 16th a fax arrived saying that my trip was cancelled or at least delayed. I think that the problem is that they are awaiting a rewrite of the script and don't therefore have a real start date for the movie. Now I begin to get concerned: after all I have turned down a lot of work. The next days are difficult. I feel as if I am stuck, paralysed. I have to try to believe that Warner Bros. are going to keep their side of the agreement, so I continue to turn away projects, yet I have terrible doubts because, via my agent, I hear that he is having a lot of trouble getting a start date for me, and I don't yet have a contract.

June 30 A fax came from LA over night. Contract is agreed and they want me to leave in three days' time!

July 5 Los Angeles. To the studios for a meeting with everyone except Tim Burton. An army of people, and all eagerly awaiting the overdue rewrite without which a lot of necessary preparations for shooting cannot be made. My initial involvement is mainly with Dan Radford, special effects co-ordinator. I am unhappy with the system he favours for shooting the film, a sort of bastard CinemaScope called Super 35, which involves enlarging the camera gate and including the soundtrack area as part of the exposed negative area. Then, in the final stage of post-production the image has to be optically reduced and squeezed in the laboratory into an anamorphic image. An extra optical process which creates extra grain, lack of sharpness and general muddiness. I won't go into all the reasons why this system is used on some films, but it doesn't look good compared with normal anamorphically shot films or with normal spherical 1.85 films. This battle will be hotly fought over the next weeks.

July 7 More meetings. I am now an employee of Warner Bros., with all its rules and regulations to obey. I have to sign pages of documents relating to subjects as diverse as safety and sexual harassment. I come to the obvious conclusion that next to failing in business, the fear of being sued for any of a multitude of reasons is the nightmare of any corporation and of many individuals. I remember reading in the *Los Angeles Times* about a man who attempted to sue a well-known actress for invading his dreams.

September 1   Since my last entry I have spent two months at the Warner studios, contributing what I could to the preparation of *Mars Attacks*. The shooting date seems to recede every week, and we look unlikely to shoot until January.

As far as the practicalities of shooting the film are concerned, my main worry continues to be the format. We shoot a comparison test between Super 35 and ordinary widescreen. The test also involves adding a separate animation component of a Martian. The two elements are then brought together in post-production using a process called 'compositing'. It takes a month for our short sequence of three shots to be composited, and probably enough money to shoot a very low-budget movie! But the results clearly show the deterioration of the image in the Super 35 mm version due to the extra phase it undergoes in the laboratory – a squeeze akin to the squeeze produced at the time of photography in anamorphic (or Cinema-Scope). Tim Burton finally agrees with me, though with sadness, that we should shoot in widescreen.

Throughout August I have also been talking with David Cronenberg who has been preparing *Crash* on a smaller budget than our preparation costs for *Mars Attacks*. Realising that *Mars Attacks* cannot really begin until January, I start to press for my release so that I could shoot *Crash*. With only a day or so to go before Cronenberg needs to take a decision, Tim Burton says he is considering the matter. The next day I wait for Tim to come to the studio, for he has been working on the storyboards. He has the whole film storyboarded and the boards have been videoed, cut and entered on an Avid editing machine, complete with dialogue, music and sound effects, albeit in a crude form. This way he will get a feel for the shape of the whole film and the proportion of special effects to live action. Every frame of stop-motion animation and 'compositing' is very costly, so if a few minutes of animation can be cut, there will be a saving of tens of thousands of dollars. Tim is, as usual, dressed in black, with his black hair in the normal unkempt look that he is known for. He wastes no time in coming to the point and simply said, 'Go and do it.' I am hugely relieved and delighted.

September 5   And so begins the next chapter. Toronto and my fourth movie with David Cronenberg. We have a very unusually strong instinctive understanding for what we need to do together when we are filming. I've never had a professional relationship – personal at the same time – quite like it.

This film feels like a particularly high-risk enterprise. On the practical level there is not enough time to shoot the overabundance of car scenes (cars are always slow to film) which are nearly all at night. On the creative and emotional side it feels very exposed and raw, but I feel it in my bones – and have done so for three years – that this film will be at the least very

111

unusual and at best quite extraordinary. It will upset many people, but not gratuitously.

I have less than three weeks to prepare. There are so many locations to see and we spend days travelling here and there across the city and along the motorways. Some of the scenes on motorways will present me with very large vistas to light at night. Luckily I have a familiar nucleus of people to work with, so all of our energies can go easily and naturally into making the film. I ask for a day or so for make-up tests because I just like to get a feel for the actors' faces and characters before I start. I can also use the opportunity to test a few ideas. I test Kodak and Fuji film stocks, shooting on a motorway at night, and decide that for this film Fuji gives me a look I prefer. The make-up tests confirm this. Scars are going to be important on this film, James Spader and Holly Hunter have their scar-face look tested and it looks good!

I will operate the camera on this film as I always do with Cronenberg. Even when I work with a camera operator I do not consider myself a 'lighting cameraman' – the English description of my craft. I work more happily with the American method in which the director and cinematographer decide how a scene should be shot, where the camera should be placed and how many angles there are going to be. The director of photography (or cinematographer) takes a rehearsal with the actors, and when he is satisfied, hands over to the camera operator. In England the custom was to leave the cameraman to light the scene, the director and operator deciding on the cuts and placement of the camera. My blood boils when I think of how I worked in the past. Never again! I feel closest to the movie when I'm behind the camera. I am the first viewer of the film as I look through the lens and feel the whole weight of what is going on. I can also see what is wrong with my own work straight away and, if I have a good and easy relationship with the director, I can sometimes point out things that can help in all sorts of ways.

September 27 We start shooting today. The first two weeks will be daytime exteriors, then it's into the night. We start with car scenes; the days are getting short and we always seem to be filming as it is getting dark. A race against time as usual, but in an acute form on this film. This film also calls for a lot of courage from the main players; from the actors, director and myself too. There's no point tackling it timidly. The actors have difficult things to do here – raw emotions, physically and mentally exposed. I too will need to find a courageous way to tackle my side of it.

October 10 To find oneself shooting the final scene of the film, at the end of week two, to find the right feeling for it, is not so easy. In the morning I know how much we have to do in the day, and that some of the shots will take a long time to do, so I ask David not to leave the last scene until late in the day. But he wants to shoot another scene first. I have worked out that we will begin shooting the main scene around 5.00 pm, and it will be too dark to shoot by 6.00 pm. David wants to shoot James Spader in his car as

112

he chases and bumps Deborah Unger (his wife in the film) in hers; her close-up; as well as some shots of the cars themselves weaving in and out of traffic. We have a piece of elevated motorway closed off to traffic. For each close-up we have to hitch the actor's car to our camera car and then fix the camera very securely on to the actor's car – this takes about forty-five minutes. We then have to position ourselves and all our drivers, and then set off on the short piece of road we have. To go to the beginning again takes ten minutes on small roads open to the public so that when we stop at traffic lights, passers-by stand and stare at us.

Finally we get all the bits and pieces which we need to make the sequence work, but by the time that I climb onto the crane from which I shall shoot the last shot of the film, it is 5.00 pm – just as I feared! I had to guess where to place the crane as one can never know what it will look like until one gets up to full height – in this case around twenty feet. It doesn't quite give us what we want so we move it a few feet. Luckily it's mounted on a truck so we only lose a precious ten minutes. In the shot we have to follow James Spader as he gets out of his old Lincoln and stumbles down the embankment to find his wife, who has been thrown from the car (he has knocked her off the road). They make love, we crane and zoom back to show a wide shot of the wrecked car and the motorways surrounding them.

By the time we have done three takes, the light is beginning to fade and we have perhaps twenty minutes to do the rest of the scene. Things go wrong – a sound cable shows in one take, a taped microphone on the abdomen of the actress in another – things we cannot afford to have happen when night is approaching. We do finish the scene, shooting until it is just too dark to continue.

Thinking back on that scene I am struck by the bizarre situations in which one finds oneself when shooting a movie. It was an astonishingly surreal moment: with dusk rapidly approaching, a camera crane hovers over a motorway verge, where a half-naked actress lies on the cold, damp grass, trying hard not to shiver. In this harsh and very real, if not banal, environment, exposed for all of us to see, two actors simulate one of mankind's most intimate moments.

October 15 We are now starting our third week of filming and from now on most of our work will be done at night.

October 24 The nights are sometimes wet and are gradually getting longer and colder. Day by day I put more clothes on until I have the proportions of a Michelin Man, making some of the contortions needed to assume the camera operating position difficult.

When we are preparing to film car stunt scenes, our discussions are aided by arrangements of toy cars, either on a table or actually on the road, as the stunt co-ordinator demonstrates how the cars will behave. Sometimes a group of people are to be seen in the middle of the road, at night, bent over these toy cars, intent on imagining a full-scale version of what looks like a boy's game.

I'm having to shoot this film in ways that are sometimes documentary-like because of a combination of factors: lack of money, a short shooting schedule for the sort of film we are making, and the huge scope of some of the night scenes which involve a couple of miles of motorway. This last week's work – all at night and sometimes in pouring rain – includes a lot of shots from a motorbike side-car. They call it appropriately, 'Moto Cam'. This method permits fast and very mobile shots, low and close to the ground. I have to do these shots with no lighting except the street lamps, and today we will see our rushes.

The laboratory, like all others, closes down at the weekend. It so happens that we have been shooting some of our most difficult scenes over those days – Friday to Sunday nights – when we are unable to see the results. On Friday night we put our huge Lincoln convertible (the sort that President Kennedy was assassinated in) on to what we call a 'process trailer' or 'low loader'. It's a platform on wheels, set as low as possible, allowing the camera to be placed alongside or in front of the car, which the actor doesn't really drive. By the time lamps are attached to the platform no one could see enough to drive, let alone manage to act at the same time.

This evening it has been raining so hard that the open car has to be covered while we are preparing for the scene. James Spader is in the driving seat and in the back seat are two other actors; one of them, Elias Koteas, is examining the half-naked body of the other, who is playing a prostitute, as we proceed on our illuminated platform, in the rain, down a road that is partially used by the public. The actress is brave indeed to expose herself to the freezing cold and the gaze of passing motorists.

Twice in the process of making this film, I have come close to having a serious accident. The first time was in the first week, as we were filming underneath this same overhead motorway. I was on the back of our camera car, standing on the camera dolly, when the car started to swerve violently from side to side, causing the dolly to career one way and then the other, its weight too heavy to hold with the G-force added to it. I was thrown to the floor, and was prevented from falling onto the road and under passing traffic only by the assistants grabbing my bulky jacket. The second time was just after filming the scene with the prostitute and the two men. The overhead motorway, or rather one side of it, was closed for us. For years the road had been only part finished, the overhead section coming to an abrupt end, the concrete supports in place, but no roadway placed on it. It was here that one of our drivers, going the wrong way on the elevated motorway nearly drove us over the edge and into the air. My diary nearly came to a sudden end that night!

I am feeling fearful at this stage that, because of the nature of the filming – on roadways, in and out of cars at night – and because there's so little time, I might not be able to do my best work on this film. Our previous movies together, *M. Butterfly*, *Naked Lunch*, and *Dead Ringers*, have all been very controlled, being almost entirely studio bound, so I have been able to do what I wanted, but this film is another case all together. I never forget that the script is wonderful, it's just that sometimes I wish that visually I could make more of it. Still, there are another five weeks or so to go, and I might be wrong about my work. It is so easy to lose sight of what one is doing and to see it as others see it.

Today, I am anxiously awaiting the screening of the last three nights' work ... Thank goodness just about everything looked the way I wanted it to, even the motorcam material shot under the worst conditions. The scene in which the heavy old Lincoln is pursuing the small Miatta sports car – at night under the yellow lights of the highway – feels charged with menace and excitement.

November 14 How the overall look of the film will feel, I cannot tell at this stage as I am too close to the details of the daily work, affected by the hour-to-hour struggle involved in working out each scene, each shot. I always find it hard at this stage to judge the film as a whole. I am aware of what I feel are its strengths and its weaknesses, but I fully expect to be surprised by the film when it is edited. Films seem to take on a life of their own which, of course, is the sum of what we do hour by hour, day by day. We become lost in the maze, unable to see the wood for the trees. The rhythm of the film, the flow of a group of sequences is one of the hardest things to discern when in the middle of shooting. One easily imagines the film when reading the script, but everything changes once it is peopled and spoken by real actors. Our film has little dialogue, but the actors, of course, bring a physical presence into the scene and every day bring surprises. Indeed it is the unpredictable nature of the act of filming that makes it so exciting, and any director who tries to prevent unpredictability creeping in is bound to deaden the result. Allowing for even welcoming, the unpredictable is an essential element of good film-making, and as long as that space for the unexpected, the surprising, is accompanied by an overall vision, one can, with a good script and cast, be on the way to a good movie. But you never can be sure. Until the very end.

By now we have reached the end of our seventh week out of the ten allotted to us. We have also reached the end of six weeks of working outside at night. Thank goodness. The weather has been getting steadily colder and nights of endless rain have given way to temperatures of minus four or five and snow – unusual so early in the year.

Last weekend we were filming a sequence in which two cars crash into each other. One was to be driven by a stunt driver and the other, a lightweight reproduction of a 50s Porsche racing car, was to be remote controlled. Unfortunately, as the remote control technician was practising, he managed to turn the car over and damage it. As our film is so low-budget, we didn't have a second car, so it had to be patched up and touched up, resulting in a delay of several hours, and much angst.

While we have been shooting *Crash*, *Mars Attacks* has continued to be on hold. Two weeks ago I was asked to meet Tim Burton in New York, so having got to bed after filming to 7.00 am on Monday (my day off), I got up at 12.30 pm and took a cab to the airport, still feeling a bit groggy and weary. At the meeting some recent animation tests were screened. We were able to discuss the look of the tests and a few other concerns. They are going to film the demolition of a hotel in Las Vegas and use it in the film. As they will be adding flying saucers to the images in post production, they have opted for the shooting to be done in VistaVision which I personally first used when shooting *The Empire Strikes Back*. Not being available for this event, I have nominated Dick Bowen, a colleague and friend whom I've known for some twenty years now, and he is to be in charge of shooting this brief event which will cost hundreds of thousands of dollars.

November 30   We are nearing the end of our shooting though we are now probably four days behind schedule. Our schedule was unrealistic to start with because cars and winter night shootings are really hard and slow. I will only summarise the last two weeks because fatigue has set in and my weekends are spent recovering from the rigours of the week. I, of course, get no break from work. There's usually a fourteen-hour working day or night. I am constantly behind the camera, organising the next shot and then shooting it, operating the camera myself, directing the dolly grip and lighting technicians. Luckily my relationship with David Cronenberg is so close and full of understanding that finding each shot and deciding how to shoot each scene is an easy and rapid process; a quick exchange of ideas and an easy agreement on what needs to be done.

I have, strangely enough, shot relatively few 'love scenes' in my life, but this movie has several of them. Simulated sex scenes would be a more appropriate expression to use in the context of *Crash* because there is little expression or evidence of love between the characters. 'Stuffed cabbage is a fatal choice of dish to eat before a sex scene,' says one of the actors as we embark on one of those scenes. It was on the menu that day, but I didn't notice any problems in this respect. The most important thing in this sort of scene is to make it so believable that there will be an element of doubt in the spectators minds as to whether it was for real or not. Impossible body positions, such as in *Damage*, just distance the audience because they know instantly that it's fake. I've always looked on Toronto as somewhat puritanical, so it's odd to be filming so many 'sex scenes'. Perhaps I was wrong about Toronto!

We had a small drama unfolding behind the scenes, something which I have been unaware of. During filming, one of the stand-ins, a woman, has accused a male colleague of sexual harassment and has gone as far as bringing the case before the tribunal of the actors' union. The alleged incident occurred while we were filming the last scene in the film, a scene that takes place in the open air under the crashed wreck of the car. The stand-ins had to lie in the same positions as the actors – the normal thing for them to do – and were simulating the sexual act, man behind woman. The female stand-in accused her male co-worker of touching her stomach in an 'inappropriate manner'. To most of us the accusation seems to be ridiculous given the context of their work and the context of the scene, but the accusation could have serious consequences for the man – he wouldn't be able to work again as an actor or stand-in. Suddenly all our attention was fixed on this dispute, and the more we thought about it, the more comic it seemed.

I have remained in contact with LA and *Mars Attacks*. The film has now been confirmed and will shoot 5 February.

December 8   One of the last scenes which we shot was the continuation of a scene that we had started eight weeks previously. Very often one has to keep in one's mind the feel, the rhythm and look of a scene partially shot, in order to pick it up again at a later date. These days we have a video record of each scene to jog our memories, but it gives only an approximation of the details of the look of the scene for the director of photography. Our scene entailed re-creating a car wash in the studio, or at least the interior of a car while in a car wash. For this purpose we had our old Lincoln cut in half breadthways for easy access for the camera, leaving only the back seat of the car. The actors duly performed their wordless embraces while soapy water was sprayed on to the windows, and the brush mechanism imported into the studio set in motion.

This has been one of my happiest shooting experiences despite the physical rigours, the cold and the nights. David and I have got on so well and the crew has been a joy to work with: there has been what I can only call a loving atmosphere on the set.

Our farewells are fond and tearful. Thus ends the filming of *Crash*. The weather on the last day recorded a low of −12°C, so people envy me my departure for LA, but I tell them that I can scarcely imagine that it will be as much fun as *Crash*. We will see.

December 28   Looking forward to the start of shooting a new film: at this stage, before a film is made, it always offers, or seems to offer, open-ended possibilities. Until the script is peopled, until the film is cast, the characters on the pages rest in one's imagination, and stylistically the film could go in a number of directions. This is the most exciting moment: akin to chaos out of which creation is made. In a few months we will be either satisfied or disappointed with what we have participated in, or, as is often the case, our feelings will lie somewhere between satisfaction and disappointment. At this moment, though, I feel the thrill of the vastness of possibility lying ahead of me.

Seamus McGarvey

The year 1995 proved to be an auspicious one for young cinematographer Seamus McGarvey. It saw the release of Butterfly Kiss, *his first cinema feature as director of photography, marking a major turning-point in his career. The following extracts concentrate on two very different projects, both located in parts of the world currently undergoing a transition from civil unrest to tentative peace.*

June Belfast. I'm here for two weeks to shoot a thirty-minute comedy drama for BBC Northern Ireland called *Out of the Deep Pan* to be directed by Kieron J. Walsh. It's a sign of the times (i.e. post cease-fire Northern Ireland) that the BBC is commissioning a lot of comedy at the moment. Belfast has changed so much in the past ten months since the cease-fire was announced. The optimism is tangible. The first day of the shoot involved us screeching around an underground car park in Belfast in a series of *Starsky and Hutch* pastiches. Unfortunately, during a rehearsal, I hadn't properly secured myself before the actor driving had sped off. We suddenly skidded to a halt and I was catapulted towards the front of the car. I emerged, bleeding profusely and ashen-faced but essentially uninjured and alive! I did, however, have to sustain the embarrassment of a 'looney tunes' bump on my head for several days.

I saw the day's rushes. It was quite difficult assessing how my visual approach was working because we are editing on Avid and at this stage we are processing negative only. This means that all the film is telecined at the laboratory by a video technician. It makes things really difficult for me because I don't have my normal visual or technical co-ordinates to work from. There are no printer lights, no film grader, no accurate trouble-shooting regarding focus, exposure, scratching or steadiness. This seems to be the situation with a lot of the films I shoot these days. I'm no Luddite but when my work is being affected adversely by technology which should only be there to enhance *all* of our work, I think we need to consider other approaches. Actually the thing I really miss is the viewing of film rushes in a room with the other crew members. Video viewings tend to be solitary affairs with the director. A communal screening of everyone's work is a very cohesive force on a film, but one which seems to be ebbing into history.

June 23 Working in a place that has effectively been an unspoken war zone for all those years is a great experience. I'm meeting lots of young film-makers here who are involved in fascinating projects. Most of these are either very low or no-budget films, but the important thing is that there are so many stories to be told. The relief of no violence has created a situation where film-makers can reappraise things in a more objective way, untrammelled by partisan allegiances.

The camera I am using is called the Aaton XTR Prod (short for production) which has led to a few jokes about what side of the fence the camera department is from ('prod' is slang for Protestant)! My focus-puller

Baz Irvine and I had an additional nameplate engraved at CineEurope which read Aaton XTR Taig (slang for Catholic) – and we quietly replaced the 'Prod' for the 'Taig'! It got a good laugh when the sparks discovered it. Such a good-humoured reaction would have been difficult to imagine ten months previously.

June 29   Today is my birthday and it is also the last day of shooting. As ever it is pedal to the metal at the last furlong and we are doing lots of pick-ups as well as our scheduled material. We finish with everything achieved with fifty feet of film to spare! Wrap is called and I am given a birthday cake and presents from the crew. Harry the gaffer gave me a 'No Surrender' tablecloth and Liz Gregg the assistant director got me a King Billy tablecloth!

September   I received a letter from Sara Prichard at Casaroto Marsh agents in London saying that she knew I was presently represented by someone but that if I ever changed my mind they would be very interested in representing me. Sandra Marsh is one of the best agents for directors of photography and she represents many of the cameramen I most admire in the world – people like Gabriel Beristain, Dick Pope and Denis Lenoir. It didn't take me too long to decide that to go with them would be a really good thing at this stage in my career. I went into their offices in Wardour Street and was very impressed with the whole set-up. I told them there and then that I wanted to join them.

The results were almost immediately apparent. I got back from a Telecine in town one evening and Sara phoned to say that Les Blair wanted to meet me with regard to shooting his next film. The problem was that he was due to leave the next day for South Africa, so tonight was the only time he had available. I walked straight back to the tube and met Les and his producer Indra de Lanerolle in a pub off Tottenham Court Road. We seemed to get on well. I had been recommended to Les by Barry Ackroyd, Ken Loach's regular cinematographer. Les explained that he had no script yet and that his normal working process consisted of taking a group of actors off for an extended period of improvisation out of which would come a scene breakdown. Unlike Mike Leigh, Les never actually writes down the dialogue so it always has a fresh, natural quality. In theory this is really exciting and I'm interested to see how it will work in practice, particularly where continuity is concerned. I'm excited at the prospect of adapting my normal working methods to Les's distinctive approach.

October   While in Sweden shooting a music video for Ace of Base with Richard Heslop, I hear that Les wants me to do the film. He wants me to travel to Johannesburg on 22 November for ten days to meet the crew, see the locations and do some stock and filter tests. My crew will all be South African, as will the cast.

November   I land at Jan Smuts airport and Indra drives me into town.

119

The heat is a stifling thirty degrees. I slept through most of the overnight flight and don't feel so distant or jet-lagged. This really compounds the sense of culture shock I feel as I drive past the scarred landscape – huge yellow slag heaps line the highway. Indra takes me on a quick drive around where we see the most amazing juxtapositions of high-tech office blocks, with mirrored glass reflecting the crumbling old shopfronts opposite. The city has no reason for its location other than the mines beneath it. The Central Business District, which during Apartheid was a whites-only area, is now being reclaimed by black people on the streets. The area has an energy that reminded me of post cease-fire Belfast. It isn't picturesque by any stretch of the imagination but it has a definite look and feel which I know will work well on film. Words and place names ring quite big bells from the Apartheid years.

I meet our actors and Les lets me sit in on a few improvisations. A scene which will probably last one minute in the final film had a three and a half hour improvisation. Some of the dialogue and situations which arose were electric and exciting. I hope Indra has made provision for extra stock! With scenes being improvised, for the most part in rooms, Les had intended to photograph them quite simply as interiors with no special camera move-ment. But through discussions with him and through my first impressions of the city, we have decided to opt for a different approach. There is energy and flux and instability in this period in Johannesburg and we aim to reflect that visually by employing more camera movement and hand-held work. This, we hope, will work with the spontaneity of the acting and the situations.

Before I went out to South Africa I had been working in Scotland, doing some second camera on Michael Winterbottom's *Jude*. The director of photography, Eduardo Serra (with whom I had worked on *Map of the Human Heart*), gave me some good suggestions as to how to deal with the high-contrast light I was going to find in South Africa. He suggested that I pull process the film. Under British lighting conditions this might produce a slightly flat look, but when I finally tested the process in Johannesburg I was really pleased with the results. I explored a range of filter possibilities which Les and I analysed. I think Les even surprised himself by taking such an interest in the photography.

I have opted to go for a local lab – The Film Lab. I normally work with Technicolor in London but for this film I really need immediate rushes reports and a close contact with a grader. Indra and I are taken to lunch by a rep who gives us the hard sell. I put my tests through them and am very impressed with the results.

My lighting company, Southern Lighting, have also been very helpful. I have heard that they were blacklisted during the Apartheid years because they worked on anti-government and anti-Apartheid films such as *A World Apart*. It is good to know that they are successful and prolific again. John Harrison, the company boss, who is originally from Belfast, is helping me to get a special light for my night scenes. I want a helium balloon which has 8kw of light inside and floats to a height of 40ft. It gives a very soft, naturalistic effect. My only worry is that a huge 10ft balloon will make perfect target practice when we are in Soweto!

December 9 I get a phone call from Leos Carax (*Mauvais Sang, Les Amants du Pont Neuf*). I thought it was my friend Dave Stewart taking the piss! Luckily I played along until I realised it was bona fide. He is shooting a new film next year and wants to meet me as a possible director of photography. It is so exciting to have the prospect of meeting, never mind working with, a director like him whose work I really admire. He gives me his home number and we arrange to meet in Paris early in the New Year before I head off to South Africa.

The Designer

John Bloomfield

Top international costume designer John Bloomfield's credits include Conan the
Barbarian, The Bounty, Robin Hood, Prince of Thieves *and* Waterworld.
*In 1995 he applied his ingenuity to the full on the production of the sci-fi
adventure,* Space Truckers.

May 5   Fly to LA for an interview with the director Stuart Gordon in a
dubbing studio in Burbank. He is doing a sci-fi movie to be shot in Ireland.
The main actor is Dennis Hopper who has recommended me. Stuart is
obviously worried that anyone who worked on *Waterworld* might be a
money waster!

May 16   Stuart offers me the job to design costumes for *Space Truckers*.
(Will my dignity allow me to do a movie with a title like that? Actually it's a
very good, tight and funny script.) They will shoot in Ireland in August and
September.

May 26   Now back home in England. Prepare my drawing space ready for
next week. I haven't worked at home for eighteen months so I find I have to
fit in around my wife Ann's drawing boards, which she has set up while
finishing another job. This is the best part of any job. No pressure, letting
ideas swim around in your head, and buying sketchbooks and pencils!

May 31–June 3   Spend these days at my drawing board at home, trying to
wrestle with the problem of making a sci-fi space movie look real. In *Space
Truckers* disparate elements, from western to road movie and political satire
have to be melded into a believable whole.

June 4   Drive to London for meeting with Stuart at the Atheneum Hotel.
Ann comes with me – she is likely to work with me on this film in July,
August and September, so I have her involved from the beginning. We
discuss the drawings, script, characters, schedule and budget. Stuart seems
pleased and the whole project is now much clearer to me.

June 7   Ireland. At Ardmore Studios to meet the producers, Alex De
Grundweld and Mary Breen Farelly, and the production designer, Simon
Murton. The studios are small and there are two other movies here already
– *Moll Flanders* and *Kidnapped* – so space is limited. The Irish government's

bid to encourage foreign film production certainly seems to be working. Interview several costume supervisors and decide on Maeve Pattison.

June 8 Scout Dublin to find out what's available – I am checking out the fabric stores, industrial safety wear, harnessing and ex-army supplies. Also looking for a place to work, to set up my manufacturing base here. There is nowhere suitable in the studios because every good workshop is booked by other productions already.

June 21 Stuart and I drive together to meet Dennis Hopper at the Berkeley Court Hotel. He has a penthouse suite – a baronial hall on top of this modern building. I know Dennis from *Waterworld* so we have a good gossip about that while looking at drawings for *Space Truckers*.

June 24 Go to Billericay in Essex with Ann to look at a scrapyard specialising in derelict aircraft bits. It has small quantities of personal rescue equipment and webbing, helmets, etc. that are of interest to me. I am trying to find this kind of stuff in Ireland, but if not, this is a back-up.

July 3 Fly to Dublin. From now on I shall now be based here. Drive to the studios in time for lunch with Maeve Pattison and two assistants whom she has employed to work with us – Colette Jackson and Ann Stokes. A warehouse space that Maeve and I looked at last week in Bray has proved to be unavailable, so we decide that we must find a space at the studios. There is a double-height room that will have to do. It is very dark and airless, so I organise to have all the internal studding walls removed, four windows put in, and a back door knocked through the breeze-block wall to give proper through ventilation and safety exits. We will also need more power, a large sink and drain, and more lights. If we paint the whole area white, it should give us a passable workshop as opposed to the depressing cave that it is now.

July 4–5 Shopping in Dublin with Colette. Digging through ex-army supplies and different types of plastic, tubing, hoses, industrial safetywear – all the basics of space movies!

July 6 Meet Graham Easton of the Completion Bond Guarantee Company. He is assessing our budget. Is it realistic? Stuart Gordon asks me to draw a Coca-Cola trucker's costume for use in a sequence in a diner in space, to send to Coca-Cola to see if they like the idea. Sounds easy, but it uses up a bit of midnight oil.

July 10 Start work in the new workshop. Take delivery of rented machinery – flatbed straight stitchers, overlockers etc. Meet Robert Lane, who has been recommended by Maeve and who will work for me as a sculptor/moulder.

July 18 Dick Spring, the Irish Foreign Minister, comes to visit the studios

– this pile of rubbish we are collecting must look very strange to an outsider. In the late afternoon I go into Dublin to meet Mr Leech, a tailor, to look for fabric, and to talk to an embroiderer about making some badges and logos that I need.

July 23 Ann is going to work with me for ten weeks on *Space Truckers*. This is her first day.

July 25 Weekly production meeting at which are expressed general worries about the slowness of the cash flow. The producer assures us that the financial regime is changing and that the completion bond is now in place.

August 2 Go to O'Neill's in Dublin, a sportswear manufacturer who are going to make some custom-made football-type shirts for me. Then on to the leather warehouse to choose some suedes and natural hides that I am going to need.

August 3 Plastic fabrics that I ordered from Italy arrive. They are beautiful – bronze and silver colours.

August 4 All day spent in the studio. We are moving the paint/dye shop to an area above the prop store because of space limitations for other departments. This can become a very good workshop but it has very poor ventilation so I insist on having new windows! Anyway, these are obligatory anyway because we need a second exit up there in case of fire. There is enough room here to put Robert Lane and his team as well. They are doing the casting of the space helmets etc. This puts all my art workers under one roof.

August 11 I do a first fitting for a space suit on myself (I am a very similar size to Dennis Hopper). We have to work out the zips etc. so that they can be put on by an actor on camera without help. In the afternoon I go into Dublin shopping with Ann and Maeve. This includes a blitz on the big charity shops to get a large stock of cheap clothing for us to cut up and convert into futuristic rags for homeless people. This is for a scene we are going to shoot outside the hospital in Dublin in September.

Later I go to the Savoy Cinema in central Dublin to see the opening of *Waterworld* in Ireland. This is the first time I have seen the movie so it is very nerve-wracking. Obviously I saw rushes on location, but that gives you little idea of the finished product. I am pleased with the way the movie looks but disappointed with the story. It was crazy to start a project of this magnitude without a finalised script and I think it shows on the screen.

August 16 The first of Dennis Hopper's jackets is finished and I can try on the whole outfit – jacket, shirt, pants, gaiters, hat and boots. It looks just like the drawing. I go into Dublin to see Mr Leech, the tailor who is making some suits for us. We measure up some of the actors in his shop.

August 17   We make some belts in the studio. They're much better than the ones available to buy. Continue work on the spacesuits. Get the second helmet out of the mould – it's great shape. The leather suits we ordered from Kawasaki arrive. They're very exciting. We are now able to start dressing up in the clothes and can really see what we've got!

August 18   The actor Shane Rimmer is measured in London by a tailor at Angels the costumers and the information is faxed to me for Mr Leech to start making his clothes. Mr Leech tells me how much he hates working with the stretch plastic fabric I am using, but says he will persevere and make up a suit so we can all see the problems. The first lot of embroidery arrives and it looks very good. This is a series of logos I am using on the uniforms and elsewhere.

August 21   Mr Leech phones. The fabric from Italy just doesn't sew, he doesn't know what to do. I go into Dublin to see the problem. He has made a suit but it looks terrible. He is very upset and so am I. I am using him because he is a very traditional craftsman, and I wanted something beautifully crafted, classic suits, but made in an unusual plastic fabric. He obviously doesn't want to continue because he feels he can't achieve his usual high standard. I take the suit home with me to try to work out what to do. The problem is to stop the plastic slipping on the machine foot.

August 22   Ann works on a piece of the dreaded Italian fabric and devises a method of sewing it by bonding it to vilene and calico and sewing through tissue paper. Back to Mr Leech to show him what we think can be achieved. It was not fair of me to expect a skilled tailor, who forms his shape with clever stitching and pressing to work in this way. Anyway, I convince him that he can do it and he agrees to carry on.

August 23   Start to fit extras at the studio. It's great to see the ideas coming to life. But it makes me realise how close we are to shooting. Panic! There is some problem financially with the Irish company making this film and we are told that from now on the production is fronted by an entirely American company. Everybody feels nervous. A change at this stage is not good.

August 24   We are told that we cannot use the word 'Transgen', which is what we were calling the company that effectively rules the world in our story. Apparently there is a French company of the same name and comparisons drawn would not be flattering. We decide to call the company just that – The Company. This saves any possible litigation, but also means that some of my embroidered logos are now useless.

August 30   There is a fitting for Stephen Dorff who arrived from LA yesterday. He is very nervous and worried and is very frightened about dressing up. It is a costume designer's job to give the actor confidence and help him see the part and get into the convention of this particular story. It is an exhausting process.

August 31   I collect the clothes from Mr Leech. He has made eight suits for the President of the company and his secret service entourage. Beautiful work on extremely difficult plastic fabric. I am delighted. Ted Mann, our writer/producer comes in and wonders if they look too plastic. I tell him no.

September 1   Start the day with a physical test of the spacesuit attached to a parachute on the beach north of Dublin. We decide that jumping from a scaffolding tower is just as effective as a crane and seems a lot safer! In the afternoon we go back to the studio to start on the costumes for George Wendt (Norm from *Cheers*). I need one of these to send to LA where the special effects are creating a blow-up dummy of him to suck through a broken spaceship window!

September 4   Continue work on spacesuits and helmets. Dennis Hopper arrives in Ireland. I show him what we have been doing and arrange a fitting for tomorrow after he has moved into his house. I then fit Shane Rimmer, who is playing the President of the world, in a plastic suit and fat padding! He seems to enjoy it. It's great to see my drawings coming to life. Stuart comes in to introduce Van Morrison who is doing a song for the movie.

September 5   In the studio we have a read-through of the script with all the actors who are in the country. I give a talk to them showing them the drawings and explaining the general concept. In the afternoon I fit Dennis Hopper. He likes his clothes – a big hurdle for me to be over.

September 6   Fit George Wendt and four other actors including Ron House who is playing the mad scientist with a peg leg, so spend a long time talking through his problems and reassuring him. Later I discover that we have the wrong respirators for the spacesuits. I bought one originally to fit on the back and send fresh air into the helmets and worked out the fittings based on that model. I then ordered four more of the same model only to find that the specification has been slightly changed and the tubes no longer fit my helmets! I ring the supplier who promises to ring round and find some old stock and change them.

September 8   Fit Debi Mazar. She comes straight from the airport after a night flight from LA, so she is pretty exhausted. She is great – lots of style and personality – and extremely pleasant. She is great fun to fit and really enjoys her clothes. This gives me a great burst of energy which I will need to get everything ready for next week.

September 11   First day of shooting. Up at 5.00 am. Drive to the beach at Bull Island. It's a beautiful day but cold even after the sun comes up. There's a light wind which will be good for the parachute. A wonderful symphony of greys as the mist clears, giving way to bright sunshine. It's even hot! I get Dennis, Debi and Stephen Dorff into their spacesuits. This looks so bizarre with the blue sky and the sand. For the first time in weeks I have nothing to do but watch.

September 14   First day of shooting in the studio. This is a scene set in the sewers of the hub spacestation. I wasn't expecting quite so much water, so we have wet feet to cope with. Cue for some *Waterworld* jokes.

September 15   We shoot what will be the final sequences of the movie: the four leads in new spacesuits strapped into a new ship blasting off from Earth. To my horror the helmets almost get cut – they can't line up the shot to see all the faces at the right angle, because when the actors turn their heads, the helmets stay put, anchored to their shoulders. I get in and adjust all the shoulder positions to line up with the camera, which leaves everybody happy, except the actors who feel very claustrophobic.

September 19   Three hours sleep. In at 7.30 am to spray down the jacket and put it straight on to Debi Mazar as she comes out of make-up. I hate this sort of last-minute panic but costumes like this are so personal that you can hardly start before you have the actor, and Debi has only been available to us for a week and is already in her fourth outfit.

September 20   In the workroom finishing truckers costumes for the diner sequence. We also work on the underwear for Dennis, Stephen and Debi, ready for a scene where they all take their clothes off as the spaceship heats up.

September 21   Hard day at the office working on the budget. I have agreed to do this movie at a certain price and now is the time to make certain that the promises I made in July were realistic. This is not a big studio-backed picture and budgets have to be rigidly adhered to. *Waterworld* it isn't. Though I must say that the only reason I went over budget on that was because the schedule was repeatedly extended.

September 22   Do the sequence with Debi and Stephen undressing and their clothes drifting away in zero gravity. Stuart doesn't like Debi's panties – he expected a G-string. But I manage to persuade him otherwise.

September 25   It's the first time Dennis Hopper has to put on his spacesuit by himself, on camera. He is finding it difficult so I do a demonstration for him and the director to show how it can be done following the right procedure. There's a fitting for Vernon Wells who has just arrived from LA to play the chief pirate/hijacker. Good rushes after shooting – I really enjoy the cartoon quality of the colour.

September 28   Pirate/hijackers on the set for the first time. The set is jacked up at an angle so it's very difficult to work. Debi panics in her spacesuit and needs help to calm down – a kiss through the helmet cheers me up too!

October 2 This is an important day for me because I have my three lead actors and the stuntmen doubles in spacesuits with the air packs working. Nobody is exactly comfortable, but nobody really complains (except Alan the soundman who has to cope with what sounds like a trio of hairdryers). A big relief. Also it's the first time on the set for a bio-mechanical warrior. They look great.

October 4 Start work on Charles Dance's costumes. This is a recast of the part of Macanudo, the bad guy in the movie. He has replaced the American actor, Ron House. They are such different personalities that this involves a rethink and fresh drawings.

October 7 Start shooting on a new set: inside the trucks that the spaceship is pulling. These are full of the genetically engineered square pigs over which with Dennis Hopper and George Wendt are disputing owner-ship. Crazy.

October 9 Shooting in the bar/diner. The set is like a hub of a wheel, with us inside it. So no area is flat. I feel quite seasick after a few minutes. But it is a unique look.

October 14 Before packing to go home Ann comes in with me to see the fitting for Charles Dance. The basic fitting is pretty successful, but in the afternoon the prosthetic work for his arm and body arrive from LA. They are so much bigger than I expected that it means a remake of the coat and dressing gown. It is ridiculous to be finding this out so late. The reason is of course the recast of Charles Dance's part.

October 16 Work all day on the Charles Dance remake. Shoot camera test on make-up and costume in the late afternoon. I hate camera tests, especially when they're not done with the main unit cameraman or the director. Actors need help and without proper support will look stupid.

October 18 We change stages today. Finish shooting in the upside-down spaceship on B stage in the morning then move to D stage for the pirate ship in the afternoon. This gives me all morning to see the pirate actors and extras dressed. A luxury indeed. Everyone is most complimentary and it does look very good. At 9.00 pm I go to the 'dailies' at the end of shooting. I see the amazing upside-down shots and then the make-up test shot on Charles Dance. He looks ridiculous – a pizza on his face and a whole steel works on his arm. It ends up as a row between me, the director and the special effects make-up department. I see no way that I can contribute to make Mr Dance look more elegant, given that he is covered in latex and fibreglass.

October 20 This is the third day of the pirate sequence and everybody has grown into their clothes. Despite the heat and smoke, there is a good atmosphere on the set, greatly helped by Charles Rotherham, the assistant director. He's very calm and efficient, with a good sense of humour.

October 23 Still on the pirate set. Check all the characters to see they still look good. It's amazing how extras, when they have been wearing clothes for a few days, can start dropping things off. You can lose the whole look if you're not careful. The set is getting smokier and dirtier. I'm sure the costumes are losing their colour. I don't see there is much I can do about it – but it's a pity.

October 25 Start work on my final sequence (in fact the opening sequence of the movie) which we will begin shooting on 9 November. There are some forty extras, six actors and eight stuntmen. I get out everything that is already prepared and work out what's missing. Have I got any money left to do anything about it anyway?

October 27 Scene 90. This is the most complicated scene in the movie where our heroes escape from the pirate spacestation. There's a lot of action, and I need both to pay attention to the actors' safety (padding etc.) and keep the look I want. After shooting I watch dailies in the studio theatre with a glass of Guinness – very civilised. Some good performances among the pirates. Very cheering.

November 2 Today we start work on the bedroom set. Charles Dance has to undress and attempt to rape Debi Mazar, with his metal leg, metal arm and plastic head. This is very complicated to choreograph. Then she has to disguise herself in his clothes and escape. So I spend a long time at rehearsal on the set showing the actors how the costumes work and making sure nothing goes wrong.

November 4 Arrive at studio at 7.30 am to find slight panic as the second unit have invented a shot that requires a new costume in duplicate for a stuntman and a dummy. So a brisk half-hour cobbling together remnants that will look good. This prompts me to do a count on how many pirate costumes we have actually done. From an original budget of fifty extras and stuntmen, we are now supplying the eighty-fourth. Then work on security troopers' badges on uniforms for next week's shoot.
    6.00 pm. Move on to C stage for the scene in which Macanudo (Charles Dance) dies, splattered over the floor, with Dennis Hopper and Stephen Dorff in spacesuits and helmets and breathing apparatus. Nobody wants to start this, late on a Saturday night, but the budget pressures are such that we have no choice.

November 6 Two units in full swing. Dennis and Stephen in spacesuits with a disintegrated Charles Dance on C stage and pirate stuntmen killing

129

each other on D stage. Deeply intellectual movie this! Spend the day fitting extras as technicians for The Company laboratory sequence on Thursday.

November 9   Big day for me. The start of my final sequence. Fifty extras and five actors all in new costumes. Once these are on I have nothing new to do on this movie. Ann flies back from London. We intend to spend a few days driving round the west coast before taking the car ferry back home next week. We get the first shot on the big new set at 8.00 pm, and then it's a wrap.

Christopher Hobbs

Christopher Hobbs is one of the most inventive production designers working in Britain. His credits include Caravaggio, Edward II, The Long Day Closes *and* The Neon Bible. *This diary finds him working on* Cold Lazarus, *the writer Dennis Potter's posthumous final work, produced jointly by Channel Four and the BBC.*

April 5 We started with an art department budget of over a million pounds – enough to make several complete Derek Jarman films! However, there have been almost inevitable reductions to this, so now at the beginning of April a great deal of time is being spent in reducing expenses. Andrew Munro, my art director, bears the brunt of the financial manoeuvring while I spend my time dreaming up new cost-saving approaches that won't compromise the look.

Andrew and I go to NEFX, a special effects firm in Wandsworth run by Tom Harris, to review the (impressively large) vehicles being built specially for us. The chassis for the first 'police van' is more or less complete and is very elaborate, with front and rear wheel steering. The 'auto orchids' mobile chairs to be used in the main laboratory set are not yet begun, but I have seen the air pads they are to skim upon – it's all becoming reality before my eyes, a very exciting moment in the development of any design. I find a whole treasury of acrylic domes etc. in a scrap-plastic firm across the way and get several hundred quid's worth of shapes for about £10 – very good going.

April 12 Drive down to Riverside Studios where Renny Rye is filming *Karaoke*, the precursor to *Cold Lazarus*. Albert Finney is there and we try make-up tests in a mock-up of the device that will (I hope) make the audience see him as a frozen severed head. Not easy, as Mr Finney is a jolly-looking man with a certain amount of flesh about his face. However, with the make-up he looks suitably haggard, so we may be able to make it work.

April 17 Set up paintings for film at home. Make good progress on the 'cabbage painting' and lay the canvas on board for other pictures. By doing all the 'fine art' paintings for sets myself I'm saving a good deal of money and get some painting in to keep me sane!

April 20 Set out for Soho to join Andrew Munro and Chris Harvey, the assistant art director, at Peerless Effects, just off St Martin's Lane. Discuss the tank shots and try a few shots on the vast motion-control rig. The difficulty is that no one has attempted the effect I have developed of building underwater models and shooting them through Dettol in order to give them atmospheric haze. The advantages are considerable in that the water acts as a lens and the depth of field is much better, meaning we can use smaller models. Parallax is not affected as much, which is good, and the haze is wonderfully consistent. On to The Asylum effects house where Martina's Palace on its DNA-altered coral plateau has been built in very beautiful miniature. The model is seven feet long with a whole little town around it. Very well made and clearly going to work in shot – rather exciting. No problems in shooting this – the nature of the shots made the underwater approach unsuitable so it will be a conventional model shot, with smoke.

April 24   Work through various lists for my horde of draughtsmen. The trouble is that no sooner are they finished than I feel the need to alter things. A tendency I must curb or we'll never finish on time. Roll on computer draughting! Last night I dreamed up the 'Siltz dining room' – I saw the gold decorative bands on the columns as much darker, almost bronze and glistening. I think they will look all the richer for it. Centrepiece on the table, a light surrounded by crystals surmounted by a huge translucent seashell.

April 26   Set up an experiment in a tiny tank (about 2ft long) to solve the problem of the 'sky' above my miniature city which may come into shot. Since the model is hung in the tank upside down, I find that cotton wool laid at the bottom of the tank appears wonderfully soft and amorphous underwater, and makes very reasonable clouds. Take some video shots of a simple mock-up city and the end result is surprisingly effective. Talk to the sound engineer about how sound would bring our city to life. Thank goodness he seems to understand how much sound would strengthen the imagery, especially the effects. I have hopes of coming up with some pretty interesting end results.

April 27   Do the props houses with our buyer, David Fyson, a charming and very experienced man, very dapper, with a white imperial beard and one glass eye. Later we drive to NEFX to check on the vehicles. They are coming on well. I drive down the road sideways in our huge four-wheel-steering police vehicle, causing fear and astonishment to at least one learner driver hoping for a quiet back road. The 'auto orchids' are coming on well too with a mechanism that clearly works and is comfortingly silent.

May 9   Drive up to Ross-on-Wye where I meet our locations manager and Renny Rye (the director). Spend the latter part of the day looking at bits of the Forest of Dean. Much of it has been municipalised by the forestry commission. The whole area we see is a filmic disappointment, the only real beauty being neat carpets of bluebells dappled with sunshine, sometimes thin as woodsmoke, sometimes like a summer sky under the trees.

May 12   Off to Nottingham where we look at a power station. It looks good for the Masdon Centre, we'll add huge domes to the tops of the cooling towers via computer. Tom Harris (special effects) meets us with Ralph, his assistant, and they show us the chassis of one of the huge police vehicles I've designed. Twenty-five feet long, with four-wheel steering, it performs splendidly, swooping and weaving round the site at considerable speeds. As ever, we learn that the place is to be vastly restored just before we film, so we may find that whole areas of texture and colours have been changed.

May 15   First day at Pinewood. Arrived to find a large, airy art department at my disposal, newly refurbished and with lots of space. Start filing my papers etc. and then go through the ground-plans for the sets with Renny. Considering he has only just finished *Karaoke* he has retained very clear memories of what we are doing.

May 26   The glass tank for the 'cityscape' arrives: 5 × 7 × 4ft of thick glass manoeuvred from the truck on a forklift. I hold my breath. The boss, Sam, a charming Italian gentleman, manages the arrangement of the tank on to its solid steel base with great clan, and it is finally fixed, much to everyone's relief.

June 1   Drive up to Coleford in the Forest of Dean. We speak to the owner of two empty shops. He is about to open them as a furniture emporium, but seems keen to let us use the façades for the film. Then up to the council estate we want to use. Forties houses, almost untouched until, that is, last month when the council began replacing all the original glazing with very unsuitable new glazing. Just our luck. There are still a few houses with old glazing, and we must just hope that the council is not too speedy with its work.

June 7   Pinewood. I go straight to the paint shop to demonstrate the alabaster effect I need for the message room. Off with David Fyson to an aircraft breaker's yard where we spend the greater part of the day crawling through monumental scrap looking for suitable bits and pieces for the film. Not easy, but we find some useful stuff, including the huge hubcaps of an old Beverly from the Southend Aircraft Museum (now defunct).

June 15   My birthday. I am fifty-four, which seems impossible.
   Drive up to NEFX where three huge vehicles are arranged for my approval. Then on to Asylum where Bob Hinks has the wrist braces which look very good. They are cast in silicone; my design for them was based on a bird's-eye view of an Arab city! The huge hanging work-stations for the laboratory are progressing well. They should look like elaborate font covers in the rather ecclesiastical set. The zoomorphic VR helmets are coming on well in the clay model, but the Siltz fountain sculpture is a sad disappointment. I quickly model a clay maquette and ask them to cast it from a clay original. That way, if there is a problem, I can come in and finish it myself. Back to the office where I am given a surprise birthday party. Cake and champagne for all. Film-making has its compensations!

June 19   Pinewood. Shed 18 now resembles an arms factory. The Siltz

133

limousine arrives – a long, black 1959 Cadillac – the uttermost peak, or nadir, of American car design. Amazing and ridiculous, with doors as heavy as vault gates and a fortress of chrome on the front. At the rear, two tall fins and twin red pointed lights over O-shaped outlets give the characteristic angler-fish look. I love it.

June 21 Renny and Remi Adefarasin (the cameraman) return from the Forest of Dean with various ideas and alterations. My biggest problem at present is the constant nibbling away at the schedule. Five days of preparation were removed without consultation, I had to ask for them back. There would have been no financial saving since I would have had to put everyone on overtime to get the job done in time.

July 4 Ross-on-Wye. Producer Ken Trodd joins us today and seems in a cheery mood. We rush round the various locations: church, miner's hall, school, council house. At the church, someone has mowed the grass to stubble though I specifically asked it to be left. I shall now have great difficulty in hiding the modern grave stones. On to the council estate, where the owners of the house we are to use have replanted their garden in appallingly garish modern blooms. They will have to go. Down the road someone has installed mustard-coloured plastic 'french' shutters in their 40s council house, with 'Elizabethan' bottle-glass windows and a small concrete cathedral in the garden. Someone else has installed french windows with rows of garden gnomes inside, looking out. I must admit to enjoying these eccentricities, but they make my job a lot more difficult!

July 6 Up to Alexandra Palace for technical recce on 'Siltz Hotel'. Walk round the people's palace: huge, vulgar, ruinous. Trees should grow through it and bird's nest in its organ pipes. The others arrive and we discuss vast drapes, fountains of fire and water, and giant statues (helium balloons draped in gauze). Mark Nelmes from CFC is there and we go into the effects, whereby an enormous superstructure created digitally, will tower above the palace.

July 10 Send coloured picture of HM the Queen circa 1957 to be laser copied, before returning her to the pizza shop where I found her.

July 12 Up to Pinewood where the Masdon Plateau model has been set on G stage. It's rather cramped, and it worries me that, to save money, we are not filming with motion control or a specialist cameraman. Whizzed back and forth on my bicycle – I'm glad I brought it in. Martina Masdon's poolside set is now in construction and looking rather impressive. I get a real thrill bicycling round the colonnades and seeing my designs for the first time full-scale.

July 14 Set up rough shots of the 'head box' with Albert Finney. Pretty good illusion, although difficult to make it as flexible as Renny would like.

We walk round the sets together and he seems pleased with what he sees. Martina's set looking pretty spectacular now, and vast! I hope we can pull it all off – certainly it's not easy. They're grabbing back the money again It's very difficult now. We are beginning to throw out major lumps of action and sets, but we are now at a stage where we cannot cut back further, since we have begun construction on so much. We have had a least a third of our budget removed, but the concept is still the same, so I have to spend far too much time inventing cheaper ways of doing things without damaging the designs which have been approved.

July 15 Ross-on-Wye. The 'antiquing' of the streets is well advanced and remarkably convincing – not at all twee or like a Hovis advert. People of the town keep trying to come into our fake shops and buy things that haven't been sold in forty years. A fine selection of cars in properly run-down condition has arrived. I reject any that look too well kept or overly preserved; this was a poor area at a poor time – most of the cars would have been pre-war. David Fyson and George Ball have dressed up the shops impeccably, and the ageing is exactly right on both old and new facades.

July 26 Pinewood. Martina's set is looking very good, glowing pink against the blue sky. Steve, the scenic artist, has finished the 'tattoos' on the bedroom walls and left. The techno team are doing very well installing their glittering gadgetry, and Colin and I paint the tree. It looks very strange, but that, of course, is the idea. Siltz's sitting-room is still suffering from problems with the carpet laying team. They are not used to carpet on the ceiling. The massage room, all in resin to suggest alabaster, looks very promising.

August 2 Working on the huge 'California' set. Martina Masdon (Dianne Ladd), robed in ever more exotic clothes, vamps her way around the fan-shaped, Hockneyesque swimming pool reduced from the existing tank on stage. Beyond the parapet, brilliant fake sunshine floods the (real) trees and the (painted) distant mountains. Behind us are the adobe walls of the house tower, pink and bulbous as terracotta pots. Today the set is full of Martina's 'bimbo boys' who cause general amusement. One is in little more than a clingfilm sarong and hair curlers, another is wearing a G-string and scarlet corset, and the third is in an abbreviated skin-tight matador costume. Renny asks me to devise a small cigarette disposal unit for tomorrow, so I rush up to Shed 18, our techno unit, and build a very small leafy triffid with large fleshy silicone lips. I shall ask make-up to lipstick them for the shoot.

August 4 On to Martina's sitting-room. The set works well though I wish I had been able to keep the terracotta walls throughout all the interiors. Increasing financial pressure has forced me to use liquid lurex in this set which is richer, cheaper, but makes a less coherent backing for the actors. Nevertheless, the overall effect is pretty good, with the huge surreal octopus/tree filled with latex weather balloons and Martina's lamp, a clear resin Medusa apparently floating free above its base, trailing cillae of dry ice.

August 10 The Masdon sets are being pulled down now and we are moving on to F stage and the 'Siltz' penthouse. I go down with David Fyson to a nearby garden centre to buy rushes and water-plants, to surround the huge bronze fountain dominating the sitting-room. It looks pretty good, hanging like a dinosaur turd over its shelf of bright green grass. The ripple effect in the massage room works well – twelve ripple trays around the exterior of the circular translucent set, with fans agitating the water, and lights bounced on to the resin dome give a lovely watery effect.

August 16 We shoot in the 'pool room'; with its wonderful pool table made in 1840 from solid slate, the base carved and painted to look like porphyry inset with black arabesques. The red matchboard walls covered in pictures and trophies look very good and Remi has put in smoke to give extra atmosphere. Milton's room coming on well despite a problem with the floor outside the door which bulged up and had to be relaid. All the paintings I did for the room are framed and in place now, and work well.

August 24 See rushes of Alexandra Palace and Becton – both look very good and suitably grandiose. Travelled down to Becton to check out the latest set-ups there. The computer trials at CFC in Soho are coming along very well though the 'golfball' tops of the Masdon Centre are still not quite right – something odd about the perspective. For the most part, however, the computer images and the live action are marrying very well.

August 31 Alan Yentob and Michael Grade come down to see where we are spending all the money and are apparently impressed, which is a comfort. The men spraying the laboratory columns with expanded polystyrene leave early because their machine has broken down but will be back tomorrow. The foam is giving a splendidly organic look to the columns which would be very difficult with plaster. Furthermore it weighs very little, so when we need to move the columns for the re-dress at the end, I shall have no weight problems, or lumps of plaster falling off.

September 8 Fyodor's drawing-room is taking up a lot of time, particularly when the vacuumform panels begin to melt under the lights. In the end I have to back the entire set with kitchen foil! The big laboratory set has been a bit hectic, especially when the foam sprays failed and the columns ground to a halt. In the end a new machine was found, but the sprayers had to works two days and a night without sleep to catch up. All the struggle paid off though.

September 12 Into work late, as I have to go to Batty's model shop to buy plastic model kits to make into buildings for the London city model. Mark Copeland has made the main miniatures, but I need some odds and ends in the background to extend the horizon. The tank is uncovered again now that Richard and the Shed 18 techno team has moved down to south dock. We have reconstructed the scaffold and will be setting it up for the model shoot at the end of the week. It should be exciting!

September 18   The Shed 18 boys, now transferred to the south dock, have returned to install the model in the tank, which is now full. Paul Wilson, the effects cameraman, is busy lighting. He is one of the best and most experienced cameramen in the country, but even he has never had to light an upside-down submerged city model before. None of the usual rules apply optically, but he seemed to be enjoying himself and appeared happy enough to consult me on the atmosphere I am after.

September 19   Resume work on the cityscape. There are some problems with chemicals in the water which for some reason are less stable than during the tests. The atmospheric haze has become a pea-souper, and we have to drain the tank and reprime it. The bubble problem can be solved (I am told) by using alcohol rather than water. In a tank our size that would be very expensive! Lose some shooting time, but Paul is well ahead, so we are perfectly safe. He had allowed one shot per day, but thanks to the flexibility of the rig we have been getting in three or four shots. Curiously enough, the gradual thickening of the haze throughout the day has helped us to vary the shots nicely.

September 28   Spent some time on the head box where Albert Finney's frozen head is to be displayed. Very subtle and difficult manoeuvring to get all the elements to work in an ambitious illusion. Renny wants more and more camera angles, which tests my ingenuity to the utmost. The basic idea is so simple, and onstage or in a carnival the audience's viewpoint can be carefully controlled, but Renny keeps going beyond the tolerance of the illusion. I think I can keep up however, and if I can, the illusion will work all the better for being shot from angles that should be impossible! I know we have succeeded when Renny is himself fooled into forgetting the presence of a mirror even though Albert was sitting there patiently and bodyless right in front of him.

October 3   First day in the big laboratory corridors. Renny seems very happy with the new set. It's very simple in look, but has a complex ground-plan and is, as he hoped, very big. The use of the mirror to double the depth of the space works well, although perhaps it could have been more brightly lit. The distantly moving figures and auto-cubes help to give it the impression of the huge space inside the Masdon Centre. Finish the day by planting light-conductive rods in foam bases on the second laboratory set. The effect, as I hoped, is like a series of crystal gardens.

October 10   Final adjustments on A stage to the second relax room and Siltz's dining-room. Both looking good. Throughout the day the dining-room in particular gets better and better, the great 'marble' table looking spectacular with its ten furry golden feet and its varicoloured 'marmoleum' inlayed top (which does look surprisingly convincing). The columns with their bronze bands and crimson leathery texture look pretty good as well. Meanwhile, over on B stage Tom Harris and his team continue to blow up the second laboratory set. Saw the rushes of the major explosion from yesterday – very spectacular, although much more violent than expected. Finish by blowing up 'Fyodor', or rather a stunt double. All goes well except for some singed hair!

October 11   The relax room on stage A has come together well. Renny decides not to have potted plants as in the script, but to substitute them with a perspex screen. Fortunately we have a lot of perspex put by, which I originally liberated from a skip at Twickenham on the off-chance that it could come in useful. The screen works well for the action, but I would have liked to have some greenery to set off the rather severe set. It is difficult to change sets at a late stage without unbalancing the look. I hope the textures and the coloured table settings will have done the job, and of course the actors themselves provide the most important element.

October 13   Last day for me, although there are some pick-ups tomorrow. The shooting goes smoothly enough, and I spend the day riding up and down saying my farewells. It really has been a very enjoyable year, though hard work. Renny has been amazingly relaxed and has allowed me a free rein with my imagination, so I think I have been able to give him something pretty interesting and I hope not too *Doctor Who*-ish (although I have always wanted to design a *Doctor Who* series). My amazing team has allowed me to concentrate on design and not get too involved in the bureaucratic details of the shoot. We seem to have kept pretty much within budget without any major problems in the shoot at all. Astonishing!

The Editor

Mick Audsley

Mick Audsley is a world-class editor, whose credits have included My Beautiful Laundrette, Dangerous Liaisons, The Grifters *and* Interview with the Vampire. *Mick Audsley's diary concentrates on the making of Terry Gilliam's* Twelve Monkeys, *a particularly complex fantasy of time travel starring Bruce Willis, Brad Pitt and Madeleine Stowe.*

January 17 London Premiere of *Interview with the Vampire*. My partner, Joke [also an editor], and I have arranged to meet everyone inside the cinema before the crowd shows. We exit as the public comes in, everyone clawing at the window of the Warner West End to get a glimpse of Tom Cruise. We have all ducked watching the movie yet again to have dinner while it plays, and put this one 'to bed' once and for all. It's been over eleven months for me . . . longer. The fans remind me it's just another 'star vehicle'. Supper with Neil Jordan, Stephen Woolley, lots of wine and *Vampire* reminiscences. I'm glad it's finished. It took enough of my blood!

January 26 A lunch with film editor Jim Clark. He's very enthusiastic about cutting on computer. I come away thinking I've missed my chance to use this on *Twelve Monkeys*. Perhaps Terry (Gilliam) and I should have considered it more. I feel like a dinosaur. Still, as I console myself, you have to know how to make a handmade dovetail joint to make a table, whatever the tools! I'm getting nervous about starting to edit a new movie (I know how to make this last one, but not the new one). It's always the same fear and apprehension: that in digesting and reforming you will somehow distort, misinterpret, misrepresent the material on the way. The trust of the cast and the host of other contributors will be, as always, overwhelming. I may well be there on the first day of shooting, but I'm always there till the bitter end (I've even ended up carrying the prints to the cinema in person). It's a very long ride.

February 9 Philadelphia. *Twelve Monkeys* shoot. The very first roll of rushes arrive in our makeshift cutting room. I sneak a look (scene 21). Bruce Willis dribbles in front of Madeleine Stowe as a result of time travel. It looks great. The actual very first shot filmed was a medium shot of a prisoner pissing into a toilet bowl (seemingly for real, over and over). I phone David and Janet Peoples, the writers, and some old friends from *Hero* [released in Britain as *Accidental Hero*] to say this is a first. I attend the evening dailies where everyone is in good cheer. I meet the crew but can't remember names. Gulp. Soon I'll have to start cutting this stuff. It's all so hard at the outset, faced with all these unrelated fragments.

February 16 Location cutting room. A day of utter frustration. Every piece of equipment that could break down has. My assistants Brian and Amanda seem heartbroken. I calm them and say it's not their fault. In spite of this, I make and show Terry an assembly of two scenes. I've used far too many close-ups – crazy, for a scene where the relationship isn't at all developed. I will have to remake. The gear problems create endless distractions. Wobbly pictures, bad sound, scratches, etc. It's always the same setting up: a *nightmare*. I stay cheerful.

February 20 I notice a slogan on the inside of the great organ which is installed in the Wannamaker department store and coincidentally designed by a relative of mine (and used as background in a movie): 'A man who uses his hands is a labourer; a man who uses his hands and his head is a craftsman; a man who uses his hands, his head and his heart is an artist.' I take note.

March 11 Talking with Terry about the 'cover' of material he's shooting, I suggest that, with a movie as complex as this, it's like 'packing for a long journey – you just have to check you've got enough pairs of socks. And for all weathers! It's so hard in the fog of production to keep a clear view of the inner core of the movie as it comes in, in its disjointed component parts. To keep the overview, I believe, is the film editor's task.

Bruce throws a party for the crew and acts as DJ. Brad Pitt comes over to say 'Hi' but I don't recognise him in his new guise. Ian Kelly, the video assistant, tells me that on set, with this Hi'8' set up, he can edit stuff straight out of the camera right there. He assumes I will be upset. He is doing quick-reference 'sketches' on site, so decisions can be made on the spot. I convince him I'm delighted. It allows me to worry about the broader scope of things. I tell him that anything he shows me that looks good I'll steal. (He's not sure whether I'm kidding or not.) I leave early – the music Bruce is playing is deafening. I fear for my eardrums.

March 28 Baltimore. Location editing continues. I sense that I'm very behind schedule for my first-cut screening deadline (usually set for a week to ten days after the completion of photography). Also the quantity of material to put together day by day seems overwhelming at the moment. All this is 'normal' panic, I tell myself. A productive day, however, recutting the mental hospital sequences and, later in the afternoon, the arrival of 'Louie', the raspy-voice character, into the movie.

Late rushes reveal serious doubts about Brad's previous day's work (the library sequence in the Goine's mansion section). He watches it with us and is very concerned. The different look required for Jeffrey (Brad Pitt's character) at this point in the movie seems to have thrown him, causing him to caricature his role at that point. Brad seems very disheartened by it and offers to pay for the sequence to be reshot himself. We all agree that it's not right, although to reshoot immediately is not possible because of the availability of the set (a real location).

I don't think anybody is serious about Brad's offer to pay, but calls to Universal will be made to investigate the possibility of setting up a reshoot.

April 20   A good day producing two little scenes. The second is complex because woven through the action is a TV story in parallel. Always tricky. At lunchtime, buying sandwiches, I overhear this: 'Experience is what you get when you don't get what you want.' H'm! Is this relevant?

May 10   London. First week after shoot spent setting up cutting room. Very jet lagged indeed. I have carried some film home with me to put together until the bulk arrives, namely the World War I sequence and scene 60. The night kidnap car sequence looks terrific. I'm struggling. My ability to absorb details is seriously impaired. The new assistants are completely lost picking up the movie at this stage. Here at home I feel exhausted but manage some progress. Great to be home.

May 15   First-cut screening for Terry and Chuck (our producer, who flies in). It seems to go well at two hours eighteen minutes and I'm pleased that the complexities of the story and time jumps can be grasped, even if clarifications are necessary in due course. The interior airplane sequence at the end works well, but I'd love to see the movie without it. The hurried work done in the last week in the panic to hit the screening date seems good nonetheless. The centre of the movie, reel seven (the 'reel from hell' as we call it) is still a big problem and the line on Railly's (Madeleine Stowe) character needs work. Kidnap cars seem ENDLESS. All players seem to work well in general, Brad especially. I think everyone is pleased with this first draft. I'm delighted to be moving onwards to the next phase. The agony of theorising the impact of the 'whole' is over. The journey get easier when you know where you are going.

June 19   The process of reassessing each of the thirteen 'assembled' reels continues, with Terry and myself analysing all parts of the writing to ascertain if they function for the whole and take the movie forward.

We've reduced the car kidnap material and will continue with what is affectionately known as the 'reel from hell' (reel 7). This is a major blockage in the flow of things, but I have ideas on how to clear the way and get to what is really important.

I am continually anxious that it is in the nature of this movie that the 'set-up' of information is complex and rather slow, in order for the conflict and resolution, i.e. the second half, to work and pay off. Will the movie engage its audience quickly enough?

August 8   Flying to Washington, DC, for the first preview screening of

Twelve Monkeys (known to us as an N.R.G: that is National Research Group).

I'm nervous and tired from making the temporary sound mix over the last few days; I wonder what impact the temporary music score will have on the film. Another worry is that some of the dark wit has been overshadowed in some way and that this toppled us too far towards 'seriousness'.

August 9 Morning set-up and rehearsal in a multi-screen theatre in Georgetown. The smell of popcorn in all US cinemas always gives me butterflies and makes my knees wobble, on account of the association with the dreaded preview screening. No escaping that one and, as the day wears on toward the 7.30 pm kick off, I realise this will be no exception.

Oddly enough the projection room has a large map of the Florida Keys, strangely relevant and a thematic idea in the movie. I hope this is a good omen.

The film plays smoothly to 450 people, seemingly all very young. As we are in a college area, I sense that they might be well educated in movies in general, but can't tell if that is in our favour or not. I sense restlessness with the opening fifteen to twenty minutes. Probably because of the slowness, the confusion, or both. Brad's arrival in the movies delights them and they just go with him completely. He can do no wrong. With Bruce, I'm not so sure.

The scenes in the car that are still 'bluescreen' (i.e. no background) hurt us badly in spite of the usual speech at the start, preparing the audience for a 'movie still in the making' they giggle at the sight of two stars pretending to drive along the road. However, by the end, Terry and I feel it has played well, with the audience attentive and positive: perhaps we *are* in good shape.

The focus group soon reveals we are not. I am shocked and somewhat confused. It did play well, *I felt it*.

As always, if things don't go well in previews, it reveals the absurdity of this strange process of inviting an audience to participate in making the movie with you. Hearing, or reading, comments and thoughts at this stage is a dangerous game if not treated with extreme caution. The real value is to witness the film with a crowd and that tells you where the bumps, bangs and confusions really are. The scales drop from one's eyes very rapidly indeed. The real needs of the film reveal themselves and shout out at you.

August 10 Meetings over breakfast with Terry, Chuck, and David and Jan Peoples reveal the following information from the research group. The audience *don't* like Bruce; *don't* believe in the relationship/attraction between Madeleine and Bruce; they *hate* the violence; they are confused by the ambiguities of the ending; they wonder why anyone would want to wipe out the world? – this makes me very suspicious and indicates that they haven't read any newspapers lately; and most amazingly they find the movie predictable. A Terry Gilliam film, predictable?

Chuck tells me that after reading the script for the first time two years ago, he felt like a swan diving off a high building on to a slab of concrete . . . and today . . . he feels much the same! I remind him of an Irish quote about producing: 'Trying to produce a movie is like trying to F*** the wind!'

I am curious to see the next screening tonight, which is essentially the same movie, but with the interior plane sequence at the end removed. My curiosity over this issue will, I hope, be resolved tonight.

Washington, DC. Second preview screening. Plays the same, without the plane interior, and comments and scores are similar to last night. H'm. The focus group discussion afterwards is also hard on us. It all seems to revolve around the plausibility of the relationship between Bruce and Madeleine. This will have to be worked on. The positive responses from the projectionists and sound crew cheer me up.

September 1   The end of a two-week stint of intense activity, recutting all the reels (of which there are now twelve – one for each monkey maybe!), to be scrutinised by Chuck as we hand them over. The brief we had set ourselves was to nail Madeleine's character and involvement with Bruce in order to allow the audience to accept her decision to stay with him, when an opportunity to leave presents itself. We've greatly accented this decision to stay in the 'reel from hell' (now reel 6). The centre of all movies are difficult for some reason.

We've also reduced the dream sequences somewhat in order to remove any fears that the prophetic dreams, dotted throughout the movie, may deflate the power of the ending, when the importance of pulling all the strings together, emotionally speaking, is paramount.

September 12   The following is overheard as the audience leave the third public preview screening in Pasadena, California: 'It will be better when it's been edited!' (ouch!) and 'Shoot the F****** writers.' I tell David and Jan. We can only laugh.

In spite of all the work the reaction to the movie has only really shifted marginally. However, the marketing people seem very enthusiastic, and it has now become clear that, with such a dense movie, reactions can swiftly alter after a screening. People need time to digest this one. Or am I kidding myself?

September 15   Received this splendid footnote to a list of thoughts from the writers, David and Jan:

> Give our love to Terry and Mick and remind them that David got out of editing and into writing in order to get upstream of the flow of shit, and even to initiate it, rather than to toil and suffer downstream in the muddy water. Love Peoples & Peoples.

September 18/19   We've continued to make picture changes which have resulted from information and thoughts from the third preview screening held in Pasadena, California. All our work has been devoted to *clarification* of time, adding date subtitles in places to speed and ease the story. Terry and I have run out of steam with cutting, but we think we've now finished the picture. Chuck finds it hard to accept that the movie is now CUT.

I go home boggled at the thought of the eight months of cutting behind me. There is still much to do and a hard deadline still ahead of us – to complete by late October. Scoring, opticals, titles, etc. and, of course, the sound mix. Everything is way behind in these areas. I feel panic once again. How will we draw all this together and deliver on time?

October 2–5   The opticals (digitally made FX) are still not arriving fast enough to allow negative cutting to complete reels. We have to make them with black spacing gaps in order for the bulk of colour grading to continue. It's now a race, against the 27 October deadline. I have little faith we'll make it, in view of the endless complications getting things right. The crew is very tense. The lateness of the opticals will be our downfall.

October 6   With most pre-mixes behind us we are due to make a final mix of reel one. Paul is working around the clock to keep writing and scoring the music ahead of us. I worry about the impact of this score. Is it too heavy? We have mix problems with the multi-track digital recorders and have to abandon today's plan. We lose a day. The schedule crisis worsens. The sound crew are very jumpy.

October 20   Somehow we have completed our first pass at a complete mix with FX, music and everything, even though some optical FX slots are still not delivered and adding sound to them is somewhat difficult. Guesswork prevails.

At 12.30 we run the movie in the dubbing theatre to see the results of all this work. The film leaves us all somewhat cold (over-exposure and exhaustion play a part). We sit in the theatre until 1.00 am discussing the endless sound alterations we have collectively amassed. There are pages and pages of notes. All my responses are somewhat dull and I worry that any spontaneity the soundtrack may currently have could get smoothed away. Rawness can be a great asset; decisions made 'on the fly' have spark and freshness. Something could slip through the net as we are all so whacked out. It's easily done, and the chances and the time to make the correct changes will run out. If only we could step back and get a fresh view. Impossible now.

October 30   Multi-track playback screening of the dub(mix) to date for Terry, on his return from a week's holiday. Terry and I both hated the film on this pass, especially the structural demands that the opening requires in order for the later part to work. It seemed dreadfully long and way too slow to engage us. Delays with the optical shots is driving all departments crazy. Hope this down view of things is just a symptom of the usual 'over-exposure' to a project. I call it 'film blindness'.

November 1 We continue with dozens of dub fixes (sound balances) and an evening recording session at CTS music studio for a revised/rewritten version of the solo violin piece Paul Buckmaster has produced, to be played by soloist Michael Davis. For the first hour of the recording, I convince myself that this isn't going to work, but, quite suddenly, it happens. When it's played against the closing sequence of the movie I feel it engage and am sure it will convincingly replace the temporary music we've had for so long. A relief. I warm towards the film once more.

November 3 The schedule has crunched. At the end of the day one more of the endless stream of crisis meetings with Chuck in the cutting room. I have Marieke (my eight-year-old daughter) with me. She sits patiently through this tense and volatile meeting, and then, on the way home, she remarks (cool as a cucumber), 'If we all spoke at the same time like that at school, we'd be put in the "incident" book.' Enough said.

November 20 *Twelve Monkeys* is nearing completion and *The Van* (for Stephen Frears) is about to start editing. As I expected, the two movies have collided. I feel panicked, I'm not ready for a new movie: *Twelve Monkeys* isn't finished. And, of course, the end titles of *Twelve Monkeys* has to be reshot – there are spelling mistakes!

November 23 Finally, three weeks late, I finish working on *Twelve Monkeys*. The early-morning screening at Rank Lab Denham with complete 'D.T.S.' soundtrack convinces me that it's done, with whatever strengths or weaknesses it might have. What a long road! I sense we will be subject to all kinds of criticisms, but now I'm just happy it's made. I hope Terry is too. We part. Wearily, having now viewed the film countless, countless times at all its different stages. It's time to let it go.

November 27 My first day on *The Van*. How strange to edit a film that is almost already completely shot. The Lightworks computer [editing facility] convinces me by mid-morning (under the careful guidance of my new assistant Nigel) that this is going to change my life. It's great!

November 30 I'm sold on the new technology. It's very fast, and thinking so speedily on to the film is breathtaking. I feel resentful of the years I've spent using a 'Hand-drill', now to discover the 'Power' version.

The new set-up allows me to gear change into another movie quite swiftly, although I realise that the speed with which one can build scenes is almost too quick. It's thinking time that counts. But it's a wonderful, wonderful tool.

I'm slow to gain independence with the machine; I'm so greedy to construct the new scenes swiftly. It takes a while to find the *rhythms*. I'm anxious to see the results made up into screening reels for the big screen. It feels like cooking a grand meal as a chef and leaving a lot of washing-up for somebody else.

December 3 We have made about four reels in script order on the Lightworks and I'm excited about the ease of manipulation. It's very direct and one's powers of concentration, removed from the physics of cutting and filing film are simultaneously increased. Comparing the takes happens so quickly that being thorough with the material is made so much easier. I have to persuade the production to keep the machine (if costs allow) as long as possible. I'm hooked!

December 29 Christmas holidays and *Twelve Monkeys* is due to open in the USA at the weekend. I'll wait until the New Year to phone and see how the first weekend went (always a good guide to the general success of the project). I hear Brad has clocked-up a Golden Globe nomination for his part as Jeffrey. Good news.

Postscript (January 18, 1996) *Twelve Monkeys* has grossed over $30 million in the USA and been the number one movie for the two weeks since its release. A great relief!

Anne Sopel

Anne Sopel is a relative newcomer to features; her credits include The Young Poisoner's Handbook *and the shorts* Tropical Fish *and* Curious. *In contrast to Mick Audsley's periodic snapshots, Anne Sopel concentrates on the day-to-day experience of cutting a feature film,* Sweet Angel Mine.

September 7   I arrived in Halifax, Nova Scotia, this afternoon. *Sweet Angel Mine*, an Anglo-Canadian co-production, begins filming on Monday. As editor I am the last of the small British contingent to arrive, the rest of the crew being made up of locals and technicians from other parts of Canada. The first assistant editor, Jay Coquillon, is already here and I'm relieved to leave the setting up of the cutting room to him.

September 11   I drove to the location with the British producer, Sam Taylor, very early this morning. The first shots of the day are pretty simple, mostly motorbike run-bys. We are editing on film. In Nova Scotia most productions are using Avid, particularly as the bulk of work here is for TV, but the local film board has some 35mm equipment and the rest comes from Toronto or London. The rushes are being processed at Film House De Luxe in Toronto and so won't be with us till the early afternoon.

September 12   Unfortunately it has been decided not to hire a projector and we are having trouble finding somewhere to see rushes on a big screen. My Steenbeck has seen better days and I know how depressing it can be not to see things properly.

September 13   We viewed rushes at 8.00 am at the University Arts Centre, a huge and impressive auditorium with a big screen. The film looks wonderful but there is nothing substantial to see yet – certainly no 'acting'.

September 14   Terrible weather today led to disagreements over re-scheduling. Sam asked me to go to the set to talk to Curtis Radcliffe, the director, and I went out to the set in the driving rain. The crew was completely drenched, huddled under inadequate cover on a beach which looked totally cut off from the mainland. The script reads, 'The sun shines, the birds twitter, it's a gorgeous day', but an elaborate platform has been built and they decided to go ahead with the scene. The camera crew donned wetsuits and took actor Oliver Milburn out to sea where he had to float face down and naked, pretending to have a good time. I didn't feel very useful and was relieved to get back to my cutting room. I talked to Sam about what to show to Gareth Jones at Handmade, one of the film's investors, who is due to arrive tomorrow. There are always scenes or shots that you prefer not to show in these cases, but with less than a week's filming done it's going to be difficult to avoid the delicate areas.

September 15   I started cutting today but it's still all very bitty, with close-ups etc. missing. There is some concern over the casting of one actor and various consultations are going on between departments. Oliver burnt his hand on a motorbike exhaust and had to go to the hospital so the crew wrapped early and came to see rushes on the Steenbeck.

September 18 My first big dialogue scene to cut and I started to enjoy myself. It was also fascinating to see a new actor in the rushes, Alberta Watson, who plays Megan. We are all impressed with her and I think she's going to bring something very individual to a part which I find rather unsympathetic in the script.

September 19 A big problem today with two shots that had a large cloudy circle in the centre of the frame. The labs didn't report it and we rely on them as we're not seeing anything till late afternoon most days. 'We didn't know what effect you guys wanted' was the response when Jay telephoned. This adds a set-up to the rapidly growing list of reshoots and pick-ups.

September 21 Chris Zimmer, the Canadian producer, talked to me about seeing cut footage but the director hasn't seen anything yet and there is a kind of protocol about this. I hope there's time this weekend.

September 23 Curtis stayed after rushes to see some cut scenes. He felt the usual disappointments with the compromises made and was pleased with some parts. He is a first-time director and I tired to reassure him that this was a normal reaction. We discussed Alberta's accent and decided to suggest that she listens to some sound takes tomorrow. She is doing a rural Nova Scotian Canadian, based apparently on the boom operator's accent, but which is making the actress playing her daughter sound too West Coast.

September 24 Alberta immediately recognised the problem and also suggested that we send an audio tape to Anna Massey in England who will be playing the grandmother. Actors are not seeing rushes – which is quite normal – but I sometimes think that it would be useful, especially for actors new to cinema, to see their performance at the end of the shooting period. Too late for the current film but possibly helpful for the next.

September 27 My first violent scene to cut. I wonder what the restaurant opposite thinks at the blood curdling screams coming from my room. At least I don't feel as ill from this footage as I did from certain shots in *The Young Poisoner's Handbook*, when I had to go onto the balcony for fresh air between takes (scenes that didn't make the final version).

September 30 Drove out to the set through great banks of fog. A stand-in was made up, wigged and dressed for some inserts and close-ups, but Witold Stok, the director of photography, decided her skin was too tanned to match Alberta Watson's. Everyone looked around for a replacement and

I was selected and sent to wardrobe and make-up to have my arms and hands 'dirtied'. Had a quick look at the wide shot on the moviola and they all seemed to enjoy the joke that if the insert won't cut in it'll be my fault as they wheeled over the video assist so I could see myself on camera.

October 2 More problems with the labs. This morning a 'no problem' report was followed with news that the negative was still sitting at the airport due to a misunderstanding with Air Canada. The prints look great but the contact service is not as good as in England.

October 3 Today's rushes with the 'Vikings', a group of men supposed to cause a drunken brawl in a bar, are hilarious but mainly for the wrong reasons. I couldn't believe the scene was complete but Curtis later told me that he'd fired all the extras and actors involved. The big fight scene to come will be filmed with proper stunt actors and today's scene, if it survives at all, will be in a brief version and no one will notice the change of cast.

October 6 Oliver broke his toe running barefoot in the woods. This is his second hospital visit and the jokes are coming thick and fast. He managed one scene hopping into frame pretending to have twisted his ankle but the rest of the day was lost and next week's schedule will be scrapped. The proposed helicopter shoot is in jeopardy; it has already been reduced in scope from the scripted version. There is a possibility that I might go up in the helicopter with a second unit cameraman if it can't be fitted around Curtis's availability, and I have decided to get a copy of *The Shining* for inspiration.

October 13 The crew has seen no rushes all week despite being based in the studio which is much closer to Halifax than previous locations. Anna Massey has been here this week, her rushes are very good and I know they must be eager to see them. More worryingly, the interior lighting is quite dark and sometimes it's hard to judge focus without seeing the film on a big screen – and it seems we can't rely on the labs. The moviola, despite its old-fashioned appearance, has the best picture of all but isn't very good for mass viewing. We decide to delay striking all sets until we see rushes projected.

Problems with finding screening time to suit everyone leads to a decision to hire a projector. Jay and I can't believe it, as the expense originally objected to was the shipping cost from Montreal, and now we will be paying for just a week-and-a-half's hire. There must have been some explosions on set to bring about this change.

October 17 A good body double is used for some of Oliver's scenes as he's still hobbling around on crutches. I can see him limping slightly in his close shots but I don't suppose anyone else would notice. They've asked me to go on set tomorrow because of the matching that needs to be done.

October 20 Filming is due to end on the 27th but I'm going to stay

149

another week or so to finish the first cut of the film. Jay and I will take the cutting copy home with us in case the film is delayed in customs. I have worked on other productions where work has stopped because customs have held on to the film. The Canadian producer is keen to extend even this time as I'm sure he's anxious to see as much as possible before everything changes. A few scenes have been dropped but otherwise we are on schedule. Shooting will finish on Friday, and the helicopter trip is on Saturday – but, unfortunately, without me.

October 23–27   The projector is set up in the producer's office and there is a large turnout for rushes. It takes so long to get the sound working properly that attendance dwindles later in the week. We have to decide if there are any last-minute crucial things to shoot and although I'd like more cover in certain scenes – editors always do – there is nothing very much missing that could easily be done this week. Meanwhile, we decide to solve the problem of the lack of blood on an actress in one scene with some digital optical work.

I was worried that the film might be too short but the first cut seems to be coming out at about two hours which gives us plenty to tighten for the desired final length of about ninety-five minutes.

The Composer

Simon Fisher Turner

One of the most innovative soundtrack composers and designers working in film,
Simon Fisher Turner is perhaps best known for his work with Derek Jarman,
including the soundtracks to Caravaggio, The Last of England, The Garden,
Edward II *and* Blue. *His most recent feature score is for Michael Almereda's*
Nadja. *The following extracts focus on the film-related work including improvised*
concerts of music and poetry inspired by Blue.

May 1   In the middle of various projects. Nothing to do with film – but
always to do with image (or imagining).

Live, Blue Roma, a CD of the group playing last year in Rome is being
compiled. I felt unable to compile it myself, as I've no idea really of what
direction to take it. Derek Jarman's poems are the core and centre of the
piece, but as it was recorded over six nights there's hours of different
mixes and versions to go through. Later in the week I also show up at the
cutting room. It's taking hours to balance John Quentin's voice and the
music, but by 10 pm it's all done. Art work next. Liam's profile shot of
Derek is on the front. Golds and yellows inside. Sleeve notes by Jon
Savage. I hope Derek would approve. This live CD of *Blue* is the end of
the road.

May 10   Finally buy my flight to Cannes. *Nadja*, a film by Michael Almareyda, is being shown by Ciby Sales, who've bought it for Europe and Japan.
It will be the first time we've seen it blown up, full-size, with final mixes etc.
Michael, Peter Fonda and Elina Lowensohn are all going too, so we're
sharing a flat.

May 20   Cannes. Sun, Ciby, BFI – oh how they've messed *Blue* up in their
'95 book. It says, 'music' by Brian Eno. What a cheek. An appalling mistake. Who do I blame and kill? Sleep under a bush by the bandstand. On
Sunday I move in with Elina, Michael and Sweeney. Beats the bush, now I
have a sofa.

Monday. *Nadja* party. Supper with Fonda. Interviews. Read, tape local
radio, meet Mr Horikoshi (producer) from Tokyo. Pink and blue feet.
Nadja screenings. Thank God for Ciby. Once a day go to British Pavilion.
Eat and chat with Michael about new films and his pixel documentary. He
needs front and end credits. Car to airport. Shop more. Home and supper
with friends.

May 29 Pick up *Live Blue* Queen Elizabeth Hall leaflets from Serious Speakout, the concert promoters. Distribute them through Soho.

June 2–3 New end credits for Michael Almareyda's film at Sundance. He didn't like the first lot. $500 please.

June 5 Usual sort of call-round. *Nadja* soundtrack still not concrete – what a waste of time.

June 6 *The Leopard* being shot in Jordan has fallen to pieces. I was doing the music. H'm. So well advised as ever by my lawyer, I bill them for work already prepared, days spent recording, lawyers fees, etc. This summer I've finally wised up – get an accountant and a lawyer.

June 7 Supposed to record Mike Newell for documentary. Cancelled. I feel depressed and lethargic as so much work in the last year has yet to be released, or has fallen through. Yet again, wonder what on earth I am doing it for.

June 10 *Live Blue*. Queen Elizabeth Hall. Set up, rehearse, play. Parents came at last, good response. God I love playing live. All band on form and Quentin's narration touching as ever. It's great to hear Derek's poetry again.

June 12 Call lawyer re my publishing contract. I am getting broke and need my next advance quickly. Speak to John Quentin (*Blue* narrator) as we're doing a show on Radio 3 live on Thursday. Try to make an appointment with Binney, my tattooist, but he's up to his eyes in work till August. Lucky bugger.

June 13 BAFTA. Screening of Ben Hopkins' film *National Achievement Day*. End up at Tim's flat at the Royal Academy after a huge Guinness fix, with Gina and Shelley. Naked men do not a party make. But oh what fun still to tumble around Soho at two in the morning. Letting off steam as it were.

June 14 Tony Peake, Jarman's biographer, comes to Brixton. It's odd telling long and old stories of the man. We first met when he'd just finished shooting *Jubilee*, and I used to help make lunch at Meglavision. Salads. Howard and James. Oh, stories, stories, stories. I'm sure I think of Jarman at least three or four times a day in one way or another.

June 15 In the evening John Quentin and I play on Radio 3's *Night Waves*. He reads his own poetry and Jarman's, and I accompany him on the piano. I took my mandola, but Quentin said he preferred my piano. It was a discussion on AIDS in the arts, and we were the musical segments. Larry Kramer was fun and so wicked. He's not lost one ounce of his anger. The BBC I praise for their fine taxi service there and back, and we got paid handsomely. Now that's a change. The programme went out live at 10.30, so mistakes and all, there's no turning back.

June 22   Fly to Lisbon. Our last *Blue* concert ever. Looking forward to it. Ian forgets his passport, but we arrive and are picked up by Sabino. Straight to the concert hall, which is in a huge bank, not unlike the Pantheon, but modern. Hotel. Meet the crew. Oh God, no smoking on stage. That's always hell. Why can't we play at the Paradiso in Amsterdam again, where it's almost compulsory to smoke on stage.

June 23   It takes till eight in the evening to set up the sound, but it's not difficult. The programme is beautiful too. Supper of fresh crabs and prawns with Quentin. We all eat separately. We don't all stay together when we travel. I had a huge argument with James Mackay. I've had it, and the lawyers will take over. So fences to be mended before we play tomorrow, otherwise ... For once the visuals look huge and are the best yet. Ironic, isn't it? Go out with a big blue bang.

July 10   Mute. I've been asked to write an article about Derek and how *Blue* was made, so I borrowed a console and typed in a rough draft which then corrects itself. I send my RCA contract to my lawyer; as I worked for free, I want to retain all rights for the music. Part of my '95 plan is to turn into a grown-up.

July 11   Train strike. I curse and panic as I bus and walk to Deptford High St to see Alnoor Deushi. He's done a BFI short and it's very funny. Hooray. The Steenbeck is in his flat, so we look at it a few times and talk about where to go from here. I want to score it, but not do general sound. So I get him to call Marvin Black to see if he's interested. He is.

July 17   Fax invoices for money owed. Meet executives from advertising team. I'm doing my first corporate video – part of the growing-up process, I suppose. I seem to call the world. God help our phone bill.

August 2   Mute. At last we are compiling the *Nadja* soundtrack. It has taken fourteen months to get it together. Rights, money, distributors, etc. What a nightmare! A fifty-minute version of the film using dialogue, FX out-takes, etc. is being released in America. A sixteen-hour day. At last, the whole project can be laid to rest.

August 3   Courier masters to New York for cutting and production. Forgot to write sleeve notes. I hope Michael can do this in New York.

August 4   Soundsuite studios with Richard Preston. A one-day write-and-make-it-up-as-we-go-along session for a corporate video. They've spent hundreds of thousands, and we get £1,000. Terrifying as I'd never done this before. A tune on the piano was first, then we were off. It turned out sounding like music for a corporate video. The director and producer sat around and their silence seemed to offer us no enthusiasm whatsoever, but it did mean that they didn't dislike it. In fact, the opposite. They're pleased.

August 11   A lawyer day on the phone and the fax. Problems with *Nadja* soundtrack. One piece of music I've used on the CD and co-written and played with a friend has not been cleared for CD. Oh hell. Drop it then, I say. No, we'll risk it. So the cut is still going ahead in New York. But as it's August everyone is on holiday, and well, the weekend's coming up again. Time to forget it. I've really done the best I can with *Nadja*.

August 26   *Nadja* opens in New York.

October 5   Mix day of *Anton and Minty*, BFI short. I'm early and Marvin and Alnoor are still on pre-mixes. So I go home via every pub in Camden Town, and never bump into any of Blur. I've got my damn key-ring from *Smash Hits* though. I hate 'em.

October 22–23   Half of the *Blue* group meet for two days and record an album. Great fun. Not blue at all. It's our soundcheck music and we eat and merry ourselves in Elephant Studios underneath the Thames at Wapping. We all decide to record it ourselves and pay for it too. All improvised with lots of variety. Reminds me if anything, of Can [rock band]. We want to edit sections in December then put it out. Fine vibes.

The Distributor

Pam Engel

Pam Engel is managing director of Artificial Eye, one of the leading film distributors in the UK. The company also owns three cinemas in London: the Lumière, the Chelsea Cinema and the twin Renoir. Since June 1994 she has also been programming another five London cinemas on behalf of Mayfair Theatres and Cinemas. The following extracts concentrate on a three-month period, at the centre of which is her experience of the Cannes Film Festival, a crucial moment in any distributor's calendar.

April 3   Checked the figures for all of the cinemas. The weekend weather had been brilliant but was pleased to see that the phenomenal *Madness of King George* was still delivering a great result at the box-office despite a substantial drop, accounted for by the fact that Goldwyn/Rank went too wide with the West End release. Our own film *Mrs. Parker and the Vicious Circle* is proving somewhat of a disappointment. I decided to move *Parker* to the Minema after it leaves the Renoir and put *Heavenly Creatures* into the Phoenix. The changes are passed on to our designers in time for *Time Out*'s mid-day deadline for the ad. During the afternoon, various artworks have to be checked for forthcoming releases *Exotica* and *Clerks*. A lot of time is spent working out the details for the campaigns and talking to the designers as well as extensive discussions for the marketing of *Clerks* (a very funny and original American indie made on a miniscule budget) with John Durie, our marketing consultant. Our strategy is releasing in the West End in several small screens and then around the country, targeting a younger audience as well as our core audience.

April 5   Buena Vista and Roger Wingate of Mayfair Entertainment have apparently planned to change the release of *Jefferson in Paris* after the film's recent bad reviews in New York, although the business is good. They want to put it in the Odeon Leicester Square, which does not seem like a good idea to me. This also gives me the problem of finding substitute films for the Curzon Mayfair and the Curzon West End, but of course it's Roger's own film and so it's very much his decision.

April 7   Checked that everything is set for *Clerks* and *Exotica*. Both films have had rave reviews in the States but as usual I am pretty nervous about the releases. Discussed booking *Butterfly Kiss* and *The Young Poisoner's Handbook* – two interesting new British first features, both very black. I really want to show both films. *Priest* is unfortunately not performing very well, as it has gone too wide and we're playing against the Warner West End which was a mistake. The Curzon West End has barely risen above its break figure. This booking was a gamble which didn't come off very well.

April 11   Decided to reduce our spend on *Clerks* and *Exotica* as we seem to have gone over the top. Must get the budgets set before proposing the advertising schedules! Worked through the magazine quotes for both films – reviews are generally very good. Apparently Fox have advised us to add 'a gun' to our design for the video-rental sleeve for *Amateur*. They want us to use our four-sheet poster campaign, and insist that the gun is needed to sell the video, thereby imitating the *Pulp Fiction* video campaign, where a gun had apparently also been added. This is fair enough for *Pulp Fiction*, but a completely wrong emphasis for *Amateur*. However, it seems it's going ahead as I was outvoted.

April 12   Meeting with David Linde and Rick Sands of Miramax. Showed them our designs for *The Neon Bible*, which I'm very pleased with – coloured press-kit covers, T-shirt and badge. We looked at their latest trailer for the film which they are making at Creative. We all thought it wasn't working (they even used music from a completely different film) and seemed to be trying to make it work like a new *Fried Green Tomatoes* instead of a Terence Davies film. Luckily Rick agreed that it would do nothing for Davies fans and so they offered to redo it, this time using music from the movie, including 'Perfidia' and the *Gone with the Wind* music.

April 24   I'm still recovering from the shock that *Three Colours Red* didn't win even a single gong at last nights BAFTA awards. The ceremony at the Palladium was excruciatingly boring and I felt helpless while Kieslowski, Piesiewicz and Irène Jacob sat patiently through the whole affair, showing barely a flicker of disappointment.

April 28   Suggested to Andi [Engel] that we pay the asking price for *Land and Freedom*, the new Ken Loach in competition at Cannes, which would hopefully secure the film for us. We had decided not to pre-buy unless it was absolutely necessary, but I felt we simply should get this film. Luckily Andi agreed and we made an offer. There were, it seems, two of our competitors on the brink and so I think we did the right thing. We'll be able to see the film soon. Of course I hope we are not disappointed. The complete list for Cannes is now announced and I spent some time working through all the titles and discussing the prospects. On the whole it looks promising but much of the product is already bought. Andi will go to Paris to see some of the Quinzaine [Directors Fortnight] films and special screenings of a few of the competition movies. We cannot afford to wait for Cannes.

May 4   Had an interesting meeting with producers Rebecca O'Brien and

Sally Hibben about *Land and Freedom*. They showed me the Spanish campaign which I really liked. We will work out our own campaign after Cannes. They thought Ian Hart would be keen to work on the film and after his great success in *Backbeat* I'm sure there'll be a lot of interest in him – and, of course, Ken Loach. The Sales Company have made a splendid pressbook and we're providing a T-shirt for Cannes. We also want to organise a drinks reception for the press. Sally seems to like my ideas of an exclusive or mostly exclusive run at the Lumière. I can't wait to see the movie.

May 11 Finally saw *Land and Freedom*. Extraordinarily moving and really good.

May 16 Arrived in Cannes. Spent the day filling out diary with a multitude of screenings, meetings and even a few parties. Had to read all those synopses and make decisions about what to see. Ended the day with our traditional first-night dinner at Mère Besson's.

May 17 Spent the morning trying to locate the girl giving out tickets for the opening night film, *The City of Lost Children*. The film, though, was very disappointing. Luckily we do not have to distribute it.

May 18 The 8.30 am competition film was *Sharaku* by Masahiro Shinoda. It looked beautiful but I thought it was rather arid. From there I rushed to see *The Confessional* which we very rashly had bought last night for quite a large sum of money. I feel a bit tense throughout the screening but am relieved that the movie is in fact very original and entertaining. This is our third pre-buy showing in competition, the other two being *The Neon Bible* and *Land and Freedom*, and all three are fine.

May 20 Today I saw an interesting movie called *Heavy* by first-timer American James Mangold. It won a prize at Sundance this year. I liked it a lot. Rather slow but beautifully made with wonderful performance by Liv Tyler. I later discovered she will be in Bertolucci's next movie and Woody Allen's! Tell Andi about it and he goes off to buy the film for the UK from our friends at Fortissimo. Also saw *Antonia's Line* (but not at the all-women's screening) and didn't like it much. We also had a meeting with the mighty Miramax to discuss the possibility of working more closely and maybe taking on some of their smaller titles which Buena Vista International are not interested in.

May 21 In the evening we had our drinks party for Terence Davies and Gena Rowlands for *The Neon Bible* which we are very happy to have. It seemed to go pretty well.

May 22 Today was the official screening of *Kids*, which we were all invited to see in a private screening, and had hated, and a later screening was the reason why several journalists arrived late at our reception for *Land*

and Freedom. But as everyone seems to absolutely love the Loach, I think everyone was very happy. It was really nice that not only Ken Loach came, but also Ian Hart, Rosana Pastor and several of the militia. Later I saw the quite amusing *Denise Calls Up*, directed by Hal Salwen in the Critics' Week.

May 24 Screening of *Ulysses' Gaze* which I thought wonderful. Although three hours long, the audience sat rapt throughout and the screening was packed. Harvey Keitel was superb. Later we bought the Angelopoulos from Bill Stephens, not too expensively, I hope.

May 25 In the morning went to see Oliveira's *The Convent* starring Catherine Deneuve and John Malkovich. I enjoyed it, though it's rather weird. Later I saw Emir Kusturica's extraordinary epic *Underground*. Some truly amazing moments, but too long.

May 26 Discussed *Underground* with Andi and Robert. We thought the price was too high but that we should make an offer. Saw *Shanghai Triad*, Zhang Yimou's gangster movie with Gong Li, which Electric/PolyGram have. A little disappointing but very watchable.

May 27 Decided to leave a day early so I saw *Dead Man Walking* in the morning, which I loved and then left for Nice airport. Not a great Cannes, but we come out of it with some good movies: *Land and Freedom*, *The Neon Bible*, *Heavy*, *Ulysses' Gaze*, *Denise Calls Up* and *The Confessional*.

June 2 The figures for Alexandre Rockwell's *Somebody to Love* at the Curzon West End are disastrous after some unkind reviews. I have to find a replacement fast, to sustain the five weeks to go until *Country Life*. I talk to Daniel at Buena Vista who, thank God, agrees that we can move over *Bullets over Broadway* to the Curzon West End when it comes on at the Odeon Haymarket. In the meantime, we'll have to move *Death and the Maiden* back again in a couple of weeks.

In the afternoon I had a meeting with Mia Matson from Creative Partnership who does design work on most of our important releases. She's working on *The Neon Bible* and had made us two beautiful roughs for the quad, and another for the proposed four-sheet poster. We're using the motif which I personally like very much too. It's reminiscent of an Edward Hopper painting and I agree with Terence that it will make a good poster. We had ourselves chosen this shot of Gena Rowlands and the actor who plays the younger boy for a four-sheet poster but had had to abandon it to keep our work within budget. So now this image will be used in the quad poster and I hope everyone is happy. We had to meet Penguin's deadline for the artwork as they are reprinting the novel with our poster campaign on the cover.

June 5 We have a distribution meeting and discuss my proposed release dates for our new acquisitions from Cannes which takes us into May 1996.

Roger Wingate, who in the last year or so has had a 50 per cent interest in our film purchases, expressed a strong interest in playing *Land and Freedom* in one of his main cinemas and so I decide to swap around my plan for *The Neon Bible* and *Land and Freedom*. The former will now open at the Lumière, exclusively for two weeks and then wider in London, while the latter will open at the Curzon West End as well as in six other cinemas in London.

June 16 Had an enjoyable lunch with Fiona Mitchell (from Ciby Sales) and Robert to discuss our offer for the Kusturica film. We outline a possible deal with her, regarding our previous offer made at Cannes which was withdrawn owing to the fact that Ciby were so long giving us an answer. Since Cannes we've slightly turned off the film and I assume Ciby are kicking themselves. The moral is always accept extravagant offers made by overexcited distributors in Cannes lest sanity returns when they get back to London!

The Exhibitor

Philip Grey

Philip Grey is manager of the Screen on the Hill in London. His diary gives a rare insight into the rhythms of the operations of a small urban, arthouse cinema.

April 1 *The Madness of King George.* 1,025 admissions. The cinema has marked the start of the hundredth anniversary of the industry's inception by posting a new box-office revenue record with *The Madness of King George*. Despite being a massive leap in revenue terms, the film fell some way short of the record for admissions, still held after all these years by *Dance with a Stranger* and *The Draughtsman's Contract*, with only one ticket separating them! Everyone in the industry from the directors through distributors and marketing personnel right down to the weekly charts in *Screen International* are obsessed with grosses. What is remarkable is that our top two grossers and five of the top six in the admissions chart are British.

The first three months of 1995 have seen a marked upturn in business, after a rather lacklustre 1994. We opened the year playing one of the

THE SCREEN ON THE HILL: Box-office Countdown

Film	Admissions
Dance with a Stranger	6452
The Draughtsman's Contract	6451
The Madness of King George	5623
My Beautiful Laundrette	5530
Sex, Lies and Videotape	5423
Peter's Friends	5392
Barton Fink	5113
The Player	5087
Orlando	5005
The Piano	4835
Homicide	4774
Postcards from the Edge	4731
Damage	4708
Nasty Girl	4690
Quiz Show	4538
Metropolitan	4321
Schindler's List	4301

most talked about films of 1994 by that man Tarantino, who, after *Pulp Fiction*'s screening in Cannes, has been in a stratospheric orbit from which he shows no sign of descending. This was followed by *Even Cowgirls Get the Blues*, Gus Van Sant's misguided, sloppy adaptation of the Tom Robbins cult classic, the less said about which the better. Business picked up considerably with Ang Lee's *Eat Drink Man Woman*, a highly entertaining examination of family mores in contemporary Taiwan. Next up was *Heavenly Creatures*, Peter Jackson's remarkable examination of a real-life adolescent relationship in 50s New Zealand between two girls that ultimately led to murder. Sadly we had to pull this off after only a fortnight to make way for Robert Redford's *Quiz Show*, which seems to have found greater favour with British audiences than it did with their American counterparts. Then came *The Madness*, in more senses than one.

April 7   601 admissions. Gary Lineker came to see the film tonight. I did a classic double take as I walked past him in the foyer; and then couldn't restrain myself from blurting out 'It's Gary Lineker!' Luckily it came out *sotto voce*. I feel celebrities in their private time ought to be treated as ordinary members of the public, neither hassled nor accorded any special privileges – queue jumping, upgraded seats or, as in the case of one local actor, a seat in a sell-out show. Most of the celebs that visit the Hill tend to come from the world of entertainment – actors, television personalities, musicians, writers – not that many sports people. Gary Lineker was certainly a big surprise.

April 8   980 admissions. I work Wednesdays through to Saturdays; Ian Jenkin, a relatively new addition to the company, manages the remaining three days of the week. There has been uncertainty all week as to whether we are to continue playing *The Madness*. The staggering box-office performance of the film has led to attempts to diplomatically extricate the cinema from its contractual obligation to show our next film, Polanski's *Death and the Maiden*. As far as I can gather, discussions only got as far as trying to get Rank – distributors of *The Madness* – to cancel its booking of the film into the nearby MGM Hampstead on the day on which it is due to come off here. Rank refused. A very embarrassing phone call to Electric Pictures – distributors of *Death and the Maiden* – did not have to be made therefore.

April 10   648 admissions. Met Tony Bloom – director of Mainline Pictures – at Columbia Pictures for a screening of *Guarding Tess*, a new comedy starring Shirley Maclaine and Nicholas Cage, which is being considered for a summer slot at the Hill. *Guarding Tess*, a story about a dead ex-presidents wife's relationship with her secret service minder, doesn't really have much relevance to us in Britain. Yet like films about ice hockey kids and baseball molls it will continue to suck sterling out of this country and into the pockets of corporate America.

April 19   409 admissions. A crew of final year students from the National Film School spent the morning and early afternoon filming a scene outside the cinema. Two hours were spent setting up the main shot – a track into the front of the building as an audience leaves a performance. They had requested that the front of house appear as though we were showing *Schindler's List*. The film, a 25-minute short called *The Wandering German*, is about a young man who on a visit to London finds himself in a number of situations that force him to reflect on his German identity.

April 21 *Death and the Maiden*. 317 admissions. Alarmingly, admissions were lower than the final night of the four-week run of *The Madness*. Often, however, the first Friday of a run can be a poor indication of how a film is going to perform. The sort of films we exhibit tend not to attract the 'must see it on the first day type of audience', coupled with the fact that a large proportion are drawn from the North London Jewish community for whom it is the beginning of the Sabbath. Electric Pictures/PolyGram can not be criticised for failing to promote the film. There has been an incredible amount of press and television coverage of the film, its director Roman Polanski, and actors Sigourney Weaver and Ben Kingsley. There has also been an extensive poster campaign – for a film only opening at three sites.

April 22 710 admissions. Had a surprisingly good turnout for the late show. The general impression from overheard comments of the leaving audiences appears favourable. The somewhat enigmatic ending ought to ensure continued discussion on the way home. Word of mouth will hopefully see the figures build through the week and an improved second weekend.

April 26 209 admissions. Spoke with Roger Austin – programmer at Mainline Pictures – who is concerned with the figures for *Death and the Maiden*. We discussed the options for a filler for the third week as it looks as if the film will need to come off. *The Madness of King George* is apparently taking a fortune at the MGM Hampstead, but we both agreed that bringing it back for one week would probably not be beneficial. He is working on trying to get *Little Odessa*, an impressive if somewhat bleak film starring Tim Roth and Vanessa Redgrave.

May 5 *Little Odessa*. 71 admissions. Very slow opening day. Only one admission for the second performance! Until five minutes before the actual film it looked as if there might not be anybody, a situation we have not encountered on the first day for quite some time. My contention that having four shows a day was pointless has been confirmed immediately. Thank God there was no late show.

May 10 75 admissions. *Little Odessa*, sadly, is really not performing. Everyone, staff and customers alike, who has seen it generally agrees it deserves to be doing better. This seems to further underline that no matter how strong the cast or favourable the reviews, the public don't seem interested in spending money on going to see 'dark' movies.

May 12 *Bullets over Broadway.* 540 admissions. A first-show attendance figure in excess of fifty saw off any fear that *Bullets* was not going to be a considerable hit. The three front-of-house staff and myself had a rather frenzied afternoon dealing with two constantly ringing telesales lines. There was a close-fought contest between the 9.10 performances on Friday and Saturday as to which would sell out first, until early evening when suddenly Friday's went.

Steven Payne (the projectionist) was concerned with the quality of the print. Once again the distributors have supplied us with a reconditioned second-hand print. This is becoming a common practice among multi-national companies who can make significant savings by recycling prints they have exhibited in America, rather than striking new ones. *Bullets over Broadway* is by no means as bad as some we have had, but some ends are dirty and there are a couple of nasty joins that interfere with the dialogue.

May 24 192 admissions. Long chat with Adam Chapman – Mainline Pictures – about poor figures for the second week. I expressed concern that the film would not last its four-week run. He agreed, but confirmed that he had spoken to Roger in Cannes who had no intention of pulling it out early. We pondered why *Bullets* has declined so markedly: I felt that there was a widespread ambivalence towards Woody Allen; many were still angered by the domestic scandal, others were simply tired of his work. Despite being one of his better light comedies, having garnered more Oscar nominations than any of his previous films and consistently good reviews, the attendances are dropping. I am particularly worried that the forthcoming Bank Holiday weekend will see an even more rapid decline – with our local audience base traditionally taking advantage of the week long school break to go away.

May 27 850 admissions. A bit of a turn-up for the books, literally; unexpectedly busy day with two sold-out evening performances. Perhaps the fact the Screen on the Green have stopped showing *Bullets* this week has had some bearing on the level of business.

June 1 252 admissions. The weekday figures show all the signs that a favourable word of mouth is spreading, as they are generally up on last week's admissions. Our three-day weekend total was the highest of any of the cinemas showing *Bullets*, according to Screen International, and this does not include the very good Monday.

June 6 128 admissions. It appears likely that we shall play *The City of Lost Children*, the new film by Jeunet and Caro, the makers of *Delicatessen*. It has been pencilled in as the movie we will open with after the forthcoming foyer refit. Tony said it received a very mixed reception at Cannes; the press seemed to like it. *Carrington* fared rather better, picking up the Best Actor award for Jonathan Pryce in his role as Lytton Strachey. I hope PolyGram – the film's distributor – will fuel the momentum from this solid base. We open it later in September.

June 10 *Six Degrees of Separation*. 548 admissions. Poor weather undoubtedly helps boost today's – Saturday's – figure, which included a sell-out 8.40 performance, and a creditable late show despite its absence from the *Time Out* listings. Watched the film, which, I felt, succeeds far better than *Death and the Maiden* in making the transition from stage to screen. Will Smith as the impostor is a revelation, proving that he is more than just a pretty rap artist. He has also drawn a far larger than usual black audience.

The print – already the second supplied – is appalling, with very dirty ends to the first and third reels, a problem made worse by the anamorphic lens required to project the film in CinemaScope, which also stretches the scratches and dust marks. I discussed this with Romaine when she called for the figures in the evening. She is most concerned and agreed it is high time something was done to discourage the increasingly widespread practice of recycling prints already exhibited in America. Understandably distributors are keen to cut their costs, but this really ought not to be at the expense of the paying public. In the case of *Six Degrees of Separation* there are only six cinemas on the initial release (and probably a fairly limited roll-out to follow); I do feel that Warner Bros. ought to have struck new prints for these showcase venues.

June 17 562 admissions. No real sign of the film building in its second week – which often occurs where there hasn't been a significant public awareness campaign in advance of an opening and a distributor is relying heavily on word of mouth. Today though – a Saturday – business was steady throughout the afternoon, despite the Rugby World Cup semi-final. The 8.40 performance scraped a sell-out at the last minute.

June 21 112 admissions. The longest day, and wasn't it just! Started with a midday meeting at the cinema with the architect, the building contractors doing the refit, Tony Bloom and Colin Payne, chief technician for Mainline Pictures.

June 28 69 admissions. The heatwave continues, temperatures rising inside and out; admissions continue to suffer. Roger Austin mentioned that the distributors of *A Man of No Importance*, which we open at the end of June, had seen sense and redesigned the poster for the film. The original does rank as one of the worst I have seen in my time in the industry! Roger warned that its replacement is not a great improvement.

June 30 *Miami Rhapsody*. 135 admissions. Disappointing opening, which to a large extent can be attributed to the extraordinary weather. Temperatures were in the high 80s, and the four-show day dragged by incredibly slowly. Only four admissions for the second show. Roger rang to check that I had put 'Air Conditioned' on the canopy. He does this every time we have a heatwave. I had to remind him that Mainline as yet has not installed it at the Screen on the Hill.

July 6 187 admissions. Tony Bloom called to let me know Mainline have confirmed that *Before the Rain* has been booked as the film that will fill the gap between the end of *Man of No Importance* and when we close for the foyer refit. I saw it in January and was impressed with the way it presented the seemingly perennial problem of ethnic and religious conflict in the Balkans, and how it effects both local people and those many miles away. Beautiful to look at and very powerful, it contains excellent performances from a largely unknown cast; it ought to be well received critically. But will it get bums on seats with the plethora of 'event' movies coming up?

Apparently we may not be reopening with Jeunet and Caro's *City of Lost Children* as Warner Bros. have brought forward the date for *The Bridges of Madison County*, which is currently taking a packet in America. Mainline had it scheduled for later in the year and had already attracted significant interest from charity committees wanting it for fundraising screenings and so are keen not to miss the opportunity to make amends for the recent lean patch. There had been concern that while *City of Lost Children* might open strongly on the back of *Delicatessen*'s success, it might not hold up as well over the three-week run as *Bridges*, which has been building consistently over its initial five-week run in America.

July 8 487 admissions. No one in the first show, eight in the second. Very galling. Such a gorgeous day that everyone working, myself included, would far rather have spent it somewhere else. Barry Humphries brightened up the late afternoon when he came in to buy tickets for the 9.00 show. He pretended to flirt with Julie in the box-office, who quite naively said after he had left that he really reminded her of Dame Edna!

July 14 138 admissions. *The Bridges of Madison County* is out. Apparently Warner Bros. have shifted its opening again to 15 September, which means we cannot fit it into the Hill schedule; it will go to the Green instead. Luckily Entertainment were prepared to let us have *The City of Lost Children* back, despite the claims of breach of contract when it was dropped.

July 20 35 admissions. Low figure as the last performance of *Miami Rhapsody* was dropped for a special performance of *A Man of No Importance* in the presence of director Suri Krishnamma. Pete Daley at D.D.A [PR and publicity company] rang to say he was concerned that the turnout might be poor owing to the hot weather, he suggested that we encourage passing trade to attend. I put up notices in the outside frames advertising the show and we told everyone that came into the cinema. In the event the auditorium was well over half-full, which under the circumstances was a reasonable figure. Suri Krishnamma arrived a couple of minutes before the film was due to start, which caused a degree of consternation. His welcoming speech was very composed and he coped well with the question-and-answer session that followed the film. I hope his film performs as well; the signs, though, suggest this is unlikely.

July 22 *A Man of No Importance.* 283 admissions. Come the evening, Emma and Hannah, who were timetabled to do the late show with me, were placing side bets in the hope that nobody would turn up so we could all go home early. Out of nowhere twenty-one appeared and dashed our expectations.

July 26 143 admissions. Monsoon-like storms in the early afternoon no doubt largely responsible for the doubling of the previous day's matinee figures. Unfortunately the trend failed to continue into the evening.

July 28 77 admissions. Romaine, Tony, Colin Payne, Ian and myself went through the cinema with a fine-tooth comb compiling schedules of responsibility for numerous tasks that require doing before, during and immediately after the refurbishment closedown.

Miami Rhapsody is back. For the next week we have alternate separate performances of it and *A Man of No Importance.* The idea was to compress two films' daily box-office into two just shows of each. The reality was somewhat different, with total admissions significantly down on any single day of the previous week.

August 16 *Before the Rain.* 123 admissions. The cinema continues to be very quiet. *Before the Rain,* despite receiving universal critical praise, is not pulling in the customers.

August 20 146 admissions. The final day of the 'old' Screen on the Hill. There was a palpable feeling akin to the end of term days at school as everybody applied themselves to packing up. After the final performance had gone in, Ian, Hervé and I boxed up the kiosk and bar stock and all the equipment we were going to keep. After the audience had left we moved everything into various cupboards in the auditorium. By 1 am the place had a decidedly derelict feel about it. It would have been lamentable, but for the knowledge of what was to come. The dawning of a new era!

September 1 *City of Lost Children.* 350 admissions. Everybody was there, builders, painters, plumbers, all doing their final snagging. By midday it looked like a cinema. 3pm: I opened the doors to the public. Hervé switched to touch-screen ticket issue and we hit our first glitch: the computer refused to respond to any commands. At the early-evening performance another and potentially far more serious problem arose. The system refused to retrieve credit card bookings. On the off-chance I went into touch-screen to discover that this was the only function it was prepared to do in that setting. At least everything was running smoothly in the kiosk. A number of customers commented how delicious the cappuccino was.

After the late show had gone in we discovered the system would not build any end-of-day reports. Fatigue and frustration were beginning to get the better of me.

September 7 142 admissions. The week ended disappointingly in terms

166

of business. For a film so heavily trailed, *City of Lost Children* is not pulling in the punters. One good thing though is that the kiosk/bar sales are on the increase. Over the week as a whole the percentage to ticket sales exceeded 15 per cent, with some days well over 20 per cent. Mainline are pleased that the new layout is having an immediate benefit.

September 15   *The Young Poisoners Handbook*. 141 admissions. An inauspicious opening. Another case of a critically acclaimed film failing to attract an audience. Despite arriving early in order to clear my desk, there was too much to do to allow me to watch the first show. Didn't even manage the second. Then the computer starting playing up again!

September 21   48 admissions. Got the staff preparing for the evening's special preview of *Carrington*; there were 500 glasses to rinse and polish All the mirrors and surfaces needed shining to meet Romaine Hart's exacting standards. Romaine arrived at around 6.00 am with the company secretary Liz. The canopy was changed and the front of house was ready by 8.00, just in time for the first guests who began arriving about a quarter past. Liz was in a bit of a flap because the driver due to collect the actor Steven Waddington had rang to say there was no answer at his home. Fortunately he turned up just before 9.00. I was to introduce him, and he was to introduce the film and tell the invited audience that the director Christopher Hampton would be present at the end for a questions-and-answers.

September 22   *Carrington*. 325 admissions. The expectation that *Carrington* is going to be a considerable box-office success was confounded. The figure was acceptable, but nothing like what was expected.

September 30   750 admissions. A very busy day, all systems working beautifully smoothly. Four weeks since we reopened and the computer performed as I always hoped it would, retrieving bookings quickly and without error. Even though both evening performances were sold out there was seldom more than a six person queue at either of the box-office positions.

October 7   723 admissions. *Carrington* is holding up very well; the third weekend figures still exceeding those of the first. It is doing an unusually large proportion of its business on Saturdays, attracting the North London middle-class go-out-one-night-a-week audience from hell. They all think they are the only people to possess a credit card, and that by booking on it the seas will part and allow them to sail, unobstructed by queues, to their seats. With the new box-office we now have an extra point-of-sale position which processes the queue that much quicker, but still they complain. There seems to be a failure to grasp that, because in the evening there are very few, if any, tickets left to sell, meaning that the bulk are credit-card booked, it is actually quicker not to have a separate credit-card queue. There is an innate disapproval of having to queue in the same line as those who have not had the foresight to book, or – shock, horror – do not possess a credit card, even if it would ultimately mean waiting longer if there were a dedicated box-office.

October 13 240 admissions. The first display material for the re-issue of Antonioni's *L'avventura* arrived. We will be showing it exclusively for a fortnight at the end of November. In the absence of any posters, Roger has had a large double-quad blow-up produced, outlining the film's history and narrative structure. I immediately noticed that the running-time was listed as 145 minutes, at least ten minutes longer than we can show without an intermission.

October 18 156 admissions. Steve said that the BFI had confirmed that the running time of *L'avventura* is indeed 2 hours 25 minutes. Apparently there is a classic stand-off taking place at Mainline, with Roger refusing to play the film with an intermission, and Romaine not prepared to agree to the installation of a platter projection system – the only way we will be able to show the film without an intermission – to replace the existing tower. Roger says he will not consider cancelling the booking. We are now waiting on the BFI to establish if the film has been printed on polyester stock, being very thin this would enable us to run it on our existing system.

October 19 428 admissions. The BFI confirmed that *L'avventura* has not been printed on polyester stock, and that they have struck all the prints they intend to. The film is only scheduled for a limited release and presumably the sites showing it will either have cakestand/platters or operate change-overs, so there was no need to consider using polyester stock. The question is who at Mainline is going to stand down first. I'm sure that if so much money had been spent recently on the Hill, Romaine would not have been so opposed to installing a new system.

Good final day rally for *Carrington*, further enhanced by a charity block-booking of the last show.

October 20 *Il postino*. 410 admissions. There has been a steady build-up in interest in *Il postino* since the posters first went up about six weeks ago, although it seemed to drop off somewhat last week. I feared Barry Norman might have killed it completely with his far from shining appraisal, and there had been very few advance sales. Today I was caught completely off guard. Fortunately the rota was created a week ago, before my pessimism set in, so I had just about enough staff to cope with the throngs and major phone activity.

October 23 345 admissions. I called in at Mainline's offices as there were a number of things I wanted to discuss with various people there. I suggested to Tony that it might prove more economical for Mainline to pay to have a polyester print struck of *L'avventura* than to install a cakestand film delivery system. They hadn't considered this option. After some discussion it was agreed that this would not be a good investment, because although cheaper in the short term, there would be nothing to show for it. Whereas although they will need to spend over £1,000 more on the cakestand, there is a long-term benefit. It will enable us to show films over 140 minutes without an intermission as well as removing the time required to rewind the film from our regular programming. With a cakestand system the film is drawn from the centre of a coil lying horizontally on a rotating platter. It travels via an elaborate sequence of pulley-wheels through the projector before returning to be wound back on to another platter.

October 28 808 admissions. By the time the first performance was on screen we were left with the front two or three rows for the 9.10 performance, and little more for the earlier show. Both had gone by 6.00 pm. I took over the box-office and almost the first person through the door was the dreaded Mrs Smithee, truly our number-one customer from hell. She has been coming to the Hill for years – God knows why, because somehow there is always something wrong with her booking: she comes at 7.00 and her tickets have been reserved for 9.00; there are only two tickets and she swears blind to having booked four; she specified left-hand aisle and her seats are on the right. I've come to the conclusion that she is someone who has a pathological need for conflict and actually engineers situations that produce a scene.

To the best of my knowledge this was her first visit since the installation of the computerised ticketing system. My heart sank. I knew we were in for a serious problem. She said she had tickets booked for the last performance, giving me her credit card, which I proceeded to swipe through the reader, praying that her tickets would be printed and there would be the correct number allocated in the right place. Nothing happened. No tickets came out. Fortunately she immediately corrected herself, saying she had only reserved the tickets. I went into cash reservation retrieval and again nothing came out. She began her complaint: 'But I came in yesterday specifically to check that the tickets were there and in the middle as I specified on the phone.' Why hadn't she taken them then and avoid the risk of us cocking up the booking, I wondered to myself. She said the tickets were definitely in the system when she came in on Friday and couldn't understand how they could disappear overnight. I checked every possible file in the booking system to see if perhaps it had been put in the wrong place, to no avail. I offered our house seats – which we always hold a number of for just such an eventuality – but they just wouldn't do. 'I specifically booked early and came in to check because I wanted seats in the middle as I have bad eyesight. I won't be able to see from the back, particularly as there are subtitles.' I was subjected to a good ten minute tongue-lashing, before Mrs Smithee finally agreed to take a pair of house seats.

October 29 530 admissions. Ian discussed the Smithee incident with Andrew, who had been cashier when she came in to check her booking. He was 99 per cent certain that she had seats reserved for the 6.40 performance and not the later one. I am at a loss as to how to deal with this recurring pathology. Any suggestions?

Jim Hamilton

*Jim Hamilton is director of the Edinburgh Filmhouse, one of the most important
and successful Regional Film Theatres in the UK. His diary confronts head-on the
problems of running such a venue in the present climate.*

April 10 Monday morning again. Weekend figures are fine considering
what's on. Should meet targets if *Amateur* holds up on its second run.

April 12 Spend the morning programming. Favourite job – more a
pleasure than work. The first-run films have been confirmed for a while.
Clerks, a film I hated, is in for two weeks. It's a strange feeling booking a
film that you despise, but I have a gut feeling that it might do well.

Spend a couple of hours working out the schedule for the Lesbian and
Gay Festival on tour. Thirteen titles to screen in two weeks. Really annoyed
that there are only three lesbian-themed titles, as we have a large audience
for this sort of material. Make a note to find out why there are so few lesbian
films so that I can deal with the complaints when they arrive. Concerned
about *Super 8 1/2*. Great film, but the scenes of hardcore gay porn may
cause us problems. I hope no one wanders in to a screening by chance and
complains. What if someone thinks that we are screening *8 1/2* and get the
blow jobs on screen and not Fellini?

April 25 9.00 am train to London for a COMEX [Consortium of Media
Exhibitors (Regional Film Theatres)] meeting which lasts four and a half
hours. We have had a constructive meeting. No raised voices, very polite
and one or two useful ideas emerging about exhibition policy. The one
major problem I have with the Exhibition Policy Paper is the insistence that
all cinemas serviced by the BFI must stick to a non-negotiable 35 per cent
box-office rental paid to distributors. I don't believe that the BFI ought to
dictate policy in this area. I agree that for most regional film theatres, the 35
per cent rule is valuable, and that it makes the actual booking process
simple for the BFI. But, in Edinburgh, where I am in direct competition
with the Cameo for product, I would like to be able, in certain circumstances, to offer more in order to secure a really big film, if I so decide. I
have decided not to broach this subject with the BFI yet. The time is not
right.

May 1 Spend the time rejigging the schedule for the building of the new
screen. Work will take four months and is bound to cause disruption. At
worst it could shut down the building altogether which I don't want to do
during January–March 1996 as this is our busiest period. Putting the
building period back till later means that it will be difficult to have the third
screen open in time for the Film Festival. Should we stall for a year? This
would give us more time to raise the necessary cash.

May 2 Arrive at work to be told that a film which I have booked for two weeks, late May–June (*A Man of No Importance*), has been pulled by the producers. So I have a two-week gap in my programme. Major problems. The film has already been advertised in the May brochure which is on the streets. Spent a frantic morning discussing options with staff and then redoing the June programme and altering all the times. Having moved a film from July into June to fill the gap, I then had to redo the July programme. Three hours' mad work later it's all done. In a way I'm quite pleased that the film did get pulled. The programme for June was a bit lacking in money-making potential and the new June programme looks stronger. Checked on the weekend figures. *Exotica* opened well-ish, and *Thin Ice* is holding it's own. We'll make targets for this week.

May 5 Italian Film Festival starts today! The usual panic over prints coming from abroad. Roberto Benigni's new film, *Il mostro*, was sent to us in an unsubtitled print. Lots of phone calls later we discover that the person in the film company who gave us permission to screen the film in the first place was a secretary, and the print she promised us, the subtitled print was not to be shown, because they want a pristine print at Cannes. To cut a long story short, another subtitled print was found in America, which as of today has been sent to Heathrow airport. There are two flights to Edinburgh on a Saturday and the courier promises to get it to us. Make contingency plans with Charlie should the print still not arrive in time. We still have an unsubtitled print in the building, so we'll screen that, if necessary.

May 6 Call into Filmhouse to get an update on *Il mostro*. The print has been delayed in customs and has missed both flights to Edinburgh. Our agent is trying to get it onto a flight to Glasgow and then transport it by van to Edinburgh. 7.00 pm – the print arrives in time for the 8.30 screening. Sold out Cinema 1.

May 15 Cannes. Well, here we are. Jim Hickey (ex-Filmhouse, now producing), Richard Findley (solicitor), Ken Ingles (Director of Glasgow Film Theatre), his partner and I go to the Petit Carlton. Walking alongside the Croisette the place has an out-of-season feel. The festival doesn't start until Wednesday night. Lots of cafés and restaurants are shut. The hundreds of poster frames are empty. The streets are almost deserted. The Petit Carlton is quiet.

May 16 What a transformation. An army of people are working to turn the town into its festival clothes. People are flyposting, cleaning and polishing everything. The fat, rich Americans in ill-fitting expensive clothes are talking rubbish into mobile phones as they waddle along the Croisette. Go back to the apartment, reassured that things are as they should be. Meet with the others for lunch, then go and get our passes for the festival and the Market. Take a moment to appreciate the festival organisation: 25,000 delegates to process, many of whom are incredibly rude to the staff. After registering, we stand about for half an hour watching the rain come down in sheets. Once it clears, I go back to the apartment and start to plan my fortnight. Make a list of all the films I need to see, and then work out which to see when. This takes the best part of three hours' solid work.

May 26 One week and thirty-three films later – only one more proper day of screenings left. In summary then the highlights were:

Madagascar Skin	A BFI-funded film which is really good.
The Usual Suspects	Old-fashioned thriller (not in the least a criticism). Keeps me guessing right to the end. Plot, acting, direction all good. Mr Tarantino take note!
Kids	Controversial teenage sex-and-drugs yarn. Should be required viewing for parents who don't understand what kids get up to. Needless to say, the largely middle-aged viewers don't like it.
Neon Bible	Everyone is being really hard on Terence Davies' film. I liked it. Gena Rowlands can do no wrong in my book.
All Men Are Liars	Another Australian comedy. I laugh all the way through. Comedies are so rare at this festival.
Safe	Todd Haynes' film is my film of the festival by far. A perfect film. The first in a very long time. I could not go to another film for hours after it.

And the low points . . . :

Three Steps to Heaven	BFI Production comes through with another turkey! It's supposed to be a black comedy – it's neither very black nor funny. Whoever wrote the screenplay should stop doing this kind of work. It's terrible, but there seems to be a concerted effort to hype this film. Presumably because it was sold for over 1 million. Money wasted as far as I'm concerned. It will make no money at the box office, I'm sure.
To Die For	Another Gus Van Sant mistake. Oh how the mighty are fallen.
Land and Freedom	Ken Loach being miserable in Spain.
Ulysses' Gaze	Theo Angelopolous's three-hour art-wank epic.
Shanghai Triad	Nothing happened in the first hour – literally nothing happened. So I leave. Apparently one or two things happen in the last forty minutes.

The festival is nearly over. What I don't have from this one is any idea where cinema is going. Trends don't seem to have come out of it, except those made up by the Miramax publicity machine. Their marketing is so 'one note'. I don't think they, and those like them, are any good for what we call art cinema. They are only interested in art if it makes money. It's the never-ending search for crossover movies. Films like *Neon Bible* and *Safe* have been criticised for being unlikely to cross over. If only *Pulp Fiction* had been a flop, we might have been spared the attentions of these American global marketeers for a bit longer. The public, I hope, will lose interest, as they usually do.

May 27   Last day of the competition and I go to the screening of *La Haine*. Like *Safe*, this moved me a lot. What a treat to see a film which is entertaining, exciting and bang up to date. And well directed. One of the films of the festival. I hope it wins something. At least that would salvage something from what has been, for me, a slightly disappointing festival overall.

June 6–7   Two days completing the July brochure. Paul Taylor (BFI) phones with a note of films opening in September/October, along with whatever Cameo is offering on two pictures, *The Usual Suspects* and *Carrington*. Seven-week bookings on both sides, so there's no point in even trying to compete. I only hope they won't be able to put in *City of Lost Children*. Tell Paul to offer three weeks on the film. We discuss various options for the rest of the month.

   The Edinburgh Film Festival is gearing up now. Lots more staff arriving, lots more activity. This is when things can get a bit fraught. When the festival operation is in full swing they tend to forget that they are working with someone else's building, and that what the festival would like is not necessarily possible or desirable for Filmhouse to deliver. This can cause tensions. However, we all get on much better now that Mark Cousins is director and most problems can be solved without too many tears.

June 30   Box-office, predictably, has been poor. The very hot weather is the cause, along with a poor quality of film available. It really is time that distributors started to release better-quality films outside the usual holiday periods. They have a major responsibility for the slumps in admissions. Don't they realise that cinemagoing is a habit? People will keep going if they are enjoying the films and seeing trailers for strong releases. The public aren't completely stupid. I was pleased to see that *Congo* was turning into a flop. Why did anyone think this would be a success?

July 3   The September programme is looking poor. The Cameo has snapped up all the major pictures. Two from PolyGram who also own the Cameo – so no surprise there. They have also secured *City of Lost Children* from Entertainment Pictures despite the distributors admitting that our offer was better than the Cameo. I suspect that Cameo has played the

'Gate' card. Because the competition for the major screens is fierce, the film booker for the Gate in London and the Cameo in Edinburgh will only book a film into the Gate if they can also get the film into the Cameo. So I am completely shut out. Often I do not get a chance to bid on films at all. So much for the MMC [Monopolies and Mergers Commission] report on film exhibitions.

July 4 Phone Metro Pictures to try and make sure that the three films they picked up in Cannes will be offered both to Filmhouse and the Cameo and that the best bid will win. Too late! Metro confirm that they have already placed *La Haine* at the Cameo, because they want the Gate for London. They have already talked to the Cameo about *Stonewall* for next March. I can hardly keep annoyance out of my voice. I phone Paul at BFI and try to piece together a September programme. I know I won't make my targets for the month – and the way the rest of the autumn looks, I will have no chance of getting those admissions back.

July 5 Meet with someone who is doing statistical work on the last audience survey at Filmhouse, comparing it with the results for the Glasgow Film Theatre (both surveys were done at the same time). Results are at any early stage, but it shows, so far, that the Filmhouse audience is under-represented by the people who go to the main art-house releases, i.e. the people who go to the Cameo. I am coming to the reluctant conclusion that I might have to start offering better box-office terms to the distributors – this will set me on a direct collision with the BFI. I'd rather not do this, but if it gets to the stage where my operation is severely compromised, then I'll have to do it. If things don't improve over the next four or five months then I think I will have reached this situation.

July 18 Time to get the head down and start to programme September seriously. At this stage it's unlikely that any new films will come into the frame, so I have to make the best of what I've got (which isn't much). I have agreed with Paul, what the main new films will be, and they are booked. I spend the morning reading about British horror/thriller films. I would like to play these because we're playing *The Young Poisoner's Handbook*, so some older British horror films would be appropriate. Check the films available, always a depressing job. There is no copy of *Hound of the Baskervilles*. The rest of the Sherlock Holmes stuff is very patchy. I plan to put in some Russian films around *Burnt by the Sun – Nostalgia* and *Unfinished Piece for Mechanical Piano*. I fill in the gaps with a random assortment of old and new features, designed to pad out the rest of the programme and, I hope, provide some box-office.

August 8 A couple of days before COMEX were due to hold their annual Cambridge Film Festival conference, leaks began to appear out of the BFI that they were about to announce (another) fundamental review of their operations. Adrian Wootton (BFI Southbank) jetted in to tell us about it.

Marion Doyen, travelling separately, came to listen and put in her two-penny worth. What Adrian said was that task forces had been set up throughout the BFI to try and rationalise how the institute does its job (and, no doubt, rationalise the number of staff that work for them). The first meeting of the task group would be 9 August. They would meet again at the end of September before going to the governors' meeting with their proposals in October. Thereafter there would be consultation on the proposals, and designing of structures and systems, with implementation of the 'new order' in April 1997.

It's difficult to put on paper what I feel about all this. Sometimes I get so angry thinking about the way that the BFI operates that I want to scream. Other times I get so depressed that 'these people' are in charge of delivering and promoting film culture in this country. It's not that I disagree with what they are trying to do, it's just that they make up their minds about what the want, then get agreement from the Governors, and then conduct the most basic consultation where there is little chance of changing things. A little tinkering here and there is usually all that is possible. Ken Ingles and I decided that we had to try and provide some input before the August deadline. This way the task force would have heard COMEX's views before they decided on their own what would be best for us. We agreed to meet in London before the 9th to try and work out a response.

August 15 Edinburgh Film Festival. So far, things are going quite well. There is a great feeling of excitement inside Filmhouse. The whole building has been redecorated. The bar is busy from 9.00 am till 3.00 am the following morning and box-office for the festival is high. There are plenty of problems (as usual) and it takes constant monitoring to keep the whole thing on track. In the middle of all this I've got to complete the booking for the October programme and get the brochure done by the end of next week. At the end of the following week, I'm off to the Toronto Film Festival to have a look. The main problem for me as a programmer is that I don't get the chance to see all the first-run films before I have to book them. This is so mad.

August 28 Well, it's all over. The festival has been a huge success, artistically, critically and at the box-office – more than ever before. This has proved to be a bit of a mixed blessing as far as Filmhouse is concerned. At times the sheer number of people in the building was overwhelming. However, a few major incidents aside – such as a fishtank cracking and showering the bar with water one hour before the lunchtime rush, things went quite smoothly. Not that there isn't room for improvement, but that can wait until we are all a bit further away from this year's event. Next year is the festival's fiftieth birthday, so it will be a biggie.

August 31 The afternoon was spent quietly trying to complete the October brochure. Meeting of the French Film Festival company to discuss this year's programme. It's much stronger than last year, in part due to the fact that we have moved the festival until after the London Film Festival. For the last three years, we played the festival in October (before London) and LFF put a bar on screening any of the titles they were screening (a prime example of two cultural organisations working together to make sure the maximum number of people see a particular film – NOT!). Who runs the LFF? Who supplies services and support to Filmhouse? Whose job is it to promote film culture across the whole country? Who should be in a position to force strategic decision making? The BFI of course!

September 10 I arrived in Toronto on the evening of Friday the 8th. Checked into the hotel and went to the Festival Centre to register. Every festival is different – different atmosphere, different ways of seeing films. First impressions of this one are good. Once I had found the registration desk, I was given my badge, a list of instructions on how to see films, and a chronological list of all the films I could get into with my pass. Also a list of all the cinemas and their addresses. So far, so good. Some of the most useful things for me to see are already past, like *Four Rooms*, while *Beyond the Clouds* doesn't screen till after I've gone. No matter. Today I've got films from 2.30 pm. Agnieszka Holland's film about the love-affair between Rimbaud and Verlaine, then Chabrol's *A Judgement in Stone*, then a piece of Czech depression to round off the day – lovely.

A Day at the Festival I dropped in at the public box-office on the off-chance. I managed to get tickets for four films I thought I would miss because the press shows were over. So it is possible to buy tickets despite what everyone says. I would have waited till the day of the screening to get free public tickets at the industry box-office, but they are usually sold out by that time. Fifty dollars is a small price to pay. Who knows, I might feel in a festival mood yet. Off to lunch on a high.

2.15 pm – While wandering about looking for something to eat, I came across a cinema that I'm going to after lunch. Shock – there's a queue of people already for the press show. So, I skip lunch, join the queue. I'm now in the cinema waiting for the film to start. Everyone is talking in loud voices. Having listened to them for fifteen minutes, I've come to the conclusion that no one knows anything about film. It's all opinion. Some of it informed, most of it personal. I'm not actually against this – too many people think they know definitively what is good and worthwhile. Most people know nothing, but so what! If you get off on a film, whatever the film, then no one can tell you it's a bad one. (A beautiful man has just walked in! Pity there isn't a seat next to me.) I'm stuck with an old bag in brown cords, trainers and what seems to me to be a bad case of psoriasis (much scratching). The lights are going down now, so bye!

4.50 pm – Same cinema, different seat. *Soul Survivor* the film. The last film, *Total Eclipse*, was very strange. Emotions I went through: interest, bore-dom, shock, bafflement. It was beautiful in parts, stupid in others. I was

177

moved a lot in parts, in others not at all. Leonardo di Caprio was great, except when he had to wear a silly moustache towards the end. He kept his cock covered – surprise. David Thewlis didn't – surprise also, although he needn't have bothered. What an ugly body, as Rimbaud (di Caprio) said. Lights down again!

6.00 pm – I leave the film – *Soul Survivor* – early. Bored out of my mind. The usual gangster story with nothing to redeem it. Dull script, very ordinary camera work, no interest whatsoever, and I'm starving. Chinese restaurant next door to the cinema is empty except for two sets of film delegates who were in the same film and obviously had the same idea as me. Sometimes I think that doing this job spoils the movies for me. I see so many that it takes a lot to surprise me, or stimulate me, or even hold my interest. Anyway, high hopes for the next one, *A Judgement in Stone* by Claude Chabrol. He's been a bit off of late. We screened his last two films at Filmhouse during the French Film Festival. *A Story of Women* was great, *Madame Bovary* terrible. But *Judgement in Stone* is at least a good book. The food is arriving so I had better stop.

7.25 pm – Feeding frenzy to get into the Chabrol. The cinema is full of American distributors – they are all wankers! (I'm trying to hide what I am writing because one of them is trying to read over my shoulder.) The conversations are all about what is a 'hot ticket', but none of them can agree. Is it possible that the film business is so unpredictable because so many of the people involved in it don't have a fucking clue? Lights go down.

9.50 pm – Abandoned the idea of a Czech end to the evening, and I have come home to sleep. The Chabrol film was well up to expectation. Isabelle Huppert and Sandrine Bonnaire were brilliant. The audience enjoyed it. It will play well in Edinburgh. Just before the start of the screening there was a huge row in the cinema because about forty people arrived too late to get seats and were standing in the aisle and refusing to leave. All the signs around the festival say first come first served, so I don't know why they were getting worked up. However, I got in by queuing for over half an hour so I don't care. Last job tonight is to plan tomorrow's schedule.

September 19 We are fast approaching the most crucial booking period, January–March, when, if the titles are right, we can earn the bulk of our annual box-office income. At the moment, there are far too many titles jostling for January slots. This can work to my advantage. If a lot of titles come out at the same time, then I am more or less guaranteed to get some because the Cameo can only take so many. On the other hand, the distributors may decide to spread the films out, making it easier for the Cameo to programme more.

November 18 The box-office doldrums continued through October.

Only *The Big Sleep* did even respectable business. After that one week it was back to very low admission figures, especially for *The Neon Bible* which had the worst first-run figures of any film at Filmhouse for years. Being over £20,000 behind in box-office targets, the budget for this year had to be radically revised – taking the £20,000 already lost out of the calculations and revising expenditure to make sure we break even (I hope!) at the end of the year. Luckily the bar is performing above its target level. Nevertheless, all non-urgent expenditure, including spending on cultural events, is frozen to the end of the financial year. The box-office collapse has shown just how fragile our economy is. The quality of films has been poor, and distributors, in trying to maximise their earning potential have been saving their releases for times of the year when they think their box-office potential will be maximised. So what we've had is bunching of titles around a few months in the year. The only benefit of bunching has been that the Cameo has been unable to book all the big titles.

December 12   What a terrible year! Box-office has been so erratic – completely unpredictable. Budgeting is so difficult in these circumstances. The only possible course of action is to spend as little as possible. Grants from the Scottish Film Council, Edinburgh District and Lothian Regional Councils are under serious threat for next year. If we lose any money from these sources, then we could all be in deep shit. We have no more fat to cut out of the operation. Staffing is at a minimum possible for this size of operation. If we have to make redundancies, it will mean a scaling down of operations.

It's a shame this diary cannot end on any sort of positive note but there is absolutely nothing positive to be said. The whole sector is miserable and under threat, and no one down in London seems to care!

The Censor

Richard Falcon

Richard Falcon is an examiner at the British Board of Film Classification. The following extract illustrates the kind of issues which he regularly faces in the course of his work.

April 4 A work diary is, for me, largely a list of films and videos viewed and written about. The basic pattern of my working week is that I view three and a half days, have a half-day weekly meeting with the other examiners and the three members of management, and the fifth day is spent on other tasks: writing replies to members of the public, co-ordinating the review function committee, writing minutes, holding student days, following longer-term projects, etc.

Today's viewing: two films on the big screen and a soft porn video. To get the porn out of the way, here's an extract from my report:

A model named Heidi Lynne introduces a series of models posing and stripping in outdoor scenarios involving water. A 'Native American' model dances for rain, a woman poses in a swimming pool, a model takes a bath in a large champagne glass, two models wash down an MG, and Heidi dances amid a mock jungle waterfall. All nudity here is perfectly acceptable at 18, with no individual shot or sequence causing any problems for this category.

The films, of course, are more interesting. *Tank Girl* and *Bombay*. The former is an example of how examiners tend to enjoy run-of-the-mill films far more than many critics seem to. My report says:

Wacky and hyperactive, but very enjoyable adaptation of Dark Horse Comic's popular 'Tank Girl' comic book series. More *Dick Tracy* than Tim Burton's *Batman*, *Tank Girl* incorporates splash panels and animated sequences from the comic books at key action sequences and lands the whole thing with a 60s Pop art feel – e.g. at one point Tank Girl is hit over the head and we are given a black screen with a speech bubble reading 'This is me unconscious'. The film doesn't take itself seriously (in the best sense of those words), even throwing in a *Rocky Horror* musical number featuring 'Let's Do It' (the only connection with the narrative being the lyric 'even educated kangaroos do it'). The self-consciousness of all this doesn't detract from the excitement, especially given the eclectic soundtrack featuring Björk among others, as well as punk originals like Richard Hell and the Voidoids, but it does strongly affect the classification of the following 'issue' moments.

Reel Two, 14 minutes. After Tank Girl has awoken out of her black panel, she finds herself on a plane and cracks tough with the troops who have captured her ('I like pain'). She flirts with one of the baddies and offers to 'change his oil'. 'Don't be stupid', says one of the others, 'she'll bite it off.' 'The moment I feel teeth, you feel lead,' says the trooper, standing up and undoing his fly below screen. This would be a strong moment of sexual threat in another context. But this is Tank Girl, the post-punk female superhero who climbs into a tank to Isaac Haye's 'Shaft' theme and sits astride the long barrel as she points it at the villains saying, 'Does this make you feel inadequate?' Tank Girl is no representation of female vulnerability in need of the paternalistic protection of a censor. Instead, she mocks the size of his penis (the villain's, that is) and breaks his neck with her thighs. Tank Girl's wisecracking invulnerability, the pow, zowee, Pop-art nature of the action and the humour here make this unproblematic at 15, as well as making the final fights seem restrained by anyone's standards. The villain here too is comic-book stuff. MacDowell stuffs the heroine inside a large chute and later tries to drown the little girl in it, but again this is more *Flash Gordon* than anything else. Similarly, the implication that the tough ten-year-old ('Don't say buttsmear, Sam, say asshole,' chides Tank Girl at one point) has been dressed up as a school girl to sell to the brothel punters is in context a part of a wider joke about rejecting the appeal to male fetishism in female dress and which typifies Tank Girl as a feisty post-feminist heroine. In any case, if this seems too highflown a piece of contextualisation, then consider that the sequence goes straight into a fullblown Cole Porter production number. The 15 classification should cover all of this (including one 'motherfucker' and one 'fuck' in dialogue).

April 5 Weekly meeting. The standard pattern of these meetings involves picking out items from a complete computer run-out of all material viewed in the previous week, separate discussion of individual 'problem' films and videos, and frequently a presentation. This one was on sex videos and distinguishing between 18 and R18 tapes. Of interest, too, today was a discussion of two very good Hindi movies: *Bombay* and *Andolan*. The latter has been heavily cut for PG [Parental Guidance] by the video distributor, ruining what was a very good film. *Bombay* is going to further viewings as very strong arguments have been put up by examiners in favour of allowing the Hindi family audience to see it. It has already passed 15 in a Tamil dub. Controversial in its homeland, the film deals with communal strife in India and contains rioting sequences which are unprecedented at PG, including children being doused with petrol and threatened with immolation.

April 6 TV movie, 50s schlock, soft porn (*Gang Bang, Lily in Winter, The Navy vs. Night Monsters* – not hard to work out which is which). Fairly typical paddle in the post-modern *Bilderflut*. An arm being ripped off on-screen by a monster plant in *Night Monsters*, too strong for PG still. Mamie Van Doren telling an alien victim 'I've seen men in deep shock before, it doesn't bother me' is beyond any kind of classification.

April 7   Another manga, two soft-porn tapes, a stultifying TV movie and a problem 70s movie about nuns. A day to point up the weird nature of the job. *The Nun and the Devil* exists in a morass of contexts: the sixteenth-century sources and the Stendahl novel it's based on; the history of representations of religious eroticism; the earlier success of *The Devils* (the film was first released in a cut form in the early 70s); and its mix of the Italian art movie and the sado-erotic exploitation movie. The problem with one scene with a naked, manacled nun astride a sharp horse being tortured. Shot with a sense of the perverse beauty of the image, it could nevertheless be seen to contravene the OPA [Obscene Publications Act]. I do not want to cut this and write a long report at home. (It later passed 18 uncut after the BBFC management weighed up the issues.)

April 10   Can't escape nuns. Early Almodóvar film, *Dark Habits*, sub-mitted on video about heroine addict nuns. Clearly 15 as this is camp stuff, unlikely to be accused of glamorising drugs. Grotesque low-budget martial arts movie (nothing against martial arts movies, this is just a particularly poor example) and a TV movie – the latter viewed with Stephen Whittle, Chief Advisor (Editorial Policy) at the BBC, who wanted to see how examiners classify material. Examiners can become fairly used to predicting the twists in formulaic narratives, Stephen seemed also able to predict when they would occur – to the minute!

April 12   Children's TV material yesterday, and catching up with replying to letters from members of the public. *Bombay* discussed again at the weekly meeting today: whether it is possible to pass this film PG when there is a sequence of near-immolation of children and when some sequences are as upsetting as *The Killing Fields*. Hindi-speaking examiner Imtiaz Karin explained what happened to the film in India, where it was withdrawn by the police the day after it opened because it was felt to be too inflammatory. The Hindi version has now been passed PG.

April 19   A rerun of a classic moment in BBFC history – 3 November 1971 to be precise, as *Straw Dogs*, submitted by the BFI, is screened on film in the theatre. Watched by the entire examining team in lieu of a meeting. Most of us are extremely familiar with the film and it has often been revived in the cinemas in its original X version (the one where, according to the myth, the BBFC's cut made the rape scene look even more like buggery). No real need for everybody to see it, apart from lodging it as a precedent in all our minds, and a key piece of history. Like the original examiners, we were enthusiastic about the film. Why did the BFI submit the much shorter US print (in which the rape scene was much shortened to get an MPAA

[Motion Picture Association of America] 'R' rating in the 70s? *Straw Dogs* passed 18, no cuts, and is still a hugely powerful cinematic experience.

April 21   Two martial arts movies – *Secret Force* and *Shaolin Martial Arts*. The latter is a Shaw Bros. epic from the 70s with typically fantastic (in both senses) fight choreography; given 18 for its gore. *Madonna – Innocence Lost* a US TV biopic with a lookalike actress playing Madonna and Dean Stockwell as her Dad sitting in the suburbs worrying about her as she goes to New York to be a superstar. I pass it as a 12 because of some mild sex scenes in which Madonna uses her sexuality to make it ('Wow, Madonna, you make love just like a man'). Then *Transgression*, a low-budget independent US thriller about a newsreader inviting a sexually sadistic serial killer to phone in and make contact with her. The heroine becomes a murderer herself in the process as the killer reveals her own dark desires to her. A bleak and depressing experience, rather like *Henry, Portrait of a Serial Killer*, but nowhere nearly as morally complex and frequently exploitative. Some examiners want a reject, although with a lot of cutting the sequences in which the sexual violence become titillatory could be removed, leaving the video less likely to be considered obscene. Some doubts about whether this can be achieved.

The Journalist

Neil McCartney

Editor of various trade newsletters, including Screen Finance, *Neil McCartney provides an account of some of the major news-stories that broke during the year.*

EFDO (European Film Distribution Office), mentioned in this diary, assists the theatrical distribution of mid- to low-budget European feature films by providing conditionally repayable interest-free loans to European distributors from at least three different countries. Audio-visual EUREKA is a programme that aims to stimulate the European audio-visual market by favouring the establishment of a network of partners around concrete projects which concern all spheres of the audio-visual sector. Euro Aim is the marketing structure of the MEDIA programme of the European Union, and helps European independent producers and distributors finance and promote their production of the international marketplace.

April 4   Start to look at the big survey that we are doing on forthcoming film releases for inclusion in this week's *Screen Finance*. This survey is always a problem because many distributors are reluctant to give information on their release plans, or to supply stills of their films – even if they are coming out in only a couple of weeks. Arrange to get hold of a press copy of the report on film by the Select Committee on National Heritage, which is due to be released this afternoon. Also start to ring round to find out what happened at yesterday's meeting of the European Union's Council of Ministers for Communications and Culture. This was a crucial meeting because it was due to discuss plans for the forthcoming five-year Media II Programme which is supposed to come into operation when the first programme expires at the end of this year. So it is important for us to carry something on it.

April 5   The most interesting story is about the council of ministers meeting. It seems that the ministers reached an agreement in principle to back the plan, which involves the allocation of Ecu400 million over five years to support initiatives in the areas of distribution, development and training but that there is still a lot of doubt about much of the fine detail. I can't say I am surprised. There does not seem to have been much analysis of the performance of the old Media programme, or enough work on how the new programme will work.

The other good story is about the select committee report. It has put forward a package of eleven measures including an accelerated system of tax write-offs for production expenditure, incentives to bring in new investment and make Britain a more attractive location for overseas producers, a new training scheme and an enhanced role for the British Film Commission (BFC). All of this has generally been welcomed by the film industry. But there must be considerable doubt as to whether any of the proposals will be taken up by the government.

April 24   The next *Screen Finance* is due in ten days time. There are a few things we can be sure to have – such as film starts in April and admissions in March (which will give us the first-quarter figures), plus our analysis of the type and performance of feature films shown on national network television in the first quarter. Not many other story ideas around. But we certainly need to get something on the Arts Council guidelines on which feature film projects will qualify for support from the National Lottery.

April 27   We have got a good story about Handmade preparing a production slate of four films – which would be its first features since *Nuns on the Run* in·1989. An early candidate for page one – if nobody else gets hold of it between now and next Wednesday.

April 28   Hamburg. I'm at a distribution seminar organised by EFDO and Audiovisual EUREKA. There is an opening speech from Gilbert Gregoire, vice-president of the Federation Internationale des Associations de Distributeurs de Films (FIAD). He criticises the notion of setting up pan-European distribution entities and also advocates that distribution support should be allocated along lines rather like those used for the automatic aid system in France – so a distributor would be awarded money according to the number of admissions it achieved for European films in European countries other than their home territories. It sounds like it would be a significant threat to the current EFDO-type system where awards are semi-automatic but where the size is related to the anticipated cost of distribution rather than the results.

April 29   The new head of the Media Programme, Jacques Delmoly, gives a closing speech in which he repeats his view that several schemes can run in parallel. He also expresses the view that there ought to be some provision in Media II for the exhibition sector – something that was not provided for in the original plan but which this month's meeting of the council of ministers agreed to bring in.

May 2   London. Spend the day subbing. There is the Handmade story, which so far has not emerged anywhere else, plus details of the Arts Council guidelines for the Lottery, and an application from the BFI for Lottery backing for three films. There is also a story about BSkyB picking up free-television rights to *Richard III*, the proposed film of Ian McKellan's version of the Shakespeare play. BSkyB was already due to take pay-television rights, as part of its output deal with British Screen Finance. But this appears to be the first time that it has taken free-television rights as well.

May 4   Tomorrow EFDO is due to consider an application backed by four subsidiaries of Twentieth Century-Fox for distribution support for *An Awfully Big Adventure*. This will almost certainly be rejected, given the new EFDO rule that applicants should be 51 per cent European-owned (a rule adopted in the wake of the row over UIP eight months ago). So there will be a story there, provided it does not appear anywhere else. We also know that the European Script Fund is trying to recover about Ecu500,000 in development loans that should have been repaid, but have not.

May 16   We have a bit of a problem over what to put on the front page of this week's issue of *Screen Finance* – the last one before we go to Cannes. The EFDO/Fox story will do for the bottom of page one, but is not really strong enough for the top. The other option is a story about the 'Paris Paper' on distribution, given that we now have a copy of it. This would be worth running anyway and is particularly important in the light of the growing row over Media II, which will clearly be a hot topic in Cannes. The problem here is that the paper is now a few weeks old. In the end decide that we really have no choice other than to go with this story.

May 19   Cannes. I gather during the day that a significant row is brewing over the French attempt to push for an automatic system for the allocation of distribution support – with the French meeting opposition from more or less everyone other than the Spanish. All in all, a rather poisonous atmosphere is threatening to develop. One cannot but feel that the primary responsibility lies with the EC and the politicians. The trouble is being caused by the fact that there is still so much uncertainty over so many aspects of Media II, only one month before its final shape is supposed to be determined.

May 22   Meeting with an Irish accountant, who says that Warner has just completed the finance for its *Michael Collins* film using £10 million worth of Section 35 money. But he adds that there is a problem with Section 35. Many of the big investors who were interested in using it have now committed themselves and will not be available again for some time, given the rule that a single company or individual cannot invest more than £1 million under Section 35 over a three-year period. So promoters of Section 35 schemes are having to look for smaller investors, and this is much more complicated and time-consuming.

May 25   London. We clearly have to do a big piece about the Media II debate and related issues (such as the French-backed proposal for a Ecu200 million guarantee fund to encourage private investment in the audiovisual sector, which was also discussed at Cannes but which looks likely to be abandoned because of funding problems).

May 30 It seems that Stephen Dorrell will reveal proposals to use National Lottery money to support the distribution of UK films, as well as their production. But he will not say anything about tax incentives, on the grounds that decisions in this area have to be handled by the Chancellor of the Exchequer. One other story that has emerged in the last few days is that Metrodome Films is planning to sell off 40 per cent of its equity for £2.3 million. This seems a lot of money, given that Nik Powell and Steve Woolley got only £600,000 when they sold 49 per cent of Scala to Chrysalis last November. Clearly the deal is going to be watched very closely by other small independents.

June 6 We don't seem to have received anything from the Department of National Heritage (DNH) about the Dorrell statement. All we have is responses from the BFC and the BFI, but it rather looks as though the statement went as expected – a big fuss about Lottery money (which was known about anyway) and all tax decisions left to the Treasury. Bit of a disappointing return from the first policy statement since 1984.

June 7 There is an interesting story brewing about the plans drawn up by Third Millennium (a subsidiary of the Malaysian-owned company George Town Holdings) to build a £40 million studio and leisure complex on the former Leavesden Aerodrome in Hertfordshire – where the James Bond film *Goldeneye* is currently being shot. Unclear whether this scheme will get planning permission – or whether it is a sensible idea, given that the current demand for UK studio space may not last.

June 24 Main story is the EU Council of Ministers meeting. Everyone seems to be unhappy with the French, who have not actually got what they wanted. So the French presidency seems to have been about as successful as the UK one a few years ago. Also stories on multiplex growth, British Screen's latest film and Screen Edge, the new low-budget video label.

July 6 It looks as though the total number of films put into production – and the aggregate investment involved – will both be slightly lower than in the same period last year. But in both cases the figures are still well above those of 1993.

July 11 Get hold of the UK admissions figures for May – which show a year-on-year drop for the fourth month in succession. Total admissions for the first five months are lower than in 1993. It is beginning to look as though figures for the year as a whole will be down for the first time in eleven years. Some exhibitors are blaming competition from the Lottery – which they say is soaking up disposable income and encouraging people to stay in on Saturday nights to watch the draw on television. But this seems implausible to me. Why aren't all leisure activities in trouble? The drop is more likely to be due to the simple shortage of crowd-pulling films.

August 7 It appears that the Isle of Man government, which drew up

187

plans for a production incentive scheme about eighteen months ago, has backed its first film – *The Brylcreem Boys*. It seems that the authorities will be providing about 25 per cent of the £4.8 million budget through a mixture of tax credits and deficit financing. So the scheme looks likely to repeat the Irish experience – drawing away UK productions – albeit on a smaller scale. Any chance that it will persuade the UK government to do something?

August 8   Late story comes in when we learn that Gary Sinyor is set to make his first medium-budget film – *Stiff Upper Lips*, which will have a budget of between £3.5 million and £5 million. It's good to see him progressing away from deferrals – which were a key element in *Leon the Pig Farmer* and also played a role in *Solitaire for Two*. It reinforces the view that deferrals can provide a way into the industry. But I wonder how many of the people who deferred their fees on the first two films have (a) got their money and (b) gone on to secure paid work in films.

September 11   Story about the Arts Council's selection procedure for film-production funding awards from the National Lottery – the first round of which are due to be announced on 21 September (just after our next issue). It concerns the potential problems caused by the fact that many of the people involved in the three advisory bodies that consider applications for Lottery funding will (inevitably) be themselves submitting applications (or be connected to others who are doing so). So the Arts Council has set up a fourth body made up largely of people drawn from the regional arts councils. But won't they have the same problem? A sidebar to this story is a report about the decision by the Scottish Lottery Fund (which acts separately) to award £1 million of lottery money to the £5 million project *Poor Things*, from Parallel Productions. One can see how important this money is going to become.

The level of production activity seems to have risen again. There were 11 film starts in August, the highest August total for five years. But the total for the year to date is still running behind the figure for 1995 – 52 compared with 60. There has also been an upturn in admissions, with July's ticket sales coming in at 15 per cent above the figure for the same month in 1995. But again the cumulative figure is still down, in this case by about 12 per cent.

September 19   We decide to manufacture a story about British Screen's tenth anniversary, setting out figures about how many films it has backed, how much it has put in and how much has come from other sources. British Screen says that it has put £23 million of government money into 124 films with a total budget of £261 million. It claims that the multiplier effect of its activity is about eleven. This is debatable, as some of the other money is accounted for by British Screen's own investment using returns from previous films. Critics would also argue that much of the remainder would have been invested anyway. But the record is a good one. And given that it has been almost the only source of government money over the last ten years it deserves to be celebrated.

October 2   Round-up of production starts in the first three quarters of the year. This shows that investment in films with UK producers is holding up well, although the actual number of films is down on last year. So average budgets are up, and there are far fewer films with a deferral element. The number and value of foreign films shooting in the UK is well down, but this is expected to rise again soon, given that the studios have so much work booked – as we reported last time.

October 16   Press release from the Arts Council of England about the latest Lottery awards. These include grants for two feature films for Picture Palace's *The Spire* (£1 million) and Edenwood Production's *A Midsummer Night's Dream* (£750,000). This means that this council has now awarded a total of more than £4 million to eight productions – six features, one short and one documentary. The Arts Councils of Scotland, Wales and Northern Ireland have provided a further £1.5 million for five other productions.

October 18   A call from the DNH to say that they are having a press conference with Virginia Bottomley tomorrow morning to announce the award of government money to trigger the start of the long-awaited London Film Commission (LFC). In the meantime, I check back to see what Stephen Dorrell said about this in his June policy paper. It seems he promised money without specifying how much. The DNH says that it is giving £100,000 as a one-off pump-priming exercise, and that London First (the business organisation set up to promote London) has agreed to cover the rest of the first-year costs not yet raised. I wonder how much this is. As I recall, it has been said that the LFC would need about £250,000 a year (possibly more in the start-up year). Christabel Albery, who is charge of raising finance, has arranged some money but I'm not sure how much.

October 27   Decide to investigate post-production facilities in Dublin. Several people have told me that Ireland's Section 35 tax-incentive scheme has been good for London's post-production facilities. Although Section 35 has pulled a lot of production work to Ireland, a lot of the post-production work has been done over here because Dublin simply does not have the facilities. But there are fears that Irish companies will expand their capacity in order to get more of the extra work.

November 1   It turns out that Michael Higgins, the Irish Minister of Culture, was speaking at the BFI a week or so ago and said that he was expecting soon to take receipt of a report commissioned by the Irish Film Board on the Irish post-production sector. Apparently the report is supposed to identify gaps in the sector and suggest ways of rectifying them. In addition, Ardmore Sound has recently announced plans to spend £1 million in the refurbishment of a defunct sound stage. So there is something going on. But the UK studios claim not be worried they say that it will take years for the Irish studios to present a real challenge.

News that Euro Aim, the Media 95–backed action line to promote independent production has almost ceased operations. It has stopped paying its staff and has cancelled its stand at next week's Mifed film market in Milan. It seems that it has simply run out of money because it has not yet received money from the European Commission to cover this year's budget (and some of last year's as well). I wonder if this is going to be the first of a number of such events. Financial problems would appear to be increasingly likely as the action lines come to the end of their funding, without any certainty as to what will happen next year.

November 17 I attend a meeting of the Lunch Club, an organisation which gets together people from the film and television industry for lunch once a month, using the hook of an after-lunch speaker. I have never been to one of these before, and I am curious to see what they are like. There is the added attraction that this month's speaker is Mark Shivas, the head of BBC Films, whom I know slightly, and who I think will be interesting. The talk is quite entertaining, and Mark makes a couple of interesting points in response to questions. He says that the BBC backs ten films a year, putting in between £250,000 and £1.2 million. When the contribution is small, it goes solely against rights. When it's about £700,000, they put about £450,000 against rights and the rest goes in as equity. He's a bit waspish about the British Screen/BSkyB deal. Also says that a lot of people have started to come to the BBC since Channel Four set up its own distribution company. Sounds as though this would be worth following up.

November 27 I notice that Stephen Dorrell's June statement says that the Arts Council of England will provide up to £70 million of Lottery money for production funding by the year 2000, and £14 million of distribution funding. So what's happened about the distribution side? Why is there no reference to the Lottery money provided by the Arts Councils of Scotland, Wales and Northern Ireland? What guidelines do these councils use anyway? Do they differ from those used by the Arts Council of England? Is it possible to get money from more than one of them?

In the evening, I go to a meeting of the New Producers' Alliance which is devoted to Channel Four's film policy. Sadly David Aukin, the head of drama, does not turn up. A little disappointing, in that not all that much emerges. Much of it is about how to approach the channel with a project. For instance, there is no point in doing a budget and schedule unless Aukin likes the script. But a few useful facts: since 1982 it has backed more than 300 films at an average budget of £2 million, of which its average contribution was £800,000; it gets 5,000 scripts a year, of which between 15 and 18 actually get commissioned; it spends £1 million a year on development. And so on.

November 28 On the Lottery, it seems that a film can get money from more than one advisory body, and that at least one film is trying to do so. *Stella Does Tricks* got money from the Arts Council of Scotland on 3 November, and is hoping to get further finance from the Arts Council of England on 7 December. There appears to be no reason why it should not do so.

As expected, nothing in Kenneth Clarke's Budget statement. It's the same every year. All this optimism and it comes to nothing. But I am a bit suspicious about the behaviour of Bottomley and the DNH. They seem to have gone out of their way to tell film industry people that they were lobbying for tax changes and that there was a good chance of success. Were they sincere? Somehow I doubt it.

About to go home when at about 10.00 pm when I get a telephone call from a friend telling me that the government has decided to pull out of Eurimages. Absolutely unbelievable. I can't believe they'd be so stupid. How depressing.

November 29   It's true. The government is pulling out of Eurimages after only three years. It says that the subscription, which costs a mere £2 million a year, was seen as less necessary because of the 'buoyancy' of the UK film industry. Talk about short sighted. There are also hints that the government thought it was already doing enough for the film industry with the European Co-production Fund (which serves a very different purpose), and the Lottery money (which is not supposed to be used to replace existing government spending, but clearly will be).

The government does not seem to realise how much the UK benefits from Eurimages membership. On the one hand, UK producers probably get more out of the fund than the government puts in (and not every country can say that). When you add in the other money invested in these projects, the amount of UK economic activity generated as a result of the Eurimages subscription must be many times higher. On the other hand, the participation in Eurimages projects has done so much to establish links between UK and continental producers. Much of this will now be thrown away.

It seems that the decision was taken without consulting anybody in the film industry. I remember how long it took to persuade the government to join Eurimages in the first place. It's so depressing to see all this reversed overnight.

191

The Television Documentarist

David Thompson

An experienced television director, David Thompson has made numerous documentaries on film-makers including Michael Powell, Peter Greenaway, Jean Renoir and Quentin Tarantino. His diary concerns the production of his latest project, a film on the controversial Hollywood-based Dutch director Paul Verhoeven.

May 2   In the afternoon, a brief visit to the BBC reveals to me that the *Omnibus* 'team' have been considering moving *Verhoeven* to 1996. I point out that the *Showgirls* opening date is still provisionally October, and I need the support of the distributor in the shape of free film clips to make the film at all.

May 17   I go to the BBC, where I now hear *Verhoeven* is definitely OK for money and the placing this season. Lorraine Silberstein, who was my trusty production assistant/researcher on *Tarantino* last year, is free to begin work with me.

June 14   I begin my concentrated reviewing of the Verhoeven oeuvre. I've always found his films compelling, but now they look really ahead of their time in their refusal to follow any kind of 'political correctness'. No false sentiment, very 'in your face', as a friend of mine once put it. Perhaps I'll use that as a title for the documentary.

June 15   I read through the first section – all that has been translated so far – of Robert Van Scheer's 'authorised' biography of Verhoeven, which Faber hope to publish in January. A fascinating childhood spent in the shadow of the war, with constant Allied bombing raids on The Hague. I also identify strongly with anyone who drew comic strips as a kid (as I did) and had parents anxious for their son to follow a respectable, safe 'professional' career (as mine were too).

June 16   Off to Putney for a 5.30 meeting with Nigel Williams. Nigel is notorious for hardly ever setting foot in the BBC, preferring to do his business from home, where somehow he also manages to write novels, plays and screenplays. He tells me he's determined to keep going with *Omnibus* despite the difficulties in Music and Arts. Nigel is tremendously supportive, intrigued by the stories I've unearthed on Verhoeven, and very happy for me to proceed much as I did with *Tarantino*, basing the film around a long interview (which is about all the access one usually gets these days). It's rare to find someone so trusting in this field, and so willing to let you make the film you want to make and then judge it on those terms.

June 19 I have begun communications again with Verhoeven's very friendly assistant Stacy, but it seems too early to confirm any filming dates other than 'in the summer'. *Showgirls* has now been brought forward to a September opening in the USA, but Guild in London can confirm nothing other earlier than possibly mid-November. This enables me to put off the start of my edit until the beginning of October.

June 22 I make contact with Robert Van Scheers, who is keen to participate in the *Omnibus* programme. He's coming to London soon to go over the book with Verhoeven, who will be here recording the music for *Showgirls* with Dave Stewart. I call Stacy to see if a meeting with Verhoeven can be arranged, but she tells me he'll be too busy. Very frustrating.

June 28 I send a fax to Guild asking for their help to meet Verhoeven while he's in London. Even if we didn't really discuss the programme, a meeting like the one I had with Tarantino before the filming could open up a lot of avenues and make me a familiar and supportive face.

June 29 Rob Van Scheers phones to say he's in London, and even informs me where they're recording the music. But I have to keep mum.

June 30 Rob calls again to say he's been up to the studio, and Verhoeven has responded positively to his manuscript. We agree to meet up on Saturday evening as Verhoeven is going to Holland that day. Guild call me to say they're aware of how useful a meeting with my subject would be, and request a list of all the *Omnibus* profiles of film directors plus cassettes! I point out that this is an awful lot of stuff to view, but I duly compile the list and send copies of the films on Sidney Lumet, Peter Greenaway and Ridley Scott – they already have Renoir and Tarantino.

July 1 Rob calls to confirm our dinner, but says that when he broached the idea to Verhoeven of my coming along to meet him at the studio (even for a few minutes), the reaction was very negative! Our dinner goes well, and I find myself much in agreement with Rob about the virtues of his fellow countryman, and his deserving status as an important contemporary film director. It seems, though, that a lot of Dutch people (especially the critics) have a very snobbish attitude towards Verhoeven; his most 'realistic' film, *Spetters* virtually caused a national scandal. *Spetters*, in its unflinching, sexually explicit look at working-class youth in provincial Holland, almost signalled an end to Verhoeven's Dutch career and remains still his most shocking film. Rob agrees to become my consultant on the *Omnibus*.

July 4 Alexis Lloyd calls to assure me that the Guild are 100 per cent behind the programme and that he is trying hard to arrange a meeting with

Verhoeven in London. When I return home, there's a message awaiting me that I can join Alexis and Verhoeven for breakfast at 8.00 am on Thursday. At last!

July 6   As instructed, I go to the Meridien Hotel at 8.15 am. After a slow start, the conversation takes wing and I find Verhoeven charming, relaxed and open to the proposed filming. He refers to *Showgirls* as 'real sleazy' and says this is to *Spetters* what *Basic Instinct* was to *The Fourth Man*. I feel I pass the litmus test when I declare my enthusiasm for *Spetters*. Before leaving him – after about thirty minutes of conversation – I meet his wife Martine, who is equally relaxed and amiable.

July 11   Lorraine and I decide to be in LA for the period 30 July to 11 August. So many people in LA will not confirm dates – 'Call me when you're in town' – that I found last year staying for at least a fortnight gave us sufficient flexibility without crippling the budget. Stacy has been very efficient sending me fax numbers for potential interviewees, so I send off a whole bunch – Arnold Schwartzenegger, Sharon Stone, Michael Douglas, Joe Eszterhas, Jan De Bont. I know many of these will be difficult to pin down.

July 14   Guild have arranged a screening for us of the showreel of *Showgirls* at 11.15 am; the scenes seem to follow the script closely, and the direction has plenty of Verhoeven bravura to it. Very 'in your face'. The big show numbers are really spectacular, no question. Alexis Lloyd again pledges his support, and I say that the only person I'm worried about is Rob Houwer, the producer of Verhoeven's Dutch films, as they're not on great terms and we need his OK over clips.

July 26   A last full day in the office before we leave for LA. So far only Alan Marshall, producer of *Basic Instinct* and *Showgirls*, Jon Davison, producer of *Robocop*, and Peter Bart, chief editor of *Variety*, have confirmed dates. We have also confirmed our plan to film Paul and Dave Stewart at Air Studios on Friday working on the music; Dave Stewart has also agreed to be interviewed then.

July 28   I leave with Lorraine for Belsize Park and Air Studios, who have been exceptionally helpful about our filming there. Eventually we are admitted to where Paul and Dave are at work, and both appear to be very preoccupied. But everyone cheerfully accepts the crew, and after a while we just blend in. Despite my initial concerns that he might do 'a moody rock star' turn, Dave Stewart gives a relaxed and sympathetic interview. At 8.00 pm I get a call from Rogers and Cowan in LA asking if we can shoot the Joe Eszterhas interview on Monday! Fortunately I get through to Bill straight away and he agrees it's possible.

July 31   LA. We drive over to film Joe Eszterhas in Point Dume, just north of Malibu. It's a pretty palatial residence and, before meeting Joe, we set up our equipment. True to his image, Joe turns up with slicked hair and wearing Hawaiian shorts, all very rock n' roll, and proceeds to light up a cigarette. He gives a straight-talking interview, only bristling at any hint of my application of the auteur theory to his Verhoeven-directed scripts. A good start!

August 2 We go to see *Showgirls* at the Carolco Building (soon, no doubt, to be renamed), finding ourselves sitting in front of Joe Eszterhas and family. The film is, no question, a roaring piece of drama, but for all the copious female nudity (only one male behind shot), it's hardly the great shocker some talk had suggested. Even the rape scene and the subsequent revenge are short and sharp. Once again though, Verhoeven has proven his talent for getting vibrant performances out of relative unknowns, and keeping the frame constantly alive, with some dazzling Steadicam work on the backstage scenes.

August 3 Back to Carolco again to film interviews with Alan Marshall and the new star of *Showgirls*, Elizabeth Berkeley. Alan is chummy, but reticent on camera, very much the diplomatic producer. Then we have to scramble to set up for Ms Berkeley in a boardroom, but after we lose time just trying to get in, she arrives thirty minutes late. At first she seems relaxed and engaged in the interview, but as it goes on a definite blandness creeps in. Afterwards our new soundman, Mike (who worked with us last year on Tarantino), tells me the PR guy, one Steve Newman, was directing her from behind my back all the way through, steering her away from certain topics. Such is Hollywood.

August 4 An interview with Marion Rosenberg, English-born (with accent intact) agent to Verhoeven and most of the Dutch acting talent. She confesses to losing Rutger Hauer to William Morris some time ago, unfortunately for us (we've been passed from agent to manager to publicist and are still waiting on a possible interview, as he's definitely in town shooting a movie). She has some sharp, intelligent observations to make on Paul's career, so we consider the interview well worth doing. That evening, I stay in and prepare for the big one – the interview with our main man.

August 5 We drive out to Pacific Palisades for the interview with Paul Verhoeven at midday, with the instructions that we have been allotted three hours. He is in an unpretentious, spacious house that at least feels 'lived in', unlike most 'celebrity' residences. Paul seems relaxed (when we arrive, he's watching a dance rehearsal tape of Sharon Stone, pondering its market value); as usual, there's little time for small talk, so it's quickly down to business. Martine, his welcoming wife, helps contribute to a comfortable atmosphere, and indeed he refers to her constantly as his guide on many an occasion (she advised him on the choices of all his American movies, it seems). After a rather offhand first answer, the interview takes wing and the tone is energetic, engaged and often outrageously funny. Although I'm not really happy that we had enough time, Bill and the others reassure me that it was a cracking interview, and so I feel able to relax at last.

August 7   In the morning Peter Bart of *Variety*, who claims to remember me from our last interview some five years ago, cannot, to my amusement, tell me what the 'R' rating in the USA actually means. In the afternoon, to the Sony studios for a joint interview with Jon Davison and Ed Neumeier, writer and producer on *Robocop*, who should be working with Verhoeven on his next film, *Starship Troopers*. It now looks as though we only have one more shooting day left in LA, as we have been promised Mario Kassar on Thursday.

August 10   Sharon Stone is a definite 'not possible now' (even though we were prepared to fly to Pittsburgh) and it seems Rutger Hauer has injured himself on set and is out of circulation for the present. Since all this is conveyed through his publicist, and Hauer and Verhoeven haven't spoken in years, it's difficult to know where the truth lies.

August 16   London. Paul Verhoeven kindly gave me a copy of the 'Special Edition' laser disc of *Basic Instinct* on the day of the interview. Verhoeven's commentary throughout the film is notable for two things: his unbounded fondness for Steadicam sequences, as in *Showgirls*, and his detailed conception of the plot, which he sees as entirely derived from the games set up by the Sharon Stone character. There goes my sense of the film's ambiguity!

August 23   I call in on Guild Films to meet David Willing. *Showgirls* is now definitely to be opened in London on 5 January, with a nationwide release on the 12th. This fortunately means that I can begin my edit the first week of October. David assures me that the materials on the Guild titles shouldn't be a problem, though nobody at Guild has seen the whole film. It seems Faber are now definitely aiming to have Robert's book available in January, and I have also signed up to write programme notes for a National Film Theatre retrospective next month. Thanks to the intercession of Paul Verhoeven, his difficult Dutch producer Rob Houwer has also agreed to give us clips, providing he can see a cassette of the finished programme beforehand.

August 25   I have a brief conversation with Nigel Williams. He is pleased our LA shoot went well, is still unperturbed about the lack of US stars, but warns me that a new edict says we cannot have the word 'fuck' on BBC1. But, I ask, can we show people doing it?

August 29   A few days remain before our filming trip to Holland. Lorraine has been able to make arrangements to film at Verhoeven's old school in The Hague (featured in his early student short *Feest*), and it looks like our timing is perfect for Leiden University too, as Monday will be their first day of term, with official ceremonies and welcoming parties to boot. Only the university club Verhoeven was a member of, the Minerva Society, whose own special initiation rituals he re-created in *Soldier of Orange*, has closed its doors to us. With the help of Robert Van Scheers, I have also made contact with an old university friend, Frits Boersma, who shot Verhoeven's student films and produced *Feest*.

September 1   Holland. We meet up with Rob Van Scheers at the car-hire desk and make our way to Hilversum to view Dutch TV archive. It's sadly thin on the ground – fragments of on-set reportage, very little in the way of shots of bomb damage in The Hague. Even the infamous TV show that covered *Spetters* is rather subdued (Rob said Paul recalled being assaulted by the audience – no such luck!). Then we pick up – and view – a Beta transfer of Verhoeven's first student film, *A Lizard Too Much*, which is self-consciously weird, very much under the influence of Buñuel.

September 2   I finally make telephone contact with Gerard Soeteman, Verhoeven's screenwriter on all of his Dutch films, and he agrees to an interview Wednesday morning (great relief!).

September 3   We drive to Leiden meet with the manager of the Academy to check out the university buildings. The amiable manager, Mr Van Der Molen, shows us the rooms of major significance, including the matriculation 'sweat room' which features Erik Hazelhoff's signature on the wall – he was the author of *Soldier of Orange* and is the character Rutger Hauer plays in the film. Then we find other places of interest – the church where Monday's opening ceremony will take place, and the cornerhouse which features in *A Lizard Too Much* and in which Verhoeven lived as a student.

September 4   First day's filming. We shoot the first interview with Frits Boersma (in Dutch, as his English is rather hesitant) in a classroom, and as Frits has kindly brought along a photo album with shots of a young Paul directing his student films (on the first three of which Frits was cameraman), we shoot those too. Off next to Leiden. Despite a completely misleading description of where the senior students will actually be processing, we get some footage of the initial pomp and circumstance before leaving for more Leiden exteriors. We then return to the canal by the university, where at 6 pm we are promised a taste of the initiation games for the new students (the infamous fraternity known as the Minerva Society, whose private ritual of abusing shaven-headed freshers is re-created in *Soldier of Orange*, even came over to question us when we filmed the exterior of their building). After a tiring day, I'm worried that nothing much is going to happen, but sure enough the freshers soon come jogging down the canal to be pelted with flour, fruit and eggs, as well as being made to crawl under nets and climb ropes.

September 5   We go off to Blaricum to interview Monique Van Der Ven. Monique is much like her characters in *Turkish Delight* and *Keetje Tippel* – very lively, open and direct. She even tries to phone Rutger Hauer for me,

197

but he's not answering in Holland. Then we return to Amsterdam for our 1.00 pm interview with Renee Soutendijk, who is quieter and more serious in manner than Monique, but also very open and friendly. We then find Jeroen Krabbe's house and just catch him on his return home. Jeroen gives a very relaxed interview, and he's even more outspoken than the others about Paul's outrageous behaviour on set.

September 6   This morning, off to visit Gerard Soeteman who lives just outside Rotterdam. Robert warns me that Soeteman can be a difficult man, but he was very funny and friendly with me on the phone, and he is just the same when we arrive. In interview he is a little rambling, but often very droll, even cynical. He is much amused by the way *The Fourth Man* was so well received in Holland – 'I wrote *The Fourth Man* to fuck the Dutch critics, and I succeeded.' As time is pressing we leave for Utrecht where we interview Robert in his apartment. We finish in just enough time for the crew to get to Schipol airport. I am sorry to be leaving Holland so soon. It has certainly been an intensive visit, but the crew have been very patient, and I feel we have some excellent material for the documentary.

September 7   Back to the office, where the next task is to sort out a list of what we want from the Dutch TV archive, and have the interviews transcribed. I make contact with Hedda Archbold; she once worked as a BBC secretary, and is not only Dutch but also acted in a small role in *The Fourth Man*. She is more than happy to translate material for us, especially as she knows something about the subject.

September 20   Aware suddenly that my editing days are looming close I start to panic that I really haven't got a handle on my material yet. Today at least I manage to stay at home and go through a number of the interviews.

September 21   In the morning I visit Hedda for a quick translation of the dialogues in Verhoeven's student films, as well as those 'missing' scenes from *Soldier of Orange* . I promise to send on to her the videos of the Dutch TV archive, which should be arriving soon.

September 22   After lunch, I go directly to Soho Square for a screening of *Showgirls*. On a second viewing, the film's weaknesses come to the fore (mainly the script), but there are still many moments that for me have the authentic Verhoeven 'edge'.

October 2   Much to my relief my eternally cheerful editor Dave Monk still has some work to do on his last film, so I have some more time in hand to look at my rushes plus the material from Dutch TV that has finally arrived. Lorraine called me last Friday to warn me that there was still no cassette or EPK (electronic press kit) of *Showgirls*, and she has collected some of the reviews for me (it opened in the USA on 22 September). They are uniformly terrible, criticising the script, the lead actress, just about everything. Above all, they hate the sleaziness of the world portrayed and the unpleasant characters – that much I could have predicted. I begin to doubt my initial positive reaction to the film, but reconcile myself that I am now so steeped in the Verhoeven world that even a relatively poor film has its interesting aspects, not least the vigour of the direction.

October 3   I am able finally to look at all the material to hand and begin marking up sections to be digitised into the Lightworks. There seems to be more than enough to cover all the films, so it's now a question of what to omit; I can see that *Keetje Tippel* and *Total Recall* are obvious candidates and am pretty certain I won't be able to integrate the laser-disc sequences.

October 4   Finally I sit down with Dave and begin discussing the film. As I still want more time to prepare an order of sync sections for him, I suggest he begins by cutting some short sequences out of the music recording and mixing sessions. I always hope that at least it gets an editor going to have something to cut rather than just laboriously assemble.

October 16   The third week of editing – in theory, over half-way! With the assembly completed, I can now begin to try out certain clips. I'm concentrating for now on the middle section, i.e. the narrative stuff. It's impossible to cover *Showgirls* at this stage without the film itself to hand (it's still not available).

October 19   Guild have now assured me that we'll get the *Showgirls* tape by Friday. The EPK has turned up, and it's pretty disappointing, as the on-set material has been jerkily cut up to avoid any nudity! The footage we have from Canal+ (the rehearsals) and the music sessions were definitely worth obtaining, even if I can see that we won't use that much of it in the end.

October 20   The *Showgirls* tape is a no-show (I'm somehow becoming immune to these situations), but at least we now have a meaningful assembly of clips and sync for the section beginning 'I was born' through to *Basic Instinct*. The war images seem to work well with the Stravinsky music I have chosen ('The Firebird' – Stravinsky is Verhoeven's idol), and the university section also fits in well with *Soldier of Orange*. The clips of the latter don't quite do the job yet, though. The other problem is conveying the true grunginess of *Turkish Delight* without feeling I'm crashing the BBC taste barrier. The *Spetters* controversy clicks, as does the *Flesh + Blood* section, where by chance I find a clip that talks about finding the sign to go in a certain direction – and Verhoeven's talking about Hollywood! *Robocop* gives us some humorous touches, and the *Basic Instinct/Fourth Man* intercutting is also pretty funny. We both laugh a lot at Jeroen Krabbe's masturbation story, which neatly takes us into *The Fourth Man*. All very promising; I make a VHS cassette to view on Sunday afresh.

October 23   The VHS of *Showgirls* finally materialises. Now we can really crack ahead with the film.

October 25 By the end of the morning, Dave and I seem to have cut together a winner of an opening sequence, rather jokily linking the rehearsal footage into the appropriate sequences in *Showgirls*. By beginning with sync from Verhoeven explaining how he still has a European sensibility, then ending with him saying he always wanted to make science fiction, thrillers and musicals but couldn't in Holland because life is so non-dramatic there, we really set up everything to begin the story. It's a genuine thrill to find a solution to the big problem (how should I begin?) so quickly! Now we have to address the ending.

October 26 Dave and I press on with trying to solve the ending problem. Robert's comment that *Showgirls* is Paul's take on America, and that it's emphasis on sex and power suggests it is his first Dutch–American film, proves particularly useful. The difficulty is integrating the exciting and funny rehearsal stuff with the music sessions; the quiet cues we film with Dave Stewart rather let the pace down. At the same time Dave has edited them most skilfully, and I'm reluctant to chop them further.

October 27 To the cutting room for a quick check on our end sequence. We've found an insinuating dialogue scene (bitchiness between the two female leads) to place before a final comment by Verhoeven, but I'm not satisfied. In the meantime we assemble the best of the EPK on-set footage for a final credits montage. In the afternoon, I bring Lorraine in for a viewing while we make a VHS cassette for me to look at over the weekend. She's impressed at how much material we've got into the finished film, and only seems troubled by the *Robocop* violence (my favourite scene in which ED 209 wastes a young executive).

October 29 I force myself to watch the documentary through, and my feelings are more positive than on Friday, when it all seemed so slow (always the danger of viewing the same material over and over again). I see some obvious cuts (we're just under an hour at present), and I decide it would be better to end with a dance sequence rather than a prolonged dialogue scene.

October 30 In the morning, high-energy editing as I put my ideas from Sunday into play. At 3.30 pm, Nigel arrives for the viewing, and I call in Anne Ellotson, the *Omnibus* researcher to join us. Things go very well, with some immediate laughter from Nigel. As before, he takes no notes but simply watches the film – so rare in the BBC these days. Afterwards he is delighted and full of praise, as is Anne. The problems as such lie in the final section, and he's right – it feels less worked out than the rest, and the pace definitely slackens. Nigel succinctly explains my film as telling you that behind these big Hollywood genre pictures, there is definitely a personality at work. He also feels that I have not raised any taste problems – though there are three verbal 'fucks' to clear if we can. Above all both he and Anne agree that Verhoeven is very engaging on screen, thereby justifying my approach of letting him tell most of the story (and thereby avoiding the need for commentary). I feel very elated, though a little devil tells me there's trouble still ahead getting all these clips in.

November 3 Final day of editing, and we've reduced the cut to fifty-three minutes, still retaining some of Dave Stewart and Paul at work together. At a Christmas lunch for *Omnibus* Nigel agrees that he'll try for a 55-minute slot.

November 28 After some tense weeks, all the film clips have arrived as requested and we begin the final week of post-production. They all seem to work without too much pain, and we're only sorry to sacrifice the Dave Stewart material in its entirety.

Postscript (January 8, 1996) The programme is transmitted at 10.40 pm, under the title *Paul Verhoeven: From Holland to Hollywood*. As it happens, we now follow *Film '96*, in which Barry Norman joins the chorus of general antipathy for *Showgirls*. The film receives a huge amount of comment, albeit passionately negative. I subsequently learn that the programme enjoyed 1.8 million viewers (good for the present late slot), but apparently failed to offend anyone (no complaints, public or corporate). Does this mean I failed in some way?

Checklist of Films Described in this Book

Before and After (1996)
Director: Barbet Schroeder; Exec. Producers: Roger Birnbaum, Joe Roth; Producer: Barbet Schroeder, Susan Hoffman; Screenplay: Ted Tally; Cast: Meryl Streep, Liam Neeson, Edward Furlong.

Before the Rain (1994)
Director: Milco Mancevski; Producers: Judy Counihan, Sam Taylor, Cat Villiers, Cedomir Kolar, Gorjan Tozija; Screenplay: Milco Mancevski; Cast: Rade Serbedzija, Grégoire Colin, Labina Mitevska.

Blue (1993)
Director: Derek Jarman; Producers: James MacKay, Takashi Asai; Screenplay: Derek Jarman.

Blue Juice (1995)
Director: Peter Salmi; Producers: Peter Salmi, Simon Relph; Screenplay: Peter Salmi, Carl Prechezer; Cast: Sean Pertwee, Catherine Zeta Jones, Ewan McGregor.

Breaking the Waves (1996)
Director: Lars von Trier; Exec. Producers: Philippe Bober, Lars Jönsson; Producers: Peter Aalbaek Jensen, Vibeke Windeløv; Screenplay: Lars von Trier, David Pirie; Cast: Emily Watson, Stellan Skarsgård, Jean-Marc Barr.

Butterfly Kiss (1995)
Director: Michael Winterbottom; Producer: Julie Baines; Screenplay: Frank Cottrell Boyce; Cast: Amanda Plummer, Saskia Reeves.

Cold Lazarus (1996)
Director: Renny Rye; Exec. Producers: Michael Wearing, Peter Ansorge; Producers: Kenith Trodd, Rosemaire Whitman; Screenplay: Dennis Potter; Cast: Albert Finney, Frances De La Tour, Ciaran Hinds.

Crash (1996)
Director: David Cronenberg; Producer: Jeremy Thomas; Screenplay: David Cronenberg; Cast: James Spader, Holly Hunter, Deborah Unger.

Dido and Aeneas (1995)
Director: Peter Maniura; Producers: Nick De Grunwald, Julie Baines; Cast: Maria Ewing, Karl Daymond.

Extreme Measures (1996)
Director: Michael Apted; Exec. Producer: Andrew Scheinman; Producers: Hugh Grant, Elizabeth Hurley; Screenplay: Tony Gilroy; Cast: Hugh Grant, Sarah Jessica Parker, Gene Hackman.

The Hollow Reed (1996)
Director: Angela Pope; Exec. Producers: Nik Powell, Stephen Woolley; Producer: Elizabeth Karlsen; Screenplay: Paula Milne; Cast: Martin Donovan, Joely Richardson, Ian Hart.

In Love and War (1996)
Director: Richard Attenborough; Exec. Producer: Sara Risher; Producers: Richard Attenborough, Dimitri Villard; Screenplay: Allan Scott; Cast: Chris O'Donnell, Sandra Bullock.

Institute Benjamenta (1995)
Directors: Brothers Quay; Producers: Keith Griffiths, Janine Marmot; Screenplay: Brothers Quay; Cast: Mark Rylance, Alice Krige, Gottfried John.

Jude (1996)
Director: Michael Winterbottom; Exec. Producers: Stewart Till, Mark Shivas; Producer: Andrew Eaton; Screenplay: Hossein Amini; Cast: Kate Winslet, Christopher Eccleston, Rachel Griffiths.

Land and Freedom (1995)
Director: Ken Loach; Exec. Producers: Gerardo Herrero, Ulrich Felsberg, Sally Hibbin; Producer: Rebecca O'Brien; Screenplay: Jim Allen; Cast: Ian Hart, Rosana Pastor, Frédèric Pierrot.

Madagascar Skin (1995)
Director: Christopher Newby; Exec. Producers: Ben Gibson, Stuart Cosgrove; Producer: Julie Baines; Screenplay: Christopher Newby; Cast: Bernard Hill, John Hannah.

Mars Attacks!
Director: Tim Burton; Producers: Tim Burton, Laurie Parker, Larry Franco; Screenplay: Jonathan Gems; Cast: Pierce Brosnan, Lukas Haas, Sarah Jessica Parker.

Michael Collins (1995)
Director: Neil Jordan; Producers: Stephen Woolley, David Geffen; Cast: Liam Neeson, Julia Roberts, Stephen Rea.

Mojave Moon (1995)
Director: Kevin Dowling; Producer: Matt Salinger; Screenplay: Len Glasser; Cast: Danny Aiello.

Moving the Mountain (1994)
Director: Michael Apted; Producer: Trudie Styler; Series Editor: André Singer.

Nadja (1994)
Director: Michael Almereyda; Exec. Producer: David Lynch; Producers: Mary Sweeney, Amy Hobby; Screenplay: Michael Almereyda; Cast: Suzy Amis, Galaxy Craze, Martin Donovan.

Nervous Energy (1995)
Director: Jean Stewart; Exec. Producer: Andrea Calderwood; Producer: Ann Scott; Screenplay: Howard Schuman; Cast: Alfred Molina, Cal MacAninch, Caroline Guthrie.

Out of the Deep Pan (1996)
Director: Kieron J. Walsh; Producer: Anthony Rowe; Screenplay: Tim Loane.

Paul Verhoeven; From Holland to Hollywood (1996)
Director: David Thompson; Series Editor: Nigel Williams.

The Perez Family (1995)
Director: Mira Nair; Exec Producer: Robin Swicord; Producers: Michael Nozik, Lydia Dean Pilcher, Julia Chasman; Screenplay: Robin Swicord; Cast: Marisa Tomei, Anjelica Huston, Alfred Molina.

The Preacher's Wife (1996)
Director: Penny Marshall; Producers: Samuel Goldwyn, Elliot Abbott, Robert Greenhut; Screenplay: Allan Scott; Cast: Denzel Washington, Whitney Houston, Courtney B. Vance.

Small Faces (1995)
Director: Gillies MacKinnon; Exec. Producers: Andrea Calderwood, Mark Shivas; Producers: Billy MacKinnon, Steve Clark-Hall; Screenplay: Gillies MacKinnon, Billy MacKinnon; Cast: Iain Robertson, Joseph McFadden, Steven Duffy.

Space Truckers (1995)
Director: Stuart Gordon; Exec. Producers: Greg Johnson, Guy Collins; Producers: Peter Newman, Stuart Gordon, Ted Mann; Screenplay: Ted Mann; Cast: Dennis Hopper, Stephen Dorff, Debi Mazar.

Stiff Upper Lips (1995)
Director: Gary Sinyor; Exec. Producer: Nigel Savage; Producers: Jeremy

Bolt, Gary Sinyor; Screenplay: Gary Sinyor, Paul Simpkin; Cast: Peter Ustinov, Prunella Scales, Georgina Cates.

Sweet Angel Mine (1995)
Director: Curtis Radclyffe; Exec. Producers: Gareth Jones, Christopher Zimmer, Sam Taylor; Screenplay: Sue Maheu, Tim Willocks; Cast: Alberta Watson, Anna Massey, Oliver Milburn.

Thunderheart (1992)
Director: Michael Apted; Exec. Producer: Robert De Niro; Producers: Robert De Niro, Jane Rosenthal, John Fusco; Screenplay: John Fusco; Cast: Val Kilmer, Graham Greene, Sam Shepard.

True Blue (1995)
Director: Ferdinand Fairfax; Exec. Producer: Allan Scott; Producers: Clive Parsons, Davina Belling; Screenplay: Rupert Walters; Cast: Johan Leysen, Dominic West, Geraldine Somerville.

Twelve Monkeys (1995)
Director: Terry Gilliam; Exec. Producers: Robert Cavallo, Dawn Steel, Robert Kosberg, Gary Levinsohn; Producer: Chuck Roven; Screenplay: David Webb Peoples, Janet Peoples; Cast: Bruce Willis, Madeleine Stowe, Brad Pitt.

The Van (1996)
Director: Stephen Frears; Producer: Lynda Myles; Screenplay: Roddy Doyle; Cast: Colm Meaney, Donal O'Kelly, Ger Ryan.

Vicious Circles (1995)
Director: Alexander Whitelaw; Exec. Producer: Nik Powell; Screenplay: Alexander Whitelaw, Stephen O'Shea.